LEVEL 3

문제로 마스터하는 중학영문법

문제로 마스터하는 중학영문법 LEVEL 3

지은이   NE능률 영어교육연구소

연구원   신유승 노지희 박서경 이강혁

영문 교열   Patrick Ferraro Nathaniel Galletta August Niederhaus MyAn Thi Le

디자인   안훈정 오솔길

맥편집   이정임

Let's grow together

NE능률이
미래를
창조합니다.

건강한 배움의 고객가치를 제공하겠다는 꿈을 실현하기 위해
40년이 넘는 시간 동안 열심히 달려왔습니다.

앞으로도 끊임없는 연구와 노력을 통해
당연한 것을 멈추지 않고

고객, 기업, 직원 모두가 함께 성장하는 NE능률이 되겠습니다.

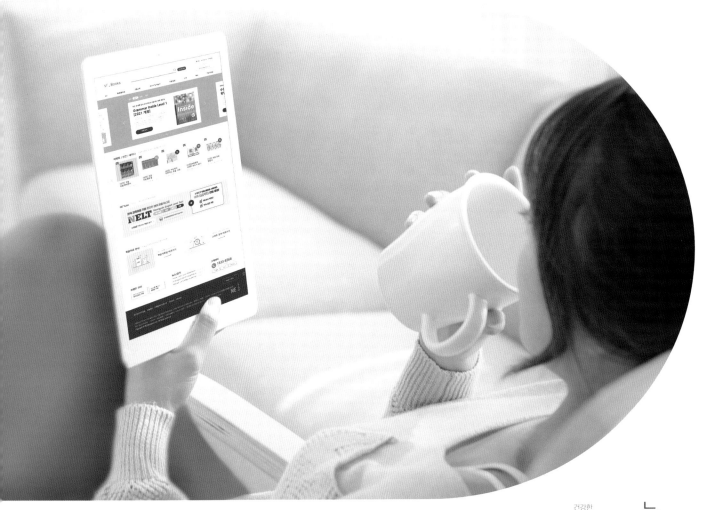

Start where you are.
Use what you have.
Do what you can.

당신이 있는 곳에서 시작하라.
당신이 가진 것을 사용하라.
당신이 할 수 있는 것을 하라.

- Arthur Ashe

Structure & Features

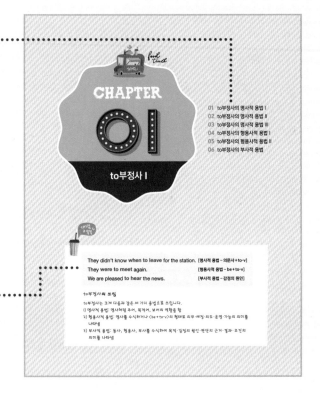

1 자세하게 나뉜 문법 POINT

문법 항목을 세분화하여 그에 따른 각각의 POINT를 제시하였습니다. 각 POINT를 차례대로 학습하면 큰 문법 항목을 보다 쉽게 이해할 수 있습니다.

2 개념 쏙쏙

각 Chapter에서 배울 문법 내용을 한눈에 보기 쉽게 정리하였습니다.

3 핵심만 담은 문법 설명

문법 설명에서 군더더기를 걷어내고, 중학교 과정에서 꼭 배워야 하는 핵심 문법 내용만을 체계적으로 제시하였습니다. <PLUS TIP>과 <내신만점 TIP>을 통해 알아두면 좋은 문법 사항과 기출 포인트를 익힐 수 있습니다.

4 문법 항목별로 주관식 위주의 문제 다수 수록

세분화된 문법 항목별로 많은 수의 주관식 문제를 수록하였습니다. 스스로 써 보는 문제를 많이 풀어 보면서 확실하게 문법에 대한 이해를 점검하고 작문 실력을 향상시킬 수 있으며, 나아가 중학 영문법을 마스터하게 될 것입니다.

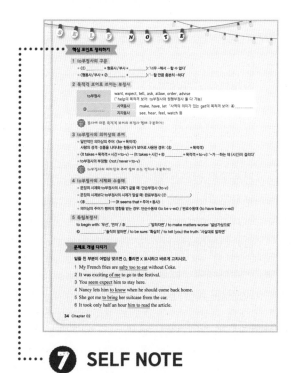

⑤ 내신대비 TEST

통합적인 문제들을 제시하여 해당 Chapter의 학습 내용을 빠짐없이 확인할 수 있게 하였습니다. 최신 기출 유형 문제들이 포함되어 있어 어려워진 학교 시험에도 완벽하게 대비할 수 있습니다.

⑥ 서술형 따라잡기

다양한 유형의 서술형 문제들을 통해 응용력과 문제 해결력을 높이고, 실제 서술형 평가를 효과적으로 준비할 수 있습니다.

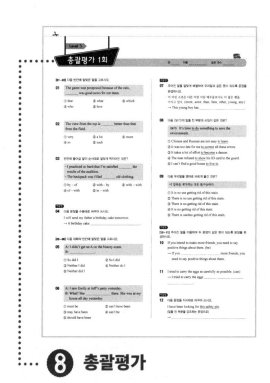

⑦ SELF NOTE

각 Chapter에서 배운 문법 사항을 스스로 정리하고, <이것만은 꼭!>을 참고하여 확인 문제를 풀어보면서 문법 실력을 탄탄하게 다질 수 있습니다.

⑧ 총괄평가

3회분의 총괄평가를 별도 제공하였습니다. 총괄평가를 통해 내신 대비에 필요한 실전 감각을 기를 수 있습니다.

Contents

Contents

CHAPTER 01

food truck

to부정사 I

개념 쏙쏙

They didn't know **when to leave** for the station. [명사적 용법 – 의문사+to-v]

They **were to meet** again. [형용사적 용법 – be+to-v]

We are pleased **to hear** the news. [부사적 용법 – 감정의 원인]

to부정사의 쓰임

to부정사는 크게 다음과 같은 세 가지 용법으로 쓰입니다.

1) 명사적 용법: 명사처럼 주어, 목적어, 보어의 역할을 함

2) 형용사적 용법: 명사를 수식하거나 <be+to-v>의 형태로 의무·예정·의도·운명·가능의 의미를 나타냄

3) 부사적 용법: 동사, 형용사, 부사를 수식하여 목적·감정의 원인·판단의 근거·결과·조건의 의미를 나타냄

to부정사의 명사적 용법 I – 주어 / 목적어 / 보어

■ to부정사가 명사적 용법으로 사용될 때는 문장 안에서 주어, 목적어, 보어의 역할을 한다.

To save the earth is important. (주어)

Sarah loves **to knit** baby clothes. (목적어)

My plan is **to master** Japanese in a year. (보어)

A 다음 〈보기〉에서 알맞은 말을 골라 빈칸에 적절한 형태로 써넣으시오. (단, 한 번씩만 사용할 것)

〈보기〉	finish	arrive	make	teach	keep	build

1 _____ a study plan before a test is useful.

2 Her job is _____ Korean to foreigners.

3 He wants _____ his work by tomorrow.

4 _____ a diary is not easy.

5 He expected _____ there on time.

6 Their goal is _____ their own house.

B 다음 우리말과 같은 뜻이 되도록 ( ) 안의 말을 이용하여 문장을 완성하시오.

1 나는 마지막 버스를 잡는 데 실패했다. (fail, catch)

_____ _____ _____ _____ the last bus.

2 나의 계획은 런던에서 유학하는 것이다. (plan, study abroad)

_____

in London.

3 그녀는 유명한 음악가가 되고 싶어한다. (want, be)

_____ a famous musician.

4 그의 소원은 그가 가장 좋아하는 축구선수를 만나는 것이다. (wish, meet)

_____ his favorite soccer

player.

5 영어 소설을 읽는 것은 재미있을 것이다. (read, an English novel)

_____ would be interesting.

6 그는 다른 문화에 대해 배우기를 희망한다. (hope, learn about)

_____ other cultures.

to부정사의 명사적 용법 II – 가주어, 가목적어 it

■ 주어나 5형식 문장의 목적어로 to부정사(구)가 쓰인 경우, 보통 가주어나 가목적어 it을 쓰고 to부정사(구)는 문장 뒤로 보낸다. 가주어나 가목적어로 쓰이는 it은 '그것'이라고 해석하지 않는다.

It is impossible **to get** to the airport in ten minutes.
가주어   진주어

I found **it** hard **to run** a marathon.
       가목적어   진목적어

★ **내신만점 TIP** ▷ 대명사 it과, 가주어나 가목적어로 쓰이는 it을 구분하자.

A 다음 문장을 가주어 It을 이용한 문장으로 바꾸어 쓰시오.

1 To ride the subway in Seoul is simple.
→ _____

2 To find information on the Internet is easy.
→ _____

3 To achieve one's goals is fantastic.
→ _____

4 To express your opinion in other languages is difficult.
→ _____

B 다음 우리말과 같은 뜻이 되도록 ( ) 안의 말을 배열하여 문장을 완성하시오.

1 규칙적으로 운동하는 것은 중요하다. (to, important, exercise, is, it, regularly)
_____

2 진정한 친구가 있다는 것은 멋진 일이다. (a, have, it, wonderful, true, to, friend, is)
_____

3 나는 아침에 공부하는 것이 더 낫다고 생각했다.
(morning, I, it, study, thought, to, in, better, the)
_____

4 그는 영어를 말하는 것이 흥미진진하다는 것을 알게 되었다.
(speak, it, English, he, exciting, to, found)
_____

5 Serena는 그에게 사실대로 말하는 것이 어렵다는 것을 알게 되었다.
(Serena, truth, it, the, hard, him, tell, to, found)
_____

to부정사의 명사적 용법Ⅲ – 〈의문사+to-v〉

- 〈의문사+to-v〉는 what, when, where, how, who(m) 등의 의문사 뒤에 to부정사를 쓴 형태로, 명사구처럼 쓰인다. (단, why는 이렇게 쓰이지 않는다.)
Maria told me **what to see** in Paris.
I didn't know **where to go**.
- 〈의문사+to-v〉는 〈의문사+주어+should+동사원형〉으로 바꾸어 쓸 수 있다.
Maria told me **what to see** in Paris. → Maria told me **what I should see** in Paris.
I didn't know **where to go**. → I didn't know **where I should go**.

★ **내신만점 TIP** 〈의문사+to-v〉와 바꾸어 쓸 수 있는 〈의문사+주어+should+동사원형〉의 어순을 익히자.

A 다음 두 문장이 같은 뜻이 되도록 문장을 완성하시오.

1 She didn't tell me when I should call her.
→ She didn't tell me _____.

2 He wrote down what he should do in his diary.
→ He wrote down _____ in his diary.

3 I don't know where to hide my pocket money.
→ I don't know _____.

4 They showed me how to decorate the Christmas tree.
→ They showed me _____.

B 다음 우리말과 같은 뜻이 되도록 ( ) 안의 말을 이용하여 문장을 완성하시오.

1 아무도 언제 시작해야 할지 몰랐다. (start)
No one knew _____ _____ _____.

2 그들은 누구를 초대할지 아직 결정하지 못했다. (invite)
They haven't yet decided _____ _____ _____.

3 이 복사기를 사용하는 법을 아세요? (use)
Do you know _____ _____ _____ this copy machine?

4 무엇을 살지 결정하기 전에 가격을 확인해라. (buy)
Check the prices before you decide _____ _____ _____.

5 이 지도는 당신이 홍콩에서 어디를 가야 할지 보여줄 것이다. (go)
This map will show you _____ _____ _____ in Hong Kong.

6 모든 음식이 근사해 보여서 나는 먼저 무엇을 먹어야 할지 몰랐다. (eat)
All the food looked great, so I had no idea _____ _____ _____ first.

to부정사의 형용사적 용법 I – 명사 수식

- to부정사는 '~하는', '~할'이라는 뜻으로 형용사처럼 명사를 수식할 수 있다. 이때 to부정사는 명사를 뒤에서 수식하는데, 특히 to부정사 뒤에 전치사가 오는 경우를 주의해야 한다.
  She has *a house* **to live in**.

- 형용사와 to부정사가 -thing, -one, -body로 끝나는 대명사를 수식하는 경우에는 〈-thing[-one/-body]+ 형용사+to-v〉의 어순이 된다.
  Do you want **something easy to read**?

★ **내신만점 TIP** to부정사의 형용사적 용법에서 자동사 뒤에 전치사가 누락되지 않았는지 반드시 확인하자.

A 다음 밑줄 친 부분을 어법에 맞게 고쳐 쓰시오.

1 There is a chair to sit.

2 He has good news tell you.

3 I need something drink to cold.

4 Can you give me a pen to write?

5 Sarah has several friends to talk.

6 They had no to travel time together.

7 What is the best to solve way this problem?

B 다음 우리말과 같은 뜻이 되도록 ( ) 안의 말을 이용하여 문장을 완성하시오.

1 당신은 지금 할 일이 있나요? (anything)
Do you have _____ _____ _____ now?

2 나는 입을 적당한 재킷이 없다. (wear)
I don't have a proper _____ _____ _____.

3 나는 거주할 완벽한 동네를 찾았다. (town, live)
I found the perfect _____ _____ _____.

4 나는 쓸 종이 한 장이 필요하다. (write)
I need a piece of _____ _____ _____.

5 의지할 누군가가 있다니 너는 운이 좋다. (depend on)
You are lucky to have _____ _____ _____.

6 Dan은 함께 놀 친구들이 많다. (play)
Dan has lots of _____ _____ _____ _____.

7 바르셀로나는 방문하기에 흥미로운 도시였다. (visit)
Barcelona was an interesting _____ _____ _____.

to부정사의 형용사적 용법 II – ⟨be+to-v⟩ 용법

■ ⟨be+to부정사⟩의 형태로 의무, 예정, 의도, 운명, 가능 등의 의미를 나타낼 수 있다.

You **are to come** back home by ten o'clock. (의무: ~해야 한다)

My family **is to travel** to China next week. (예정: ~할 예정이다)

If you **are to be** a guitarist, you must practice a lot. (의도: ~하려고 하다)

The girl **was to become** a famous figure skater. (운명: ~할 운명이다)

Nothing **was to be** heard in the town at midnight. (가능: ~할 수 있다)

A 다음 우리말과 같은 뜻이 되도록 ⟨보기⟩에서 알맞은 말을 골라 ⟨be+to-v⟩ 구문을 이용하여 문장을 완성하시오.

> ⟨보기⟩ end   be   succeed   visit   see

1 구름 한 점 보이지 않았다.

Not a cloud ＿＿＿＿＿ ＿＿＿＿＿ ＿＿＿＿＿ ＿＿＿＿＿.

2 너는 어두워지기 전에 여기로 돌아와야 한다.

You ＿＿＿＿＿ ＿＿＿＿＿ ＿＿＿＿＿ back here before dark.

3 네가 성공하고자 한다면 최선을 다해야 한다.

If you ＿＿＿＿＿ ＿＿＿＿＿ ＿＿＿＿＿, you must do your best.

4 대통령은 이번 주말 프랑스를 방문할 예정이다.

The president ＿＿＿＿＿ ＿＿＿＿＿ ＿＿＿＿＿ France this weekend.

5 로미오와 줄리엣의 사랑은 슬프게 끝날 운명이었다.

The love of Romeo and Juliet ＿＿＿＿＿ ＿＿＿＿＿ ＿＿＿＿＿ sadly.

B 다음 두 문장이 같은 뜻이 되도록 ⟨be+to-v⟩ 구문을 이용하여 문장을 완성하시오.

1 He was destined to lead the country.

→ He ＿＿＿＿＿, ＿＿＿＿＿ the country.

2 You have to finish this report by next week.

→ You ＿＿＿＿＿ this report by next week.

3 No one could be found in the desert.

→ No one ＿＿＿＿＿ in the desert.

4 They are going to fly to Australia tomorrow morning.

→ They ＿＿＿＿＿ tomorrow morning.

5 If you intend to be a writer, you must experience many things.

→ If you ＿＿＿＿＿, you must experience many things.

to부정사의 부사적 용법

- to부정사는 부사처럼 동사, 형용사, 부사를 수식할 수 있다.

He wakes up at six o'clock **to go** jogging. (목적: ~하기 위해서)

Brian was glad **to hear** the news. (감정의 원인: ~해서)

They were stupid **to do** such a thing. (판단의 근거: ~하다니)

She grew up **to be** a diplomat. (결과: (…해서) ~하다)

To see her dance, you would take her for a professional dancer. (조건: ~한다면)

This book is difficult **to understand**. (형용사 수식: ~하기에)

★ PLUS TIP
- 〈in order to-v〉와 〈so as to-v〉는 to부정사의 부사적 용법에서 목적의 의미를 강조하기 위해 쓴다.
- to부정사 앞에 only가 쓰인 경우 결과의 의미를 나타내며, '~지만 (결국) ~했다'로 해석한다.
  He left home early, **only to miss** the train.

A 다음 주어진 문장과 같은 뜻이 되도록 문장을 완성하시오.

1 They saw snow. So they were excited.
→ They were excited _____ _____ _____.

2 She was kind. She let us stay at her house.
→ She was kind _____ _____ _____ _____ at her house.

3 If you saw him, you would think he was an actor.
→ _____ _____ _____, you would think he was an actor.

4 I'm saving money because I want to go to Latin America.
→ I'm saving money _____ _____ _____ Latin America.

5 Scott tried his best but failed to win the prize.
→ Scott tried his best, _____ _____ _____ to win the prize.

B 다음 우리말과 같은 뜻이 되도록 ( ) 안의 말을 배열하여 문장을 완성하시오.

1 나는 중국어를 배우러 중국에 갈 것이다. (learn, to, I'm, to, Chinese, China, going)
_____

2 그녀는 그 콘서트를 놓쳐서 실망했다. (disappointed, miss, she, to, the, was, concert)
_____

3 그의 조언을 따르다니 너는 현명했다. (wise, were, to, his, follow, you, advice)
_____

4 티셔츠와 반바지를 입기에는 너무 춥다.
(too, shorts, cold, is, it, to, and, a T-shirt, wear)
_____

내신대비 TEST

[01-03] 다음 빈칸에 알맞은 말을 고르시오.

01

> My health secret is _____ for 30 minutes a day.

① exercises   ② exercised
③ to exercise   ④ be exercised
⑤ to exercising

02

> It is not easy _____ your habits in a day.

① change   ② changes
③ changed   ④ to change
⑤ to be changed

03

> Would you like some chopsticks _____?

① eat   ② eating
③ to eat   ④ eat with
⑤ to eat with

04

다음 대화의 빈칸에 알맞은 말은?

> A: Can you tell me _____?
> B: Please be here by 10 a.m.

① when to come   ② what to come
③ how to come   ④ where to come
⑤ which to come

[05-07] 빈칸에 들어갈 말이 순서대로 알맞게 짝지어진 것을 고르시오.

05

> • _____ is necessary to make a shopping list.
> • I planned _____ three languages at university.

① It – learn   ② It – learned
③ It – to learn   ④ That – learn
⑤ That – learning

06

> • I ran away but didn't know _____ to go.
> • She found _____ hard to become a fashion designer.

① where – it   ② how – that
③ who – that   ④ when – that
⑤ what – it

07

> • He has something _____ her.
> • They hurried, only _____ late for school.

① tell – be   ② to tell – be
③ to tell – to be   ④ telling – to be
⑤ what – it

08

다음 밑줄 친 부분의 쓰임이 나머지와 다른 것은?

① It was a nice shirt, wasn't it?
② It sounds very interesting to me.
③ It will be over before he knows it.
④ It is right next to the bookstore.
⑤ It is useful to go to school by bicycle.

09

다음 〈보기〉의 밑줄 친 부분과 용법이 같은 것은?

〈보기〉 He turned on the light to find his glasses.

① I'm glad to find you here.
② He failed to find a proper job.
③ It is not easy to find four-leaf clovers.
④ She was upset to find you lied to her.
⑤ She went to five shops to find a simple white blouse.

10

다음 두 문장이 같은 뜻이 되도록 할 때 빈칸에 들어갈 말로 알맞은 것은?

Can you let me know whom to choose for my partner?
→ Can you let me know _____?

① to choose whom for my partner
② whom I should choose for my partner
③ whom should I choose for my partner
④ whom you should choose for my partner
⑤ whom to choose someone for my partner

11

다음 빈칸에 공통으로 들어갈 말은?

- _____ was a mistake to give you my phone number.
- She found _____ important to be honest.

① This[this]　　② That[that]　　③ All[all]
④ It[it]　　　　⑤ What[what]

12

다음 우리말을 영어로 바르게 옮긴 것은?

그는 김치를 만드는 것이 쉽다는 것을 알았다.

① He found easy to make kimchi.
② He found to make kimchi easy.
③ He found it to make kimchi easy.
④ He found it easy to make kimchi.
⑤ He found it easily to make kimchi.

[13-14] 다음 밑줄 친 부분의 용법이 나머지와 다른 것을 고르시오.

13

① My goal is to be a lawyer.
② He is brave to do such a thing.
③ I got up early to make breakfast.
④ I'm proud to be a team leader.
⑤ We did our best, only to lose the game.

14

① We decided to take a taxi.
② He wants something hot to drink.
③ I didn't mean to lose your camera.
④ My plan was to see the sunrise.
⑤ It was amazing to look at the stars outside.

15

다음 〈보기〉의 밑줄 친 부분과 쓰임이 같은 것은?

〈보기〉 I found it hard to finish reading this book.

① How far is it from Seoul to Paris?
② It was difficult to get the concert tickets.
③ It was very sunny, so we went on a picnic.
④ Carrie likes yoga because it helps her relax.
⑤ I made it a rule to get up at six in the morning.

[16 – 17] 다음 밑줄 친 부분이 어법상 틀린 것을 고르시오.

16

① I was stupid to trust him.
② Nothing was to be found there.
③ He was to fall in love with me.
④ They haven't decided whom to hire.
⑤ Bring me a piece of paper to write.

17

① I'm sorry to trouble you.
② I promised to give it back.
③ I thought important to set goals.
④ There are many people to help you.
⑤ She is to finish the paper by today.

고난도
18

다음 중 어법상 옳은 문장을 모두 고르면? (2개)

① That is important to save money for the future.
② They believed it safe to hide in the basement.
③ She has two sisters to take care.
④ He didn't know how to do for his friends.
⑤ The baseball game is to start at 7 p.m.

19

다음 두 문장이 같은 뜻이 되도록 할 때 잘못된 것은?

① I don't know where I should go.
  → I don't know where to go.
② The boss is going to arrive at 11 o'clock.
  → The boss is to arrive at 11 o'clock.
③ I'm looking for a bench because I want to sit on one.
  → I'm looking for a bench to sit.
④ I want to learn English in America. So I'm going there.
  → I'm going to America to learn English.
⑤ If you heard him play the guitar, you'd think he was a professional.
  → To hear him play the guitar, you'd think he was a professional.

고난도
20

다음 중 어법상 옳은 것끼리 짝지어진 것은?

(a) He couldn't find a hotel to stay at.
(b) The boy grew up be a great artist.
(c) She thought it impossible jump rope.
(d) I don't know what to bring to the party.
(e) She was happy to find out the test results.

① (a), (b), (c)　　② (a), (d), (e)
③ (b), (c), (d)　　④ (b), (c), (e)
⑤ (c), (d), (e)

서술형 따라잡기

01

주어진 말을 이용하여 우리말과 뜻이 같도록 문장을 완성하시오.

(1) 그들은 그의 노래를 듣고 놀랐다.

(surprised, hear)

→ They were _____ _____ _____
his singing.

(2) 그는 그의 나라로 결코 돌아가지 못할 운명이었다.

(go back)

→ He _____ never _____ _____
_____ to his country.

02

주어진 말을 알맞게 배열하여 우리말과 뜻이 같도록 문장을 완성하시오.

(1) 그녀를 기다리게 하다니 그는 무례했다.

(wait, he, make, to, her, rude, was)

→ _____

(2) 너는 함께 일할 누군가를 찾았니?

(did, to, find, work, someone, with, you)

→ _____

03

다음 계획표를 보고, 문장을 완성하시오.

계획	목표	목표 달성 여부
(1) Eat breakfast	Improve my health	O
(2) Study English every day	Get an A	X

(1) I ate breakfast _____ _____ _____
_____.

(2) I studied English every day, but it was
impossible _____ _____ _____
_____.

04

다음 두 문장이 같은 뜻이 되도록 빈칸에 알맞은 말을 쓰시오.

To eat at night is not good for your health.

→ It _____ _____ _____ _____
_____ _____ _____ _____
_____ _____.

05

다음 그림을 보고, 주어진 말과 가목적어 it을 이용하여 문장을 완성하시오.

(easy)

(difficult)

(1) She found _____ _____ _____
_____ _____ _____.

(2) She thought _____ _____ _____
_____ _____ _____.

고난도

06

다음 조건에 맞게 우리말을 영어로 옮겨 쓰시오.

〈조건〉 1. to부정사와 의문사를 이용할 것
2. 어휘 show, cook, the meat, important, apologize를 이용할 것
3. 필요하다면 가주어 It을 이용할 것

(1) 내가 고기를 요리하는 법을 너에게 보여줄게.

→ _____

(2) 언제 사과할지 아는 것은 중요하다.

→ _____

핵심 포인트 정리하기

— to부정사의 용법

① _____ 용법	주어, 목적어, 보어 역할
	가주어, 가목적어 ② _____ : 주어나 5형식 문장의 목적어로 to부정사(구)가 쓰인 경우, 보통 가주어나 가목적어를 쓰고 to부정사(구)는 문장 뒤로 이동
	〈의문사+to-v〉 → ③〈_____ + _____ + _____ + _____〉
형용사적 용법	명사 수식
	형용사와 to부정사가 〈-thing, -one, -body〉로 끝나는 대명사를 수식하는 경우: 〈-thing[-one/-body]+④ _____ + _____〉
	⑤〈_____ + _____〉 용법: 의무, 예정, 의도, 운명, 가능의 의미를 나타냄
⑥ _____ 용법	동사, 형용사, 부사 수식
	⑦ _____, 감정의 원인, 판단의 근거, 결과, 조건 등의 의미를 나타냄

시험에 꼭!
to부정사의 서로 다른 용법 구분하기!
to부정사(구)가 주어나 5형식 문장의 목적어로 쓰인 경우, 보통 가주어나 가목적어 it을 쓴다는 것 기억하기!
대명사 it과 가주어 it의 쓰임 구분하기!
to부정사의 형용사적 용법에서 자동사와 함께 쓰여야 하는 전치사를 빠뜨리지 말기!

문제로 개념 다지기

밑줄 친 부분이 어법상 맞으면 O, 틀리면 X 표시하고 바르게 고치시오.

1 I found difficult it to stay in shape.

2 She asked him how to open the bottle.

3 We need strong someone to carry those boxes.

4 I checked if there were any chairs to sit in the room.

5 Megan stopped by a bakery to buy some bread.

6 He was brave to save the child from the river.

7 That is wise to pay for these shoes by credit card.

CHAPTER 02

to부정사 II

Kate was **too busy to look** after her daughter.

→ Kate was **so busy that she couldn't look** after her daughter.

To tell the truth, I saw you walking with someone in the park yesterday.

He seems to be a reporter. (→ It seems that he is a reporter.)

He seems to have been a reporter. (→ It seems that he was a reporter.)

to부정사의 구문

- ⟨too + 형용사 / 부사 + to-v⟩ '너무 ~해서 …할 수 없다'
- ⟨형용사 / 부사 + enough + to-v⟩ '~할 만큼 충분히 …하다'
- 독립부정사: 문장 전체를 수식하는 부사 역할을 함

to부정사의 시제

to부정사의 시제는 단순부정사(to-v)와 완료부정사(to have v-ed)로 나타냅니다.

too ~ to-v / ~ enough to-v

■ 〈too+형용사/부사+to-v〉는 '너무 ~해서 …할 수 없다'라는 뜻이고, 〈형용사/부사+enough+to-v〉는 '…할 만큼 충분히 ~하다'라는 뜻이다.

She was **too tired to go** out last night.
→ She was **so tired that she couldn't go** out last night.
He was **rich enough to travel** around the world.
→ He was **so rich that he could travel** around the world.

★ 내신만점 *TIP* 〈too ~ to-v〉와 〈~ enough to-v〉 구문에서 형용사/부사의 위치를 기억하자.

A 다음 두 문장이 같은 뜻이 되도록 문장을 완성하시오.

1 Cindy is so tall that she can reach the top of the bookcase.
→ Cindy is _____ .

2 Lucas was so tired that he couldn't move.
→ Lucas was _____ .

3 She is smart enough to solve that difficult problem.
→ She is _____ .

4 They are too busy to go on vacation.
→ They are _____ .

B 다음 우리말과 같은 뜻이 되도록 ( ) 안의 말을 배열하여 문장을 완성하시오.

1 이 수프는 너무 뜨거워서 먹을 수 없다. (eat, soup, is, to, too, this, hot)

_____

2 여기는 책을 읽을 수 있을 만큼 충분히 밝다.
(a, read, to, enough, book, bright, it, is)
_____ here.

3 그 지갑은 너무 커서 내 주머니에 넣을 수 없다.
(big, wallet, in, the, is, put, pocket, to, my, too)

_____

4 Julie는 너무 수줍음을 타서 사람들 앞에서 노래를 부르지 못한다.
(sing, can't, that, shy, Julie, so, is, she)
_____ in front of people.

5 Tim은 혼자서 여행을 할 만큼 충분히 용감하다. (travel, brave, is, Tim, enough, to)
_____ by himself.

목적격 보어로 쓰이는 to부정사

■ to부정사는 목적어를 보충 설명해주는 목적격 보어로 사용되기도 한다. to부정사를 목적격 보어로 취하는 동사에는 want, expect, tell, ask, allow, order, advise 등이 있다.
My parents **want** me **to stay** healthy.
She **told** her sister **to bring** her clothes back.

★ PLUS TIP help는 목적격 보어로 to부정사와 원형부정사 둘 다를 취할 수 있다.
They **helped** me **(to) move** the boxes.

A 다음 밑줄 친 부분이 어법상 맞으면 O, 틀리면 X 표시하고 바르게 고치시오.

1 I told her <u>stay</u> with me.

2 I asked Mike <u>to pick</u> me up.

3 They expected him <u>become</u> a professor.

4 The boss ordered John <u>for wait</u> for him.

5 Laura helped me <u>get</u> a house in Seoul.

6 The boss allowed me <u>take</u> the day off.

7 The dentist advised him <u>brushing</u> his teeth three times a day.

B 다음 우리말과 같은 뜻이 되도록 ( ) 안의 말을 이용하여 문장을 완성하시오.

1 우리는 네가 늦을 것이라고 예상했다. (be)
We _____ _____ _____ _____ late.

2 그는 그의 개에게 앉으라고 명령했다. (sit)
He _____ _____ _____ _____ _____.

3 당신은 그에게 전화를 그만하라고 말했나요? (stop)
Did you _____ _____ _____ _____ calling?

4 그녀는 나에게 수영을 하라고 조언했다. (swim)
She _____ _____ _____ _____.

5 내가 당신과 함께 여행하기를 원하나요? (travel)
Do you _____ _____ _____ _____ with you?

6 아무도 그녀가 회의를 준비하는 것을 도와주지 않았다. (prepare)
Nobody _____ _____ _____ for the meeting.

7 그들은 우리가 그 건물에 들어가는 것을 허가하지 않았다. (enter)
They didn't _____ _____ _____ _____ the building.

목적격 보어로 쓰이는 원형부정사 I – 사역동사

■ make, have, let과 같은 사역동사는 목적격 보어로 원형부정사를 사용한다.
He **made** me **stop** eating sweets.
She **had** her husband **wait** in front of the shop.
My brother **let** me **use** his laptop.

★ *PLUS TIP* get은 '~하게 하다'라는 사역의 의미를 갖지만 목적격 보어로 to부정사를 취한다.
She **got** him **to pick** her up.

A 다음 ( ) 안에서 알맞은 말을 고르시오.

1 Martin made his children (go / to go) to bed.

2 They let her (know / knowing) when to meet.

3 Linda told her boyfriend (get / to get) some dessert.

4 He had his friend (return / to return) the expensive jacket.

B 다음 ( ) 안의 말을 빈칸에 적절한 형태로 써넣으시오.

1 She made me _____ her the truth about the accident. (tell)

2 He got his sister _____ his file to him. (bring)

3 That dress makes you _____ lovely. (look)

4 Laura let me _____ her washing machine. (use)

5 My mother had me _____ some milk and bread. (buy)

6 James asked us _____ to his birthday party. (come)

C 다음 우리말과 같은 뜻이 되도록 ( ) 안의 말을 이용하여 문장을 완성하시오.

1 그는 내가 빨래를 하게 했다. (have)
He _____ _____ _____ the laundry.

2 Peter는 그녀가 약속을 취소하게 했다. (make)
Peter _____ _____ _____ her appointment.

3 Miranda는 그가 정장을 입게 했다. (get)
Miranda _____ _____ _____ _____ a suit.

4 어머니는 내가 춤 동아리에 가입하는 것을 허락하지 않으셨다. (let)
My mother _____ _____ _____ the dance club.

5 우리는 그에게 우리의 사진을 찍어 달라고 부탁했다. (ask)
We _____ _____ _____ _____ a picture of us.

목적격 보어로 쓰이는 원형부정사 II – 지각동사

- see, hear, feel, watch 등과 같은 지각동사는 목적격 보어로 원형부정사를 사용한다. 진행의 의미를 강조하는 경우 목적격 보어로 현재분사를 쓰기도 한다.
  I **saw** the couple **dance** in the park.
  I **saw** the couple **dancing** in the park. (진행의 의미 강조)

A 다음 ( ) 안의 말을 빈칸에 적절한 형태로 써넣으시오.

1 He watched me _____ on the stage. (sing)

2 Jenny helped the lady _____ the street. (cross)

3 She asked the waiter _____ a dessert. (bring)

4 I felt someone _____ my head. (touch)

5 They watched Jack _____ the ball. (kick)

6 All the teachers let everyone _____ home early. (go)

7 He heard me _____, but he didn't say anything. (cry)

B 다음 밑줄 친 부분을 어법에 맞게 고쳐 쓰시오.

1 I watched her to stealing a pen.

2 Kevin saw the child to laugh.

3 Nobody felt the earth to move.

4 He expected her coming to see him.

5 Did you hear Paul to play the guitar?

6 He made us training harder before the match.

C 다음 우리말과 같은 뜻이 되도록 ( ) 안의 말을 이용하여 문장을 완성하시오.

1 너는 바람이 부는 것을 느낄 수 있니? (blow)
Can you _____ _____ _____ _____?

2 그녀는 그들이 서로에게 미소 짓는 것을 보았다. (smile)
She _____ _____ _____ at each other.

3 그는 그의 아들이 소리 지르는 것을 들었을 때 화가 났다. (shout)
He got angry when he _____ _____ _____ _____.

to부정사의 의미상의 주어 I

- to부정사의 의미상의 주어가 문장의 주어 혹은 목적어와 같거나 막연한 일반인인 경우에는 의미상의 주어를 쓰지 않는다.
- to부정사의 의미상의 주어를 쓰는 경우, 일반적으로 〈for+목적격〉의 형태로 쓴다.
  It is dangerous **for children** *to travel* alone.
- 사람의 성격이나 성품을 나타내는 형용사(kind, nice, foolish, rude, clever, careless 등)가 보어로 사용된 경우에는 〈of+목적격〉의 형태로 쓴다.
  It was very kind **of you** *to say* so.

A 다음 ( ) 안에서 알맞은 말을 고르시오.

1 It is impossible (for / of) her to succeed.

2 It is hard (for / of) him to read for a long time.

3 It was clever (for / of) you to think of the great idea.

4 It was careless (for / of) her to make the same mistake.

5 It was important (for / of) them to get good grades.

B 다음 밑줄 친 부분을 어법에 맞게 고쳐 쓰시오.

1 Thomas wanted for himself to be a doctor.

2 I asked of him to lend me his cell phone.

3 They expected of me to come back later.

4 It was unkind for you to leave her alone.

C 다음 우리말과 같은 뜻이 되도록 ( ) 안의 말을 배열하여 문장을 완성하시오.

1 자신의 가방을 잃어버리다니 Helen은 어리석었다.
  (it, Helen, was, of, lose, to, bag, silly, her)

_____

2 그가 영어를 말하는 것은 어려울 것이다.
  (for, be, speak, it, English, him, to, difficult, will)

_____

3 네가 이 주변에서 약국을 찾는 것은 쉬울 것이다.
  (you, be, to, it, find, will, around here, for, easy, a drugstore)

_____

Point 06 to부정사의 의미상의 주어 II / 부정

- 〈It takes+목적격+시간+to-v〉의 구문은 '~가 …하는 데 (시간)이 걸리다'라는 뜻으로, 목적격이 의미상의 주어가 된다. 〈It takes+시간+for+목적격+to-v〉로 나타낼 수도 있다.
  It takes *me* an hour **to get** there.
  → **It takes** an hour *for me* **to get** there.
- to부정사의 부정형은 to부정사 앞에 부정어(not, never 등)를 쓴다.
  She told me **not to be** late again.

A 다음 밑줄 친 부분을 어법에 맞게 고쳐 쓰시오.

1 It took <u>of him</u> a week to read this book.

2 They warned me <u>to not touch</u> the button.

3 It took a month <u>us</u> to finish the project.

4 Doctors advise people <u>to skip not</u> meals.

5 It took <u>for a few minutes</u> for her to eat the chocolate.

B 다음 밑줄 친 부분을 to부정사의 부정형으로 바꿔 문장을 완성하시오.

1 I promised <u>to miss</u> the class again.
→ I _____.

2 She told me <u>to read</u> the story.
→ She _____.

3 He decided <u>to buy</u> an outdoor jacket.
→ He _____.

C 다음 우리말과 같은 뜻이 되도록 (   ) 안의 말을 이용하여 문장을 완성하시오.

1 우리는 산을 오르는 데 5시간이 걸렸다. (climb)
It _____ _____ _____ _____ _____ _____
_____ the mountain.

2 오디션을 통과하다니 그녀는 운이 좋다. (lucky, pass)
It is _____ _____ _____ _____ _____ the audition.

3 당신은 당신 아들에게 파티에 가지 말라고 말했나요? (tell, go)
Did you _____ _____ _____ _____ _____
to the party?

to부정사의 시제와 수동태

■ to부정사의 시제는 문장의 시제와 같은 때나 그 이후를 나타낼 경우에는 〈to-v〉의 형태로, 문장의 시제보다 앞설 경우에는 〈to have v-ed〉의 형태로 나타낸다.

Alex seems to be in a hurry. (단순부정사: to-v)

← **It seems that Alex is** in a hurry.

Alex seems to have been in a hurry. (완료부정사: to have v-ed)

← **It seems that Alex was** in a hurry.

■ to부정사의 수동태는 의미상의 주어가 행위의 영향을 받는 경우에 쓴다.

Justin likes **to be chosen** as a team leader. (단순수동태: to be v-ed)

She was happy **to have been named** MVP of that game. (완료수동태: to have been v-ed)

★ **PLUS TIP** 〈seem to-v〉는 '~인 것 같다'라는 의미로, 〈It seems that 주어+동사〉 형태로 바꾸어 쓸 수 있다.

A 다음 두 문장이 같은 뜻이 되도록 문장을 완성하시오.

1 He seems to have a secret.

→ It seems _____.

2 Paul is sorry that he made a mistake.

→ Paul is sorry _____.

3 It seems that she is a good teacher.

→ She _____.

4 It seems that my parents enjoyed the movie.

→ My parents _____.

5 It seems that visitors are allowed here.

→ Visitors _____.

B 다음 우리말과 같은 뜻이 되도록 ( ) 안의 말을 배열하여 문장을 완성하시오.

1 그들은 오랜 친구들인 것 같다. (old, seem, friends, to, they, be)

_____

2 Matthew는 그들이 걱정하지 않기를 바랐다. (not, Matthew, them, worry, to, wanted)

_____

3 Alice는 살이 빠진 것 같다. (weight, Alice, have, to, lost, seems)

_____

4 네 방은 청소될 필요가 있다. (be, needs, your, to, room, cleaned)

_____

독립부정사

■ 독립부정사는 관용적인 표현으로, 문장 전체를 수식하는 부사의 역할을 한다.

to tell (you) the truth	'사실대로 말하면'	to begin with	'우선', '먼저'
to make matters worse	'설상가상으로'	so to speak	'말하자면'
strange to say	'이상한 이야기지만'	needless to say	'말할 필요도 없이'
to be frank	'솔직히 말하면'	not to mention	'~은 말할 것도 없이'
to be sure	'확실히'	to make a long story short	'간단히 말하면'

To tell the truth, I lost your camera.
To make matters worse, it began to rain.

To begin with, you should follow the rules.
Needless to say, this is for you.

A 다음 우리말과 같은 뜻이 되도록 문장을 완성하시오.

1 말하자면, 그는 천재예요.
He is a genius, _____.

2 우선, 이 방은 너무 작아요.
_____, this room is too small.

3 설상가상으로, 버스가 늦게 왔다.
_____, the bus came late.

4 솔직히 말하면, 나는 네가 옳다고 생각하지 않아.
_____, I don't think you are right.

5 이상한 이야기지만, 나는 가끔 내 개가 무섭다.
_____, I'm sometimes afraid of my dog.

B 다음 문장을 밑줄 친 부분에 유의하여 우리말로 해석하시오.

1 He is smart, <u>not to mention</u> handsome.
_____

2 <u>To tell the truth</u>, he asked me for your name.
_____

3 <u>To make a long story short</u>, I need some time alone.
_____

4 <u>Needless to say</u>, he will come to see me soon.
_____

5 <u>To be sure</u>, this is not my favorite film.
_____

Chapter 02

[01-03] 다음 빈칸에 알맞은 말을 고르시오.

01

Robert is _____ to win in a TV quiz show.

① so smart   ② too smart
③ enough smart   ④ smart enough
⑤ enough to smart

02

It is possible _____ to run 100 meters in 12 seconds.

① him   ② to him   ③ of him
④ with him   ⑤ for him

03

He made his friend _____ to the concert with him.

① to go   ② go   ③ went
④ going   ⑤ to going

04

다음 빈칸에 공통으로 들어갈 말은?

- It took two months _____ her to finish her novel.
- It was important _____ him to find a solution.

① to   ② of   ③ for
④ with   ⑤ by

[05-06] 다음 빈칸에 들어갈 수 <u>없는</u> 말을 고르시오.

05

It was _____ of her to do such a thing.

① kind   ② wise
③ nice   ④ necessary
⑤ careless

06

She _____ me play the piano.

① made   ② heard
③ let   ④ watched
⑤ ordered

[07-09] 빈칸에 들어갈 말이 순서대로 알맞게 짝지어진 것을 고르시오.

07

- It is _____ cold to play outside.
- Tony had his brother _____ the soccer ball.

① so – bring   ② too – bring
③ so – to bring   ④ too – to bring
⑤ not – bringing

08

- Her poem is good enough _____ to win the prize.
- There are more exciting stories _____ by Amy.

① for her – to be told   ② for her – to tell
③ of her – to be told   ④ of her – to tell
⑤ to her – to be told

09

- _____ with, I don't like the food at this restaurant.
- Strange _____, I suddenly forgot my ID number.

① Begin – say   ② To begin – say
③ To begin – to say   ④ Beginning – to say
⑤ Beginning – saying

10

다음 빈칸에 to가 들어갈 수 <u>없는</u> 것은?

① It is great _____ travel alone.
② He felt the building _____ shake.
③ She asked him _____ join the club.
④ I helped them _____ wrap the presents.
⑤ We didn't know how _____ open the bottle.

기출응용

11

다음 우리말과 같은 뜻이 되도록 주어진 말을 배열할 때, 네 번째에 올 단어는?

Brian은 사랑에 빠졌던 것 같다.
(to, in love, fallen, seems, Brian, have)

① to   ② seems   ③ fallen
④ love   ⑤ have

12

다음 중 의미가 나머지와 <u>다른</u> 것은?

① I was too angry to talk to him.
② I was very angry, so I couldn't talk to him.
③ I was so angry that I could talk to him.
④ I was so angry, so I couldn't talk to him.
⑤ I couldn't talk to him because I was very angry.

13

다음 우리말을 영어로 바르게 옮긴 것은?

그녀는 나에게 그것에 대해 생각하지 말라고 조언했다.

① She advised me not think about it.
② She advised me to think not about it.
③ She advised me not to think about it.
④ She didn't advise me to think about it.
⑤ She didn't advise me not to think about it.

14

빈칸에 들어갈 말이 나머지와 <u>다른</u> 것은?

① It was nice _____ him to pay for me.
② It is necessary _____ us to drive there.
③ It is possible _____ me to eat with my hands.
④ It took five years _____ them to build the house.
⑤ It is difficult _____ her to speak in front of others.

15

다음 밑줄 친 부분을 바르게 고치지 <u>않은</u> 것은?

① <u>Begin with</u>, I didn't touch anything here.
   → To begin with
② The fairy tale is <u>too</u> funny that children love it.   → so
③ It takes three hours <u>getting</u> to Busan by KTX.
                    → get
④ <u>He</u> seems that he has a high fever.
   → It
⑤ Mr. Kim makes his students <u>cleaning</u> the classroom.   → clean

[16 – 17] 다음 밑줄 친 부분이 어법상 **틀린** 것을 고르시오.

16
① She made them wash her car.
② He expected her to accept his proposal.
③ It was cruel of her to say nothing to you.
④ I heard someone to come into the house.
⑤ To tell the truth, I don't know anything about it.

17
① He seems to be a police officer.
② I watched her swim in the lake.
③ She is kind, not to mention cute.
④ Susan had Mike to fix her hair dryer.
⑤ They allowed us to attend the meeting.

18
(A), (B), (C)의 괄호 안에서 알맞은 것끼리 바르게 짝지어진 것은?

(A) We saw a dance team [to wait / waiting] to go on stage.
(B) The English teacher made us [speak / to speak] clearly.
(C) Billy seems [having / to have] trouble memorizing his lines.

	(A)	(B)	(C)
①	to wait	speak	having
②	to wait	to speak	having
③	waiting	speak	having
④	waiting	to speak	to have
⑤	waiting	speak	to have

고난도

19
다음 두 문장이 같은 뜻이 되도록 할 때 잘못된 것은?

① It seems that he was a musician.
  → He seems to be a musician.
② You are too weak to go backpacking.
  → You are so weak that you can't go backpacking.
③ She showed them how to use chopsticks.
  → She showed them how they should use chopsticks.
④ To turn off one's cell phone in a theater is essential.
  → It is essential to turn off one's cell phone in a theater.
⑤ She sang loudly enough to wake up her son.
  → She sang so loudly that she could wake up her son.

기출응용

20
다음 중 어법상 틀린 문장의 개수는?

(a) To be frank, I'm very busy right now.
(b) This cap is too small for an adult to wearing.
(c) I am so glad to have been given this opportunity.
(d) It took one and a half hours for us to get to Jeju Island.
(e) He helped me organize my desk.

① 1개   ② 2개   ③ 3개   ④ 4개   ⑤ 5개

01

주어진 말을 이용하여 우리말과 뜻이 같도록 문장을 완성하시오.

(1) 그는 나에게 그 화초에 물을 주라고 말했다. (tell, water)

→ He _____ _____ _____

_____ the plants.

(2) Stella는 그가 그녀의 집까지 태워다 주도록 했다. (get, drive)

→ Stella _____ _____ _____

_____ her home.

02

주어진 말을 알맞게 배열하여 우리말과 뜻이 같도록 문장을 완성하시오.

(1) 나는 도서관에 가는 데 한 시간이 걸렸다.

(get, an hour, me, to the library, it, to, took)

→ _____

(2) 내가 지금 떠나는 것은 불가능하다.

(for, impossible, now, me, is, to, it, leave)

→ _____

03

주어진 말을 이용하여 대화를 완성하시오.

(1) A: Where's his wallet?

B: He seems _____ _____

_____ _____. (lose it)

(2) A: Why did they keep silent?

B: Julie asked _____ _____

_____ _____ anything. (not, say)

04

다음 두 문장을 한 문장으로 만들 때, 빈칸에 알맞은 말을 쓰시오.

(1) He wants to learn how to play the violin.

I can help him.

→ I can help him _____.

(2) You told him a lie.

You were stupid.

→ It was stupid _____.

05

다음 그림을 보고, to부정사를 이용하여 문장을 완성하시오.

(1) The dog runs _____ _____ _____

_____ _____ _____ _____.

(fast, the boy, follow)

(2) The bag is _____ _____ _____

_____ _____ _____.

(light, her, carry)

06

다음 표를 보고, 문장을 완성하시오.

Name	Time	What
Maria	10 a.m. - 11 a.m.	Run 10 km
Judy	3 p.m. - 6 p.m.	Read the book

(1) It took an hour _____ _____ _____

_____ _____ _____.

(2) It took Judy _____ _____ _____

_____ _____ _____.

S E L F   N O T E

핵심 포인트 정리하기

1 to부정사의 구문

- 〈① _____ + 형용사 / 부사 + _____〉: '너무 ~해서 …할 수 없다'
- 〈형용사 / 부사 + ② _____ + _____〉: '…할 만큼 충분히 ~하다'

2 목적격 보어로 쓰이는 부정사

to부정사		want, expect, tell, ask, allow, order, advise (* help의 목적격 보어: to부정사와 원형부정사 둘 다 가능)
③ _____	사역동사	make, have, let *사역의 의미가 있는 get의 목적격 보어: ④ _____
	지각동사	see, hear, feel, watch 등

동사에 따른 목적격 보어의 부정사 형태 구분하기!

3 to부정사의 의미상의 주어

- 일반적인 의미상의 주어: 〈for + 목적격〉
  사람의 성격·성품을 나타내는 형용사가 보어로 사용된 경우: 〈⑤ _____ + 목적격〉
- 〈It takes + 목적격 + 시간 + to-v〉 → 〈It takes + 시간 + ⑥ _____ + 목적격 + to-v〉: '~가 …하는 데 (시간)이 걸리다'
- to부정사의 부정형: 〈not / never + to-v〉

to부정사의 의미상의 주어 앞에 쓰는 전치사 구분하기!

4 to부정사의 시제와 수동태

- 문장의 시제와 to부정사의 시제가 같을 때: 단순부정사 〈to-v〉
- 문장의 시제보다 to부정사의 시제가 앞설 때: 완료부정사 〈⑦ _____〉
- 〈⑧ _____〉 → 〈It seems that + 주어 + 동사〉
- 의미상의 주어가 행위의 영향을 받는 경우: 단순수동태 〈to be v-ed〉 / 완료수동태 〈to have been v-ed〉

5 독립부정사

to begin with: '우선', '먼저' / ⑨ _____: '말하자면' / to make matters worse: '설상가상으로'
⑩ _____: '솔직히 말하면' / to be sure: '확실히' / to tell (you) the truth: '사실대로 말하면'

문제로 개념 다지기

밑줄 친 부분이 어법상 맞으면 O, 틀리면 X 표시하고 바르게 고치시오.

1 My French fries are salty too to eat without Coke.

2 It was exciting of me to go to the festival.

3 You seem expect him to stay here.

4 Nancy lets him to know when he should come back home.

5 She got me to bring her suitcase from the car.

6 It took only half an hour him to read the article.

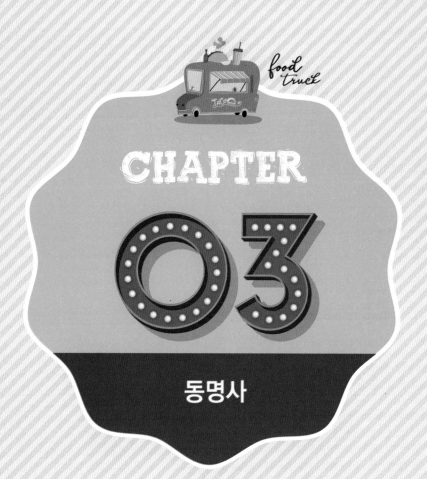

CHAPTER

03

동명사

I keep **thinking** about the novel that I read.
They <u>forgot</u> **meeting** their tennis coach.　　[forget+동명사: ~한 것을 잊다]
They <u>forgot</u> **to meet** their tennis coach.　　[forget+to부정사: ~할 것을 잊다]

동명사

<동사원형+-ing>의 형태로, 문장 안에서 명사처럼 주어, 보어, 목적어 역할을 합니다. 동명사는 현재분사와 형태는 같지만 동명사가 명사, 현재분사는 형용사의 역할을 한다는 점에서 차이가 있습니다. 동명사와 to부정사가 문장 안에서 목적어 역할을 할 경우, 동명사만을 혹은 to부정사만을 목적어로 취하는 동사들이 있으니 기억해 두어야 합니다. 둘 다를 목적어로 취하는 동사들도 있는데, 이 경우에는 각각의 의미가 다를 수도 있다는 것을 알아 두세요.

동명사의 역할 – 주어 / 보어 / 목적어

■ 동명사는 〈동사원형+-ing〉의 형태로 문장에서 주어, 보어, 목적어 역할을 한다.

Exploring new places is very interesting. (주어)
= To explore

My job is **creating** ads. (보어)
　　　　= to create

Children *enjoy* **celebrating** Halloween. (동사의 목적어)

She is scared *of* **staying** home alone. (전치사의 목적어)

★ PLUS TIP　주어로 쓰인 동명사(구)는 단수 취급한다.

A 다음 주어진 문장과 같은 뜻이 되도록 문장을 완성하시오.

1 To walk around the lake is relaxing.

→ _____ is relaxing.

2 My hobby is to do puzzles.

→ My hobby is _____.

3 It is rude to send text messages during class.

→ _____ is rude.

4 Helen started to take yoga classes in the morning.

→ Helen started _____ in the morning.

5 The couple left the restaurant. They didn't have any dessert.

→ The couple left the restaurant without _____.

B 다음 우리말과 같은 뜻이 되도록 ( ) 안의 말을 이용하여 문장을 완성하시오.

1 규칙적으로 운동을 하는 것은 건강에 좋다. (exercise, regularly)

_____ _____ is good for one's health.

2 너는 소풍 가는 것에 관심이 있니? (interested in)

Are you _____ _____ _____ on a picnic?

3 내가 제일 좋아하는 것은 산에 오르는 것이다. (climb)

My favorite thing _____ _____ mountains.

4 나는 매주 금요일마다 피아노 치는 것을 연습한다. (play)

I practice _____ _____ _____ every Friday.

5 John은 너무 많이 말하는 것을 좋아하지 않는다. (talk)

John _____ _____ _____ too much.

Point 02 동명사의 의미상의 주어 / 부정

- 동명사의 의미상의 주어는 동명사가 말하는 행위의 주체를 나타내는 것으로 동명사 앞에 소유격이나 목적격을 써서 나타낸다.
  I don't like **your[you]** eating snacks too much.
- 동명사의 의미상의 주어가 문장의 주어 혹은 목적어와 같거나 일반인인 경우에는 의미상의 주어를 쓰지 않는다.
- 동명사의 부정형은 동명사 앞에 부정어(not, never 등)를 쓴다.
  I'm thinking about **not leaving** this week.

A 다음 밑줄 친 부분을 어법에 맞게 고쳐 쓰시오.

1 I'm sorry for <u>she</u> laughing at you.

2 I'm worried about <u>he</u> being late.

3 Mark was surprised by <u>I</u> shouting at him.

B 다음 두 문장이 같은 뜻이 되도록 〈보기〉와 같이 바꾸어 쓰시오.

〈보기〉 She hates that he wastes time. → She hates his[him] wasting time.

1 We feared that he might return to the hospital.
→ We feared _____ .

2 Do you mind if I turn off the light?
→ Do you mind _____ ?

C 다음 우리말과 같은 뜻이 되도록 ( ) 안의 말을 배열하여 문장을 완성하시오.

1 너무 과속하지 않는 것이 중요하다. (too, driving, not, fast)
_____ is important.

2 그녀는 그가 서울로 오는 것에 들떴다. (his, to, about, Seoul, coming)
She was excited _____ .

3 나는 그가 내 전화를 받지 않아서 혼란스러웠다. (my calls, not, by, answering, his)
I was confused _____ .

4 내가 제시간에 오지 않은 것을 용서해 줘. (not, on time, coming, for)
Forgive me _____ .

5 그는 그녀가 자신의 생일을 기억하지 못하는 것에 화가 나 있다.
(her, remembering, not, about, his birthday)
He's angry _____ .

동명사의 시제와 수동태

■ 동명사의 시제는 문장의 시제와 같을 때나 그 이후 시점인 경우 〈동사원형+-ing〉의 형태로, 문장의 시제보다
앞선 시점인 경우 〈having v-ed〉의 형태로 쓴다.
I am proud of **being** her best friend. (단순동명사: v-ing)
Matt denied **having seen** the accident. (완료동명사: having v-ed)
■ 동명사의 수동태는 동명사가 나타내는 의미가 수동인 경우에 쓴다.
We are tired of **being treated** poorly. (단순수동태: being v-ed)
He complained about **having been insulted** in front of others. (완료수동태: having been v-ed)

A 다음 두 문장이 같은 뜻이 되도록 〈보기〉와 같이 동명사를 이용하여 문장을 완성하시오.

> 〈보기〉 I dislike that I am treated like a fool.
> → I dislike being treated like a fool.

1 We suggest that we have a barbecue party tonight.
→ We suggest _____.

2 She complained that she was stuck in traffic.
→ She complained about _____.

3 Annie regrets that she didn't take care of herself.
→ Annie regrets _____.

4 I am sorry that I spilled water on your notebook.
→ I am sorry for _____.

B 다음 우리말과 같은 뜻이 되도록 동명사와 ( ) 안의 말을 이용하여 문장을 완성하시오.

1 그는 시험에서 실수했던 것을 인정한다. (make a mistake)
He admits _____ _____ _____ _____ on the test.

2 Jean은 공부하는 동안 방해받는 것을 싫어한다. (bother)
Jean hates _____ _____ while she studies.

3 Ellen은 어제 운동장에서 넘어졌던 것이 창피하다. (fall down)
Ellen is ashamed of _____ _____ _____ on the playground
yesterday.

4 나는 파티에 초대받는 것이 기쁘다. (invite)
I'm happy about _____ _____ to the parties.

동명사와 현재분사

- 동명사와 현재분사는 둘 다 〈동사원형+-ing〉의 형태이지만 동명사는 명사 역할을, 현재분사는 형용사 역할을 한다는 점이 다르다.

  His job is **playing** the guitar in a band. (동명사: ~하는 것(이다))

  Steven is **playing** the guitar. (현재분사: ~하고 있는)

- 동명사와 현재분사가 명사 앞에 오는 경우, 동명사는 뒤에 오는 명사의 용도나 목적을, 현재분사는 수식하는 명사의 진행 및 능동을 나타낸다.

  I need to bring a **sleeping** bag on our camping trip. (동명사: ~을 위한, ~로 사용되는)

  She looked at the **sleeping** baby in the bed. (현재분사: ~하고 있는)

★ **내신만점 TIP** 형태가 동일한 동명사와 현재분사의 역할과 의미를 구분하자.

A 다음 밑줄 친 부분이 동명사인지 현재분사인지 〈 〉 안에 쓰시오.

1 A <u>rolling</u> stone gathers no moss. 〈   〉

2 We should respect all <u>living</u> things. 〈   〉

3 I saw a <u>crying</u> girl in the playground. 〈   〉

4 Andrew works for a <u>broadcasting</u> company. 〈   〉

5 Serena is <u>reading</u> mystery stories on the sofa. 〈   〉

6 I don't know how to use this <u>washing</u> machine. 〈   〉

7 One of my hobbies is <u>taking</u> pictures and <u>posting</u> them on my blog. 〈   〉

8 I love <u>teaching</u> classical music to my students. 〈   〉

9 <u>Translating</u> a language accurately is not easy. 〈   〉

10 The boy <u>putting</u> on his shoes over there is David. 〈   〉

11 I just finished <u>writing</u> my English essay. 〈   〉

12 Dad is <u>hanging</u> our new curtains on the windows. 〈   〉

B 다음 문장을 밑줄 친 부분에 유의하여 우리말로 해석하시오.

1 The girl <u>drawing</u> the cartoon is my friend.

2 It can be dangerous to take <u>sleeping</u> pills.

3 There are a lot of people <u>swimming</u> in the sea.

4 One of his hobbies is <u>cooking</u> Italian food.

5 He found his name on the <u>waiting</u> list.

6 There isn't a <u>smoking</u> area in this restaurant.

동명사 목적어 vs. to부정사 목적어

- 동명사만을 목적어로 취하는 동사에는 enjoy, keep, mind, avoid, finish, deny, quit, give up, consider 등이 있다.
  He *kept* **asking** Jane to participate in the meeting.
- to부정사만을 목적어로 취하는 동사에는 want, hope, wish, decide, expect, plan, promise, refuse 등이 있다.
  They *decided* **to help** their teacher decorate their classroom.

A 다음 ( ) 안의 말을 빈칸에 적절한 형태로 써넣으시오.

1 Paul wanted _____ her to open a restaurant. (persuade)

2 Do you mind _____ a message for Jason? (leave)

3 I've finished _____ the article about new technology. (read)

4 My parents decided not _____ me drive their car. (let)

5 Brad promised _____ Julie to the festival. (take)

6 Julia tried to avoid _____ him the secret. (tell)

7 I refused _____ to his advice. (listen)

8 Mary hoped _____ a famous writer in the future. (become)

9 Please consider _____ with me here a little longer. (stay)

10 She expected _____ to the final round of the audition. (make it)

B 다음 우리말과 같은 뜻이 되도록 ( ) 안의 말을 이용하여 문장을 완성하시오.

1 우리 형은 새 자동차를 사는 것을 포기했다. (buy)
My brother _____ _____ _____ a new car.

2 Neil은 이번 일요일에 집들이할 계획이다. (have)
Neil _____ _____ _____ a housewarming party this Sunday.

3 그들은 주말에 쇼핑하러 가는 것을 피한다. (go shopping)
They _____ _____ _____ on weekends.

4 너는 왜 계속 나에게 전화를 하니? (call)
Why do you _____ _____ _____ ?

5 Sue는 그녀의 외국인 친구들과 대화하는 것을 즐긴다. (talk to)
Sue _____ _____ _____ her foreign friends.

6 그녀는 밤에 더 잘 자기 위해서 커피 마시는 것을 그만뒀다. (drink)
She _____ _____ _____ to sleep better at night.

동명사와 to부정사를 목적어로 취하는 동사

- 동명사와 to부정사를 모두 목적어로 취하고, 서로 의미 차이가 거의 없는 동사에는 like, love, hate, start, begin, continue 등이 있다.
  Dana *started* **doing[to do]** the laundry.
- 동명사와 to부정사를 모두 목적어로 취하지만, 의미 차이가 있는 동사에는 remember, forget, regret, try 등이 있다.
  Tony *remembered* **meeting** Jennifer. (동명사: ~한 것을 기억하다)
  Tony *remembered* **to meet** Jennifer. (to부정사: ~할 것을 기억하다)

★ 내신만점 *TIP* 동사 stop 뒤에는 동명사와 to부정사가 모두 올 수 있지만, 동명사는 stop의 목적어로 쓰이는 반면, to부정사는 목적을 나타내는 부사적 용법으로 쓰인다는 것을 알아두자.
Greg *stopped* **listening** to music. (동명사: ~하는 것을 멈추다)
Greg *stopped* **to listen** to music. (to부정사: ~하기 위해 멈추다)

A 다음 두 문장이 같은 뜻이 되도록 문장을 완성하시오.

1 Suddenly it started raining.
→ Suddenly it started _____.

2 Justin has begun to learn to swim.
→ Justin has begun _____ to swim.

3 He continued to give lectures until he died.
→ He continued _____ lectures until he died.

4 They like eating bread with honey and butter.
→ They like _____ bread with honey and butter.

B 다음 우리말과 같은 뜻이 되도록 (   ) 안의 말을 이용하여 문장을 완성하시오.

1 그녀는 그를 비웃은 것을 후회했다. (laugh at)
She _____ _____ _____ him.

2 나는 살을 빼려고 노력했다. (lose)
I _____ _____ _____ weight.

3 Jenny는 길을 물어보기 위해 멈추었다. (ask)
Jenny _____ _____ _____ for directions.

4 Martin은 저녁식사 후에 숙제할 것을 기억했다. (do)
Martin _____ _____ _____ his homework after dinner.

5 Michelle은 그에게 책을 돌려줄 것을 잊었다. (return)
Michelle _____ _____ _____ the book to him.

동명사 주요 구문 I

I **feel like** *walking* down the street. (feel like v-ing: ~하고 싶다)
The boy **is used to** *using* chopsticks. (be used to v-ing: ~하는 것에 익숙하다)
It's no use *crying* over spilt milk. (It's no use v-ing: ~해 봐야 소용없다)
They **were busy** *preparing* for the festival. (be busy v-ing: ~하느라 바쁘다)
Paul sometimes **goes** *fishing* with his father. (go v-ing: ~하러 가다)
I **look forward to** *working* with you. (look forward to v-ing: ~하기를 고대하다)
The Rocky Mountains **are worth** *visiting* at least once. (be worth v-ing: ~할 가치가 있다)

A 다음 우리말과 같은 뜻이 되도록 ( ) 안의 말을 이용하여 문장을 완성하시오.

1 이번 주말에 등산하러 가는 게 어때? (climb)
Why don't we _____ _____ this weekend?

2 그는 전화를 받느라 바빴다. (answer)
He _____ _____ _____ phone calls.

3 그 영화는 다시 볼 가치가 있다. (watch)
The movie _____ _____ _____ again.

4 그녀는 혼자 먹는 것에 익숙하지 않았다. (eat)
She _____ _____ _____ _____ alone.

5 저는 당신의 부모님을 만날 것을 고대합니다. (meet)
I _____ _____ _____ _____ your parents.

B 다음 우리말과 같은 뜻이 되도록 ( ) 안의 말을 배열하여 문장을 완성하시오.

1 그녀는 자러 가고 싶었다. (going, like, she, bed, to, felt)

_____

2 나는 중국어를 읽는 것에 익숙하다. (Chinese, to, used, I'm, reading)

_____

3 그 사안은 논의할 가치가 있다. (worth, the issue, discussing, is)

_____

4 우리는 주방을 청소하느라 바빴다. (were, the kitchen, we, cleaning, busy)

_____

5 이 호텔에서는 서비스에 대해 불평해 봐야 소용없다.
(the service, use, complaining, no, about, it's)

_____ in this hotel.

동명사 주요 구문 II

I **spent three hours** *writing* a letter. (spend+시간[돈]+(on) v-ing: ~하는 데 시간[돈]을 쓰다)
There is no *looking* back now. (There is no v-ing: ~할 수 없다, ~하는 것은 불가능하다)
He **had trouble** *finding* a part-time job. (have trouble[difficulty] (in) v-ing: ~하는 데 어려움을 겪다)
Keep the kids **from** *touching* the glass. (keep[prevent]+목적어+from v-ing: ~가 …하는 것을 막다)
On *receiving* his call, I went out to meet him. (On[Upon] v-ing: ~하자마자)
How about *eating* out for dinner? (How[What] about v-ing?: ~하는 게 어때?)
It is quiet, but I **can't help** *laughing*. (can't help v-ing / can't (help) but+동사원형: ~하지 않을 수 없다)

A 다음 두 문장이 같은 뜻이 되도록 문장을 완성하시오.

1 It is impossible to avoid tests.
→ _____ tests.

2 Why don't we eat Japanese food?
→ _____ Japanese food?

3 I couldn't help but skip class that day.
→ I _____ that day.

4 It is difficult for many people to speak to strangers.
→ Many people _____ to strangers.

5 The airplane couldn't take off because of the storm.
→ The storm _____ .

B 다음 우리말과 같은 뜻이 되도록 (   ) 안의 말을 이용하여 문장을 완성하시오

1 Julia는 아파트를 얻는 데 어려움을 겪었다. (get)
Julia _____ _____ _____ an apartment.

2 그를 돕는 것은 불가능하다. (help)
_____ _____ _____ _____ him.

3 Steven은 그의 휴대전화를 고치는 데 많은 돈을 썼다. (much, fix)
Steven _____ _____ _____ _____ his cell phone.

4 집에 돌아오자마자, 그 소년은 엄마에게 달려갔다. (return)
_____ _____ _____ , the boy ran to his mom.

5 나는 너를 봤을 때 네 이름을 부르지 않을 수 없었다. (help, call)
I _____ _____ _____ _____ _____ when I saw you.

Chapter 03

내신대비 TEST

[01-03] 다음 빈칸에 알맞은 말을 고르시오.

01

David enjoys _____ badminton every Sunday.

① play
③ playing
⑤ with playing

② to play
④ be playing

02

Christine spent her vacation _____ abroad.

① travel
③ traveling
⑤ to traveling

② to travel
④ of traveling

03

They talked about _____ quitting his job.

① he
③ them
⑤ him

② your
④ hers

[04-05] 다음 빈칸에 들어갈 수 없는 말을 고르시오.

04

She _____ talking on the phone.

① hoped   ② started   ③ stopped
④ began   ⑤ kept

05

Mark _____ to send Christmas cards to his friends.

① loved   ② wanted   ③ gave up
④ remembered   ⑤ forgot

[06-07] 다음 밑줄 친 부분의 쓰임이 나머지와 다른 것을 고르시오.

06

① <u>Visiting</u> small towns is very fun.
② I'm sorry for <u>making</u> you wait so long.
③ I like <u>playing</u> basketball with my friends.
④ He is <u>learning</u> French these days.
⑤ I don't mind <u>opening</u> the window.

07

① Jane wanted to take a <u>cooking</u> class.
② We want better <u>working</u> conditions.
③ Do you know where the <u>waiting</u> room is?
④ I went to the <u>swimming</u> pool.
⑤ There are many <u>sleeping</u> people on the bus.

08

다음 대화의 빈칸에 알맞은 말은?

A: How was the Great Wall of China?
B: Amazing. _____

① I forgot to see it.
② I'll never forget to see it.
③ I'll never forget seeing it.
④ I'll never remember to see it.
⑤ I'll never remember seeing it.

09

- _____ hearing his voice, I knew it was Ted.
- What _____ having a sandwich for lunch?

① In – on
② On – for
③ In – for
④ On – about
⑤ For – about

10

- He is used _____ very salty food.
- The national park is worth _____ at least once in your lifetime.

① eating – visiting
② to eat – to visit
③ to eat – visiting
④ to eating – to visit
⑤ to eating – visiting

11

- We decided _____ some money.
- I regret _____ to her, so I'll apologize.

① saving – lie
② saving – to lie
③ saving – lying
④ to save – lying
⑤ to save – to lie

12

다음 우리말을 영어로 바르게 옮긴 것은?

나는 그가 그녀를 슬프게 하는 것이 걱정된다.

① I'm worried about making her sad.
② I'm worried about his making her sad.
③ I'm worried about he made her sad.
④ I'm worried about he making her sad.
⑤ He's worried about making her sad.

[13-15] 다음 밑줄 친 부분이 어법상 틀린 것을 고르시오.

13

① I failed to finish the project on time.
② He kept practicing for the recital.
③ Frank hates not being on time.
④ I am considering to run a race next week.
⑤ On answering John's call, she smiled happily.

14

① I'm tired of waiting for you.
② She denies to make a mistake.
③ Her dream is winning the Nobel Prize.
④ He remembered seeing her before.
⑤ These balloons will be used to decorate the room.

15

① It continued to snow.
② She is busy preparing lunch.
③ The man had difficulty to breathe.
④ I didn't expect to meet him there.
⑤ He started learning salsa dancing as a hobby.

16

다음 중 어법상 옳은 것끼리 짝지어진 것은?

(a) She avoids to go on a date with Jim.
(b) He began riding a bike when he was five.
(c) We're looking forward to opening our own bookstore.
(d) Don't forget taking the medicine after meals.

① (a), (b)   ② (a), (c)   ③ (b), (c)
④ (b), (d)   ⑤ (c), (d)

17

다음 중 어법상 <u>틀린</u> 문장의 개수는?

(a) I'm not used to wear glasses.
(b) She is ashamed of be rejected by the company.
(c) Kyle hates lending his things to others.
(d) Do you mind me turn down the volume?

① 0개   ② 1개   ③ 2개   ④ 3개   ⑤ 4개

18

다음 우리말을 영어로 바르게 옮긴 것은?

① 나는 오후 7시 이후에 먹지 않으려고 노력 중이다.
   I'm trying not eating after 7 p.m.
② 그의 위대한 작품들을 잊는 것은 불가능하다.
   There is no forgetting his great works.
③ Bill은 그녀가 오기를 고대하고 있다.
   Bill is looking forward to her to come.
④ 나는 외출하고 싶지 않다.
   I don't feel like to go out.
⑤ 그녀는 새로운 언어를 배우는 데 어려움을 겪었다.
   She had trouble to learn a new language.

19

(A), (B), (C)의 괄호 안에서 알맞은 것끼리 바르게 짝지어진 것은?

(A) They refused [to vote / voting] for her.
(B) The movie started, so we stopped [to talk / talking].
(C) They were surprised at [me / for me] passing the exam.

	(A)	(B)	(C)
①	to vote	to talk	me
②	to vote	talking	me
③	to vote	talking	for me
④	voting	to talk	for me
⑤	voting	talking	for me

20

다음 밑줄 친 부분을 바르게 고치지 <u>않은</u> 것은?

① Ted was busy <u>to treating</u> patients all morning.   → to treat
② He denies <u>have cheated</u> on the exam.
          → having cheated
③ Her daughter is afraid of <u>fly</u> in airplanes.
          → flying
④ Dad promised <u>take</u> me to the amusement park.   → to take
⑤ I was disappointed with <u>they</u> not coming to the meeting.   → their

01

주어진 말을 이용하여 우리말과 뜻이 같도록 문장을 완성하시오.

(1) 나는 생일 선물을 받는 것이 기쁘다. (given)

→ I'm happy about _____ _____ a birthday gift.

(2) 그녀에게 계속해서 사과해 봐야 소용없다.

(no use, apologize)

→ It's _____ _____ _____ to her over and over again.

02

다음 주어진 문장과 같은 뜻이 되도록 동명사를 이용하여 빈칸에 알맞은 말을 쓰시오.

(1) He worked at a restaurant. Jenny knew about it.

→ Jenny knew about _____ _____

_____ _____ _____.

(2) It was too noisy, so I couldn't help but speak loudly.

→ It was too noisy, so I _____ _____

_____ _____.

03

주어진 말을 이용하여 대화를 완성하시오.

A: I _____ _____ _____ _____

_____ in the room.

(keep, my son, run)

B: Why did you do that?

A: Because there was a complaint from a neighbor.

04

다음 Paul의 수첩을 보고, 문장을 완성하시오.

해야 할 일	실행 여부
(1) send an email	X
(2) play tennis	X
(3) run for an hour	O

(1) Paul forgot _____ _____ _____

_____.

(2) The rain prevented Paul _____ _____

_____.

(3) Paul spent _____ _____ _____ _____.

05

다음 대화를 읽고, 같은 뜻이 되도록 문장을 완성하시오.

(1) Maria: I don't eat vegetables.

Dr. Lee: That is not good for your health.

→ _____ _____ _____ isn't good for your health.

(2) Maria: I got an A in science.

Mother: I'm proud of you.

→ Maria's mother is proud of Maria for

_____ _____ _____ _____

_____ _____.

고난도

06

다음 이메일을 읽고, 틀린 부분을 모두 찾아 바르게 고쳐 쓰시오. (3군데)

Dear Mina,

Are you used to live in the U.S.? Do you have difficulty speaking English at school? We promised keeping in touch, right? I look forward to hear from you soon.

Sincerely, Junho

핵심 포인트 정리하기

1 동명사: 〈동사원형+-ing〉
- 역할: 주어, 보어, 동사나 전치사의 목적어
- 의미상의 주어: ① _____이나 _____으로 나타냄
- 동명사의 부정형: 〈not/never + 동명사〉
- 완료동명사: 〈② _____〉
- 동명사의 수동태: 〈being v-ed〉, 〈having been v-ed〉

2 동명사 vs. 현재분사
- 동명사: 명사 역할(~하는 것(이다)), 뒤에 오는 명사의 용도나 목적(~을 위한, ~로 사용되는)을 나타냄
- 현재분사: ③ _____ 역할, 수식하는 명사의 진행이나 능동(~하고 있는)을 나타냄

3 동명사 목적어 vs. to부정사 목적어

enjoy, keep, mind, avoid, finish, deny, quit, give up, consider	+ ④ _____
want, hope, wish, decide, expect, plan, promise, refuse	+ ⑤ _____
like, love, hate, start, begin, continue	+동명사/to부정사 (의미 차이 없음)
remember, forget, regret, try	+동명사/to부정사 (의미 차이 있음)

 동명사와 to부정사를 각각 목적어로 취하는 동사, 동명사와 to부정사를 목적어로 취할 때 의미가 달라지는 동사 알아두기!

4 동명사 주요 구문

〈feel like + 동명사〉 '~하고 싶다'

〈⑥ _____ + _____〉 '~하는 것에 익숙하다'

〈look forward to + 동명사〉 '~하기를 고대하다'

〈⑦ _____ + _____〉 '~할 가치가 있다'

〈It's no use + 동명사〉 '~해 봐야 소용없다'

동명사 주요 구문의 형태와 의미 복습하기!

문제로 개념 다지기

밑줄 친 부분이 어법상 맞으면 O, 틀리면 X 표시하고 바르게 고치시오.

1 I regret <u>having not visited</u> my grandfather.

2 It is not easy to stop <u>to run</u> in the middle of a race.

3 Brian decided to continue <u>to study</u> English next year.

4 <u>Not to recycling</u> pollutes our environment.

5 The kids are used to take a nap between 2 and 3 p.m.

6 My mother <u>kept me from to waste</u> electricity.

CHAPTER 04

분사 I

Cindy heard someone **using** a copy machine.　　　　[현재분사]

The manager had the food **served** to the guests.　　[과거분사]

Being on a diet, I try not to eat anything after 6 p.m.　[분사구문]

분사

분사는 문장에서 형용사처럼 명사를 수식하거나 보어 역할을 하는 말로, 능동·진행의 의미인 현재분사(v-ing)와 수동·완료의 의미인 과거분사(v-ed)가 있습니다.

분사구문

분사를 이용하여 〈접속사+주어+동사〉 형태의 부사절을 부사구로 줄여 쓴 분사구문은 문맥에 따라 때, 이유, 동시동작, 연속상황, 조건, 양보의 의미를 나타냅니다.

현재분사 / 과거분사

■ 분사는 문장에서 형용사처럼 명사를 수식하거나 주어·목적어를 설명하는 보어 역할을 한다. 능동·진행의 의미가 있는 현재분사(v-ing)와 수동·완료의 의미가 있는 과거분사(v-ed)가 있다.
The **smiling** girl came and stood by me. (현재분사)
There are **fallen** leaves on the street. (과거분사)

A ( ) 안의 말을 빈칸에 적절한 형태로 써넣으시오.

1 The man opened the _____ door. (lock)

2 I know a tall man _____ Teddy. (name)

3 Who is the girl _____ next to the tree? (stand)

4 The dog was _____ loudly. (bark)

5 Is this a _____ car or a new one? (use)

6 These chairs need to be _____. (repair)

7 The boy _____ on the bench is Brian. (sit)

8 The doctor said my leg was _____. (break)

9 We were _____ together for a while. (walk)

10 The chocolate was _____ in Belgium. (make)

11 The book was _____ by a famous ballerina. (write)

12 The plane _____ for Canada took off from the airport. (leave)

B 다음 우리말과 같은 뜻이 되도록 ( ) 안의 말을 이용하여 문장을 완성하시오.

1 너의 전화가 울리고 있다. (ring)
Your phone _____ _____.

2 이 궁은 1600년대에 지어졌다. (build)
This palace _____ _____ in the 1600s.

3 나는 토스트가 탔기 때문에 먹지 않았다. (burn)
I didn't eat the toast because it _____ _____.

4 이것들은 실종된 아이들의 사진이다. (lose)
These are the photos of _____ _____.

5 그 정치인은 떨리는 목소리로 연설을 했다. (shake)
The politician gave a speech in a _____ _____.

6 많은 유명 인사들이 어젯밤 파티에 초대되었다. (invite)
Many celebrities _____ _____ to the party last night.

능동의 v-ing vs. 수동의 v-ed

■ interest, bore와 같이 감정을 나타내는 동사는 분사형으로 자주 쓰인다. 이때 수식 받는 대상이 '감정을 유발하는' 주체(보통 사물)로 능동의 의미일 때는 현재분사를, '감정을 느끼게 되는' 주체(보통 사람)로 수동의 의미일 때는 과거분사를 쓴다.

I think fashion shows are **interesting**. (현재분사: 감정을 유발하는)
I'm **interested** in fashion. (과거분사: 감정을 느끼는)

★ **내신만점 TIP** 감정을 나타내는 분사를 쓰는 경우 수식하는 대상과의 관계가 능동인지 수동인지 반드시 확인하자.

A ( ) 안의 말을 빈칸에 적절한 형태로 써넣으시오.

1 The lecture was very _____. (bore)
  I was _____ with doing homework.

2 I'm _____. What day is it? (confuse)
  His explanation was really _____.

3 They were _____ at the results. (disappoint)
  My math grades are _____.

4 The food at the restaurant is _____. (satisfy)
  We were _____ with the service.

5 The director's most recent film is quite _____. (excite)
  She was _____ about his coming to see her.

B 다음 우리말과 같은 뜻이 되도록 〈보기〉에서 알맞은 말을 골라 빈칸에 적절한 형태로 써넣으시오.

| 〈보기〉 | tire | embarrass | depress | shock | amaze |

1 그것은 내가 여태껏 본 것 중에 가장 놀라운 공연이었다.
  It was the most _____ performance that I've ever seen.

2 Mary는 넘어지자 창피했다.
  Mary was _____ when she fell down.

3 지난주 뉴스는 우울한 기사들로 가득했다.
  The news was filled with _____ stories last week.

4 우리는 TV에서 재난 현장을 보고 충격을 받았다.
  We were _____ to see the disaster site on TV.

5 그 아이들은 밖에서 놀아서 피곤해졌다.
  The children became _____ from playing outside.

분사의 역할 I – 명사 수식

- 분사는 문장에서 형용사처럼 명사를 수식한다. 분사가 명사를 단독으로 수식할 경우에는 앞에서, 수식어구와 함께 쓰일 경우에는 뒤에서 수식한다.

The children are looking for the **hidden** treasure.

The candles **burning** on the table are beautiful.

A 다음 주어진 문장과 같은 뜻이 되도록 문장을 완성하시오.

1 A girl was hurt in the accident. She is my friend.
→ The girl _____ is my friend.

2 There are many people. They are waiting for the bus.
→ There are many people _____.

3 Do you know the man? He is sitting next to Julie.
→ Do you know the man _____?

4 A green car is parked outside. It is my father's car.
→ The green car _____ is my father's car.

5 She showed me some photos. They were taken by her husband.
→ She showed me some photos _____.

B 다음 우리말과 같은 뜻이 되도록 (   ) 안의 말을 배열하여 문장을 완성하시오.

1 저 미소 짓고 있는 소녀는 누구니? (who, girl, is, smiling, that)
_____

2 그는 영어로 쓰인 이메일을 받았다. (got, English, an email, written, he, in)
_____

3 그녀는 깨진 창문을 보고 놀랐다. (see, broken, surprised, a, she, window, to, was)
_____

4 Laura는 은행에서 일하는 오빠가 있다. (a brother, a bank, Laura, in, working, has)
_____

5 파티에 초대된 사람들이 오지 않았다. (to, invited, didn't, the people, the party, come)
_____

6 그들은 피카소가 그린 그림을 가지고 있다. (a painting, Picasso, they, by, painted, have)
_____

분사의 역할 II – 보어

- 분사는 문장에서 주격 보어나 목적격 보어의 역할을 한다. 또한 현재분사는 진행형(be v-ing)에, 과거분사는 완료형(have v-ed)과 수동태(be v-ed)에 쓰이기도 한다.
  They got **excited** when Johnny scored. (주격 보어)
  I found him **drinking** water. (목적격 보어)
- 과거분사는 지각동사나 사역동사의 목적어와 목적격 보어의 관계가 수동일 때 사용된다.
  She *had* her room **cleaned**. (그녀의 방이 '깨끗해지는' 것이므로 수동의 관계)

A　다음 ( ) 안에서 알맞은 말을 고르시오.

1　Did you hear my name (calling / called)?

2　Everyone looked (tiring / tired) after the class finished.

3　Mike will have his hair (cutting / cut) as short as he wants.

4　This book was so (boring / bored) that it made me fall asleep.

5　He realized that his new job was (interesting / interested).

6　All the people were (surprising / surprised) at George's behavior.

7　We know that the restaurant is (closing / closed) on Sundays.

8　She got (depressing / depressed) when she lost her job.

9　He saw his girlfriend (waving / waved) to him.

10　Jane had her laptop (repairing / repaired), so now she can start working again.

B　다음 우리말과 같은 뜻이 되도록 ( ) 안의 말을 이용하여 문장을 완성하시오.

1　Sarah는 내 공연을 놓쳐서 실망한 것처럼 보였다. (disappoint)
　　Sarah ＿＿＿＿＿＿ ＿＿＿＿＿＿ to miss my performance.

2　그녀는 그녀의 치아를 뽑히도록 했다. (have, pull out)
　　She ＿＿＿＿ ＿＿＿＿ ＿＿＿＿ ＿＿＿＿ ＿＿＿＿.

3　나는 주방에서 뭔가 타고 있는 냄새를 맡았다. (burn)
　　I ＿＿＿＿ something ＿＿＿＿ in the kitchen.

4　그는 그의 여동생이 놀이터에서 놀고 있는 것을 발견했다. (find, play)
　　He ＿＿＿＿ his sister ＿＿＿＿ in the playground.

5　나는 그가 나의 이름을 부르는 것을 들었다. (call)
　　I ＿＿＿＿ ＿＿＿＿ ＿＿＿＿ my name.

6　그 남자는 그 문이 흰색으로 칠해지게 했다. (have, paint)
　　The man ＿＿＿＿ the door ＿＿＿＿ ＿＿＿＿.

분사구문 만드는 법

- 분사구문은 〈접속사+주어+동사〉 형태의 부사절을 부사구로 줄여 쓴 것으로, 만드는 방법은 다음과 같다.
  ① 접속사를 없앤다. ② 부사절의 주어가 주절의 주어와 같으면 생략한다.
  ③ 부사절의 시제가 주절의 시제와 같으면 부사절의 동사를 v-ing 형태로 바꾼다.
  When he saw his new sports car, he shouted with joy.
  → **Seeing** his new sports car, he shouted with joy.

★ PLUS TIP 〈Being+과거분사/형용사〉로 시작하는 분사구문에서 Being은 생략할 수 있다.

A 다음 문장을 분사구문으로 바꾸어 쓰시오.

1 As she was tired, she took a nap.
→ _____, she took a nap.

2 When she came home, she found the light on.
→ _____, she found the light on.

3 Because he found the keys, he stopped worrying.
→ _____, he stopped worrying.

4 If you turn right, you'll see the department store.
→ _____, you'll see the department store.

5 As I knew them both, I introduced them to each other.
→ _____, I introduced them to each other.

6 While he cooked his dinner, he listened to the radio.
→ _____, he listened to the radio.

7 Since she was angry with me, she didn't say hello.
→ _____, she didn't say hello.

B 다음 우리말과 같은 뜻이 되도록 ( ) 안의 말을 이용하여 문장을 완성하시오.

1 작업을 저장한 후, 그녀는 컴퓨터 전원을 껐다. (save)
_____ her work, she turned off the computer.

2 더웠기 때문에, 나는 외투를 벗었다. (feel hot)
_____ _____, I took off my coat.

3 숙제를 하면서, 그는 졸리기 시작했다. (do one's homework)
_____ _____ _____, he started to become sleepy.

4 그녀와 나는 재미있는 이야기들을 기억하면서 과거에 대해 얘기했다. (remember)
She and I talked about the past, _____ funny stories.

분사구문의 의미 I – 때 / 이유

- 분사구문은 '~할 때', '~하는 동안', '~한 후에'와 같이 때나 '~하기 때문에'와 같이 원인이나 이유의 의미를 나타낼 수 있다.

Playing football, I hurt my leg. (때)

(→ While I was playing football, I hurt my leg.)

Knowing a lot about computers, she fixed my laptop in just five minutes. (이유)

(→ As she knew a lot about computers, she fixed my laptop in just five minutes.)

★ PLUS TIP 분사구문의 의미를 명확히 나타내기 위해 분사 앞에 접속사를 남겨두기도 한다.

A 다음 문장을 분사구문으로 바꾸어 쓰시오.

1 While I was watching TV, I fell asleep on the sofa.

→ While _____, I fell asleep on the sofa.

2 Because he is interested in pets, he volunteers at a pet store.

→ _____, he volunteers at a pet store.

3 After Kate finished her work, she went home.

→ After _____, Kate went home.

B 다음 〈보기〉에서 알맞은 접속사를 골라 분사구문을 부사절로 바꾸어 쓰시오. (단, 한 번씩만 사용할 것)

〈보기〉	while	when	because

1 Leaving home, he took an umbrella with him.

→ _____, he took an umbrella with him.

2 Being very sick, he couldn't go on the field trip.

→ _____, he couldn't go on the field trip.

3 Waiting for my homeroom teacher, I drank a glass of water.

→ _____, I drank a glass of water.

C 다음 문장을 밑줄 친 부분에 유의하여 우리말로 해석하시오.

1 <u>Talking to her</u>, I felt nervous.

_____

2 <u>Having too much work to do</u>, he couldn't go out.

_____

3 <u>After paying the bill</u>, you should get a receipt.

_____

분사구문의 의미 II – 동시동작 / 연속상황

■ 분사구문은 '~하면서'라는 동시동작이나 '~하고 나서'라는 연속상황의 의미를 나타내기도 한다.
Drinking a cup of tea, she wrote in her diary. (동시동작)
(→ While she was drinking a cup of tea, she wrote in her diary.)
Standing up, he walked away. (연속상황)
(→ He stood up and then walked away.)

A 다음 문장을 분사구문으로 바꾸어 쓰시오.

1 He took off his shoes and then entered the room.
→ _____, he entered the room.

2 While he was listening to music, he thought about his girlfriend.
→ _____, he thought about his girlfriend.

3 She put on her swimming goggles and then jumped in the pool.
→ _____, she jumped in the pool.

4 As I waved to the driver, I got out of the car.
→ _____, I got out of the car.

B 다음 우리말과 같은 뜻이 되도록 ( ) 안의 말을 배열하여 문장을 완성하시오.

1 문을 열고 그는 걸어 들어갔다. (the door, walked in, opening, he)
_____

2 소파에 앉아서 나는 책을 읽었다. (a book, the sofa, sitting, read, on, I)
_____

3 그는 노래를 불러 모든 이들을 감동시켰다. (sang, everyone, a song, impressing, he)
_____

C 다음 문장을 밑줄 친 부분에 유의하여 우리말로 해석하시오.

1 <u>Getting out of the car</u>, she gave me a smile.
_____

2 <u>Playing baseball</u>, he suddenly felt dizzy.
_____

3 The train departs at five, <u>arriving in Seoul at nine</u>.
_____

분사구문의 의미 Ⅲ - 조건 / 양보

■ 분사구문은 '~하면'이라는 조건이나 '~에도 불구하고'라는 양보의 의미를 나타내기도 한다.

Turning left, you'll find the bus stop. (조건)

(→ If you turn left, you'll find the bus stop.)

Though being very sick, she prepared for the meeting. (양보)

(→ Though she was very sick, she prepared for the meeting.)

★ *PLUS TIP* 양보의 의미를 나타내는 분사구문 앞에는 접속사(though, although 등)를 남겨두는 것이 일반적이다.

A 다음 문장을 분사구문으로 바꾸어 쓰시오.

1 Though she was driving a car, she was talking on the phone.

→ _____, she was talking on the phone.

2 Though he was breathing heavily, he kept running.

→ _____, he kept running.

3 If you make a blog, you'll meet many people online.

→ _____, you'll meet many people online.

4 Though he has a bicycle, he doesn't ride it.

→ _____, he doesn't ride it.

5 Though I enjoy taking pictures, I'm not that good at it.

→ _____, I'm not that good at it.

6 If you get some fresh air, you will feel much better.

→ _____, you will feel much better.

7 If you look to your left, you will see the oldest church in this country.

→ _____, you will see the oldest church in this country.

B 다음 문장을 밑줄 친 부분에 유의하여 우리말로 해석하시오.

1 <u>Taking this bus</u>, you'll get to the amusement park.

_____

2 <u>Though being younger than me</u>, she acts like my older sister.

_____

3 <u>Turning right</u>, you'll see the shop on your left.

_____

내신대비 TEST

[01-03] 다음 빈칸에 알맞은 말을 고르시오.

01

> Who's the man _____ to Emily?

① talk　　　　② talks
③ talking　　　④ talked
⑤ to talking

02

> I had three _____ eggs and a sandwich for lunch.

① boil　　　　② boiling
③ boils　　　　④ to boil
⑤ boiled

03

> _____ home in the rain, I caught a cold.

① Walk　　　　② Walks
③ Walked　　　④ To walk
⑤ Walking

04

다음 우리말을 영어로 바르게 옮긴 것은?

> 그녀는 그녀의 지갑을 도난당했다.

① She stole her wallet.
② She had her wallet steal.
③ She had her wallet stealing.
④ She had her wallet stolen.
⑤ She made her wallet steal.

[05-06] 빈칸에 들어갈 말이 순서대로 알맞게 짝지어진 것을 고르시오.

05

> • _____ the tickets, we went into the theater.
> • Somebody _____ Robert came to see you.

① Buy – named　　② Buying – names
③ Buying – named　④ Bought – naming
⑤ Bought – named

06

> • The jazz concert was _____.
> • The teacher was very _____ with the student's answer.

① amazing – satisfying
② amazing – satisfied
③ amazed – satisfied
④ amazed – satisfying
⑤ to amaze – satisfying

[07-08] 다음 밑줄 친 부분의 쓰임이 나머지와 <u>다른</u> 것을 고르시오.

07

① <u>Being</u> pleased, I smiled.
② <u>Being</u> an astronaut is great.
③ <u>Being</u> tall, she can reach the shelf.
④ <u>Being</u> kind, he helped the elderly man.
⑤ <u>Being</u> nervous, I began to sweat.

08

① She was used to <u>getting</u> up early.
② Who is the girl <u>sitting</u> on the bench?
③ Look at the children <u>swimming</u> in the lake.
④ The people <u>waiting</u> outside are their fans.
⑤ Look at the tree <u>standing</u> on the hill.

[09 - 10] 다음 두 문장이 같은 뜻이 되도록 빈칸에 알맞은 말을 고르시오.

09

Being a foreigner, Susan needs a visa to work here.
→ _____ she is a foreigner, Susan needs a visa to work here.

① As
② If
③ When
④ Though
⑤ While

10

Using this coupon, you'll get a discount.
→ _____ you use this coupon, you'll get a discount.

① Until
② If
③ Even if
④ Though
⑤ While

11

다음 문장의 밑줄 친 부분과 바꿔 쓸 수 있는 것은?

Putting down his bag, he lay on the bed.

① He put down his bag
② If he put down his bag
③ Because he put down his bag
④ After he put down his bag
⑤ Though he put down his bag

12

다음 밑줄 친 분사구문의 의미가 바르지 않은 것은?

① Eating a hot dog, I watched the movie.
(동시동작)
② Hearing his name called, he turned around.
(조건)
③ Being young, she can't get a driver's license.
(이유)
④ Visiting Norway, you'll be able to see beautiful scenery. (조건)
⑤ Holding hands, they smiled at each other.
(동시동작)

[13 - 14] 다음 〈보기〉의 밑줄 친 부분과 쓰임이 같은 것을 고르시오.

13

〈보기〉 Having no money, I ate nothing.

① Putting down my book, I closed my eyes.
② Watching TV, they ate Chinese food.
③ Being sick, he went to see a doctor.
④ Having dinner, we heard Jessica crying.
⑤ Using this method, you can solve the problem.

14

〈보기〉 Studying together, you'll learn more.

① Eating frequently, I'm gaining weight.
② Feeling tired, she went to bed early.
③ Taking the medicine, you'll start to feel better.
④ Diane walked around the town, taking photographs.
⑤ Waiting for the subway, I played a smartphone game.

15

다음 밑줄 친 단어의 쓰임이 올바른 것은? (2개)

① I was <u>moved</u> by his advice.

② It has been a long and <u>tired</u> day.

③ The traffic jam made us <u>annoying</u>.

④ These are the most <u>boring</u> novels ever.

⑤ Jeremy was <u>interesting</u> by the question.

[16-17] 다음 밑줄 친 부분이 어법상 <u>틀린</u> 것을 고르시오.

16

① The news was <u>shocking</u>.

② He got his hair <u>cut</u> yesterday.

③ The basketball game was <u>exciting</u>.

④ <u>Shook</u> my hand, she introduced herself.

⑤ <u>Though being</u> full, I didn't stop eating.

17

① Why do you look <u>bored</u>?

② I heard my name <u>called</u>.

③ She saw them <u>dancing</u> in the hall.

④ He found the information <u>confused</u>.

⑤ <u>Saying goodbye</u>, he left the classroom.

18

다음 우리말과 뜻이 같도록 빈칸에 들어갈 말로 알맞은 것을 모두 고르면? (2개)

> 그 단어들을 소리 내어 읽으면, 당신은 그것들을 더 잘 외울 수 있을 것이다.
> → _____ the words aloud, you will be able to memorize them well.

① Read   ② Reading

③ You reading   ④ If you read

⑤ Though you read

19

다음 분사구문을 부사절로 바꿀 때 <u>잘못된</u> 것은?

① Having lots of work to do, I can't help you.

　→ As I have lots of work to do, I can't help you.

② Being free, she was able to meet her friends.

　→ Because she was free, she was able to meet her friends.

③ Washing the dishes, she sang a song.

　→ While she washed the dishes, she sang a song.

④ Knowing what happened, I can help her.

　→ Since I know what happened, I can help her.

⑤ He read a fashion magazine, eating some bread.

　→ He read a fashion magazine while he eats some bread.

20

(A), (B), (C)의 괄호 안에서 알맞은 것끼리 바르게 짝지어진 것은?

> (A) [Go / Going] to a movie, I happened to see him.
> (B) The service at the café was [satisfying / satisfied].
> (C) The test results made me [depressing / depressed].

	(A)	(B)	(C)
①	Go	satisfying	depressing
②	Go	satisfied	depressed
③	Going	satisfied	depressed
④	Going	satisfied	depressing
⑤	Going	satisfying	depressed

서술형 따라잡기

01
다음 밑줄 친 부분을 분사구문으로 바꾸어 쓰시오.

<u>While I was running along the river</u>, I made up my mind.

→ _____, I made up my mind.

02
다음 그림을 보고, 주어진 말과 분사구문을 이용하여 문장을 완성하시오.

(1) The man is sitting on the bench, _____ _____ _____. (read)

(2) The woman is talking on the phone, _____ _____ _____. (hold)

03
어법상 틀린 부분을 모두 찾아 바르게 고쳐 쓰시오.

(1) Moving into a new house, Keeran decided to have it painting. (1군데)

(2) Look out the window, you'll see a little girl. She is jumping rope, counts the number of jumps. (2군데)

04
주어진 말을 알맞게 배열하여 우리말과 뜻이 같도록 문장을 완성하시오.

(1) 그녀는 클래식 음악을 들으면서 잠이 들었다.
(she, classical music, asleep, listening to, fell,)
→ _____

(2) 사무실에 당신을 기다리는 고객 한 분이 계십니다.
(a client, you, is, for, there, waiting, in the office)
→ _____

05
다음 영화 감상평을 보고, 문장을 완성하시오.

Maria	It was really moving.
Yujin	I'll ask my brother to download the video file.
Sora	I fell asleep during the movie because I was bored.

(1) Maria found the movie _____.

(2) Yujin will have the video file _____ by her brother.

(3) _____ _____, Sora fell asleep during the movie.

06
다음 조건에 맞게 우리말을 영어로 옮겨 쓰시오.

〈조건〉 1. 분사를 이용할 것
2. 표현 cross the road, thirsty, drink a glass of water를 이용할 것

(1) 나는 그녀가 길을 건너고 있는 것을 보았다.
→ _____ (6단어)

(2) 목이 말라서, 그녀는 물을 한 잔 마셨다.
→ _____ (8단어)

핵심 포인트 정리하기

1 현재분사와 과거분사

분사 종류	의미	쓰임	
현재분사 〈v-ing〉	① _____	'감정을 유발하는' (주체: 보통 사물) 능동의 의미 ex) exciting	진행형
과거분사 〈v-ed〉	수동·완료	'감정을 느끼게 되는' (주체: 보통 사람) 수동의 의미 ex) excited	– 완료형 – ② _____ – 지각동사나 사역동사의 목적어와 목적격 보어의 관계가 ③ _____일 때

 현재분사 / 과거분사와 수식하는 대상과의 관계 파악하기!

2 분사의 역할

- 명사 수식 (수식어구와 함께 쓰이는 경우에는 명사 ④ _____에서 수식)
- 보어 역할 – 주어나 목적어 설명

3 분사구문의 의미

때	⑤ _____	동시동작	연속상황	조건	양보
'~할 때' '~하는 동안' '~한 후에'	'~하기 때문에'	'~하면서'	⑥ _____	'~하면'	'~에도 불구하고'

 분사구문 만드는 법 익히기!
분사구문의 서로 다른 의미 알아두기!

문제로 개념 다지기

밑줄 친 부분이 어법상 맞으면 O, 틀리면 X 표시하고 바르게 고치시오.

1 My brother found his toy <u>breaking</u>.

2 Do you know the boy <u>carry</u> the flag?

3 I was <u>embarrassing</u> when I made a mistake on stage.

4 My parents were <u>pleased</u> that I got an A on the test.

5 <u>Stood up</u>, everyone cheered me during my performance.

6 <u>Though got wet</u>, she kept dancing in the rain.

7 <u>Being the strongest person in the class</u>, Mike won the arm wrestling competition.

CHAPTER 05

분사 II

Not having made pizza before, she doesn't know how.
[Not+having+과거분사]

It being a warm day, I feel like going for a drive.
→ As it is a warm day, I feel like going for a drive.

여러 가지 분사구문

분사구문에는 주의해서 사용해야 하는 몇 가지 형태들이 있습니다. 분사구문의 부정형은
〈not/never+분사〉의 형태이며, 부사절의 시제가 주절의 시제보다 앞선 경우에는 완료 분사구문
〈having+과거분사(v-ed)〉로 나타냅니다. 부사절의 주어가 주절의 주어와 다를 경우에 분사 앞에
주어를 남겨두는 독립분사구문도 있습니다.

분사구문의 부정

- 분사구문의 부정은 분사 앞에 not이나 never를 써서 나타낸다.
  Not having enough money, I couldn't buy a tablet PC.
  (= As I didn't have enough money, I couldn't buy a tablet PC.)

A 다음 문장을 분사구문으로 바꾸어 쓰시오.

1 Because I didn't want to go there alone, I waited for them.
→ _____, I waited for them.

2 As I don't get enough sleep, I can't focus on studying.
→ _____, I can't focus on studying.

3 Because he doesn't have a car, he goes to work by bus.
→ _____, he goes to work by bus.

4 Though I didn't like the food, I ate it anyway.
→ _____, I ate it anyway.

5 As she didn't have enough time, she had trouble enjoying her vacation.
→ _____, she had trouble enjoying her vacation.

6 Because he didn't know the passcode, he couldn't get into the room.
→ _____, he couldn't get into the room.

7 As I didn't want to disturb others, I moved quietly.
→ _____, I moved quietly.

B 다음 우리말과 같은 뜻이 되도록 (   ) 안의 말을 이용하여 문장을 완성하시오.

1 몸 상태가 좋지 않아서 그녀는 일찍 집에 갔다. (feel well)
_____ _____, she went home early.

2 배가 고프지 않아서 나는 저녁을 전혀 먹지 않았다. (feel hungry)
_____ _____ _____, I didn't have any dinner.

3 표가 없어서 그들은 콘서트에 갈 수 없었다. (have, tickets)
_____ _____ _____, they couldn't go to the concert.

4 어디를 가야 할지 몰라서 우리는 벤치에 앉았다. (know, where to go)
_____ _____ _____ _____, we sat on a bench.

완료 분사구문

■ 완료 분사구문은 〈having+과거분사(v-ed)〉의 형태로, 부사절의 시제가 주절의 시제보다 앞선 경우에 쓴다.

Having spent my holiday there, I know a lot about Jeju Island.
(= As I spent my holiday there, I know a lot about Jeju Island.)

A 다음 문장을 분사구문 또는 부사절로 바꾸어 쓰시오.

1 As he forgot his lines in the play, he is now embarrassed.

→ _____, he is now embarrassed.

2 As they had great fun in Japan, they plan to visit again.

→ _____, they plan to visit again.

3 Having written an email to him, I'm waiting for his reply.

→ _____, I'm waiting for his reply.

4 Because she left home when she was young, she is independent.

→ _____, she is independent.

5 Since I left my cell phone at home, I want to borrow yours.

→ _____, I want to borrow yours.

6 Having studied history in university, he knows a lot about the subject.

→ _____, he knows a lot about the subject.

B 다음 우리말과 같은 뜻이 되도록 ( ) 안의 말을 이용하여 문장을 완성하시오.

1 그가 준 선물을 잃어버렸기 때문에 나는 우울하다. (lose)

_____ _____ the present he gave me, I'm depressed.

2 많은 돈을 벌었기 때문에 나는 내가 원하는 만큼 기부할 수 있다. (earn)

_____ _____ a lot of money, I can donate as much as I want.

3 런던에서 자랐기 때문에 그녀는 영국식 억양을 가지고 있다. (grow up)

_____ _____ _____ _____ London, she has a British accent.

4 아직 졸업을 하지 않았기 때문에 그는 여전히 학생 할인을 받을 수 있다. (graduate)

_____ _____ _____ yet, he can still get a student discount.

5 그 노래를 여러 번 들었기 때문에 나는 그것을 거의 다 외웠다. (listen to)

_____ _____ _____ the song several times, I have almost

memorized it.

being / having been의 생략

- 〈being/having been＋과거분사〉 형태의 수동형 분사구문에서 being이나 having been은 생략할 수 있다.

(Being) Excited, they jumped and shouted.

(→ As they were excited, they jumped and shouted.)

Though (having been) warned before, he still drives fast.

(→ Though he was warned before, he still drives fast.)

★ **PLUS TIP** being 뒤에 형용사가 오는 분사구문에서 being을 생략하고 형용사만 남겨두는 경우도 있다.

A 다음 문장을 분사구문으로 바꾸어 쓰시오.

1 As she was surprised at the news, she started to cry.

→ _____, she started to cry.

2 As I was confused, I went to the wrong place.

→ _____, I went to the wrong place.

3 Though he was accepted by the university, he can't afford to study there.

→ _____, he can't afford to study there.

4 Because you were given an invitation, you can enter this building.

→ _____, you can enter this building.

5 Since she is interested in photos, she wants to go to the exhibition.

→ _____, she wants to go to the exhibition.

B 다음 우리말과 같은 뜻이 되도록 ( ) 안의 말을 이용하여 문장을 완성하시오.

1 사적인 질문을 받았기 때문에 그 배우는 기분이 상했다. (ask)

_____ a personal question, the actor became upset.

2 내 일에 만족하기 때문에 나는 불만이 없다. (satisfy with)

_____ _____ my job, I have no complaints.

3 학급 회장으로 선출되었기 때문에 그는 많은 책임이 있었다. (elect)

_____ class president, he had many responsibilities.

4 어떤 실수도 하지 않으려고 주의했기 때문에 그는 그것을 완벽하게 해냈다. (careful)

_____ _____ to make any mistakes, he did it perfectly.

5 준비운동을 하지 않았기 때문에 너는 수영장에 들어갈 수 없다. (warm up)

_____ _____ _____ _____, you cannot go into the pool.

독립분사구문

- 독립분사구문이란 부사절의 주어가 주절의 주어와 다를 경우, 분사구문을 만들 때 부사절의 주어를 생략하지 않고 분사 앞에 남겨두는 분사구문을 말한다.
  The snow beginning to fall, we went back to the base camp.
  (→ As the snow began to fall, we went back to the base camp.)

A 다음 문장을 분사구문으로 바꾸어 쓰시오.

1 As the weather was getting hotter, we went swimming.
  → _____, we went swimming.

2 Because the rain was heavy, we never left the house.
  → _____, we never left the house.

3 As my brother took my car, I have to go to work by bus.
  → _____, I have to go to work by bus.

4 Because it was my turn to sing, I took the microphone.
  → _____, I took the microphone.

5 Because nobody wanted to talk, the meeting ended.
  → _____, the meeting ended.

6 As there was no one in the office, I waited for an hour.
  → _____, I waited for an hour.

B 다음 우리말과 같은 뜻이 되도록 ( ) 안의 말을 이용하여 문장을 완성하시오.

1 그 개가 시끄럽게 짖어서 나는 공부를 할 수 없었다. (bark, loudly)
  _____ _____ _____ _____, I couldn't study.

2 교통 사정이 나빠서 그는 학교에 늦었다. (the traffic, bad)
  _____ _____ _____ _____, he was late for school.

3 사람이 많아서 나는 무대 위에서 불안했다. (there, be)
  _____ _____ _____ _____, I was nervous on the stage.

4 길이 어두워서 그녀는 혼자 걷는 것이 무서웠다. (the road, dark)
  _____ _____ _____ _____, she was scared of walking alone.

5 아이들이 낮잠을 자서 나는 차를 한 잔 만들기로 결정했다. (the children, take a nap)
  _____ _____ _____ _____ _____, I decided to make a cup of tea.

비인칭 독립분사구문

- 비인칭 독립분사구문이란 분사구문의 주어가 막연한 일반인인 경우, 주절의 주어와 다르더라도 생략하는 분사구문으로, 관용적으로 쓰이는 표현이다.

Strictly speaking, this answer is not correct. (엄밀히 말해서)
Judging from his accent, he's from Australia. (~로 판단하건대)
Roughly speaking, I will be traveling for about a month. (대강 말하자면)
Considering her age, she is very brave. (~을 고려하면)
Generally speaking, people like movies with happy endings. (일반적으로 말해서)
Speaking of Marie, she knows a lot about music. (~ 이야기가 나왔으니 말인데)
Frankly speaking, I forgot to call him last night. (솔직히 말해서)
Taking everything into consideration, you should come. (모든 것을 고려해 볼 때)

A 다음 ( ) 안에서 알맞은 말을 고르시오.

1 (Considering / Strictly speaking), she isn't tall enough to be a model.

2 (Judging from / Speaking of) traveling, I want to go to Spain.

3 (Generally speaking / Speaking of), men run faster than women.

4 (Generally speaking / Roughly speaking), he is 30 years old.

5 (Taking everything into consideration / Considering), you should start to exercise.

6 (Considering / Roughly speaking) what he said yesterday, his decision is surprising.

B 다음 우리말과 같은 뜻이 되도록 위의 표현들을 이용하여 문장을 완성하시오.

1 엄밀히 말해서, 이것은 불법이다.
_____ _____, this is illegal.

2 일반적으로 말해서, 서울이 도쿄보다 춥다.
_____ _____, Seoul is colder than Tokyo.

3 대강 말하자면, 나는 프랑스에 두 달 동안 있을 것이다.
_____ _____, I will be in France for two months.

4 수학 시험 이야기가 나왔으니 말인데, 시험이 언제지?
_____ _____ the math exam, when is it?

5 그녀의 표정으로 판단하건대, 그녀는 사탕을 먹고 싶어 한다.
_____ _____ her expression, she wants to have some candy.

6 솔직히 말해서, 그는 야외 활동에 관심이 없는 것 같다.
_____ _____, he doesn't seem to be interested in outdoor activities.

with+(대)명사+분사

■ 〈with+(대)명사+현재분사〉는 '~가 …한 채로'의 의미로 (대)명사와 분사가 능동의 관계이고,
〈with+(대)명사+과거분사〉는 '~가 …된 채로'의 의미로 (대)명사와 분사가 수동의 관계이다.
He was jogging **with his dog following** him.
She sat **with her legs crossed.**

★ **PLUS TIP** being은 보통 생략되어 〈with+(대)명사+형용사/부사/전치사구〉의 형태가 된다.
He talked **with his mouth (being) full.**

★ **내신만점 TIP** 〈with+(대)명사+분사〉 구문에서 (대)명사와 분사의 관계가 능동인지 수동인지 반드시 확인하자.

A 다음 두 문장이 같은 뜻이 되도록 문장을 완성하시오.

1 I fell asleep, and the TV was turned on.
→ I fell asleep _____ the TV _____ on.

2 She read a book, and her cat was sitting next to her.
→ She read a book _____ next to her.

3 Kate walked away, and her mother was calling her name.
→ Kate walked away _____ her name.

4 They got in the car, and their fans were waving to them.
→ They got in the car _____ to them.

5 Lewis was playing the piano, and his friends were singing.
→ Lewis was playing the piano _____.

B 다음 우리말과 같은 뜻이 되도록 with와 ( ) 안의 말을 이용하여 문장을 완성하시오.

1 그녀는 자신의 옷을 단정하게 개어둔 채로 방을 나갔다. (clothes, fold)
She left the room _____ _____ _____ _____ neatly.

2 그 택시가 기다리는 가운데 그들은 작별인사를 했다. (wait)
They said goodbye _____ _____ _____.

3 나는 그 문을 닫아둔 채 오후 내내 잤다. (close)
I slept all afternoon _____ _____ _____ _____.

4 그는 그 세탁기가 돌아가게 두고 외출했다. (washing machine, run)
He went out _____ _____ _____.

5 내 친구들이 식탁에 앉아 있는 가운데, 나는 스파게티를 만들었다. (sit)
I made spaghetti _____ _____ _____ _____ at the table.

내신대비 TEST

[01-03] 다음 빈칸에 알맞은 말을 고르시오.

01

_____ lived in many countries, she can speak three languages.

① It   ② Being
③ Having   ④ Having been
⑤ As

02

_____ who she was, I made a mistake.

① Not know   ② Not knowing
③ Not known   ④ Knowing not
⑤ Known not

03

_____ cloudy, we couldn't see the stars.

① Being   ② Having been
③ To be   ④ The sky being
⑤ The sky been

[04-05] 다음 빈칸에 공통으로 들어갈 말을 고르시오.

04

- Those girls danced _____ their hands held high.
- Jane slept _____ the fan turned on.

① to   ② for   ③ of
④ with   ⑤ from

05

- _____ of smartphones, which brand do you recommend?
- Generally _____, women are more sensitive than men.

① Being[being]   ② Doing[doing]
③ Speaking[speaking]   ④ Judging[judging]
⑤ Having[having]

[06-08] 빈칸에 들어갈 말이 순서대로 알맞게 짝지어진 것을 고르시오.

06

- The band was playing with the audience _____.
- _____ at the news, he didn't say anything.

① clap – Surprised
② clapping – Surprised
③ clapping – Surprising
④ clapped – Surprised
⑤ clapped – Surprising

07

- All the money _____, he borrowed some from his father.
- _____ the ticket price, the concert isn't worth going to.

① being spent – Consider
② being spent – Considered
③ having spent – Considering
④ having been spent – Considering
⑤ having been spent – Considered

08

- _____ cold water, I felt much better.
- _____ in French, the book looked difficult.

① Drinking – Writing ② Drinking – Written
③ Drunk – Writing ④ Drunk – Written
⑤ Drink – Being written

[09-10] 다음 두 문장이 같은 뜻이 되도록 빈칸에 알맞은 말을 고르시오.

09

As I didn't have a pen, I had to buy one.
→ _____ a pen, I had to buy one.

① As having ② Not having
③ Didn't having ④ Had not
⑤ Having not

10

Because she was born in Germany, she is used to German culture.
→ _____ in Germany, she is used to German culture.

① Born ② Having born
③ Being born ④ Been born
⑤ Was born

11

다음 빈칸에 being이 들어갈 수 <u>없는</u> 것은?

① It _____ a sunny day, we went to the zoo.
② _____ sick, Dan stayed in bed all day.
③ Though _____ young, she is a great cook.
④ _____ sleepy, I couldn't focus on my class.
⑤ _____ late for work yesterday, I got up early this morning.

기출응용

12

다음 문장을 분사구문을 이용하여 바르게 바꾼 것은?

As she worked at a café, she knows how to make coffee.

① Being worked at a café, she knows how to make coffee.
② As worked at a café, she knows how to make coffee.
③ Worked at a café, she knows how to make coffee.
④ Having working at a café, she knows how to make coffee.
⑤ Having worked at a café, she knows how to make coffee.

13

다음 우리말을 영어로 바르게 옮긴 것은?

버스가 급정거해서 그녀는 넘어졌다.

① The bus stop suddenly, she fell down.
② The bus stops suddenly, she fell down.
③ The bus stopped suddenly, she fell down.
④ The bus stopping suddenly, she fell down.
⑤ The bus being stopped suddenly, she fell down.

14

다음 밑줄 친 부분과 바꿔 쓸 수 있는 것은?

<u>Not needing</u> his car anymore, he decided to sell it.

① Before he didn't need
② If he didn't need
③ Because he didn't need
④ While he didn't need
⑤ Though he didn't need

15

다음 대화의 빈칸에 알맞은 말은?

A: Why didn't you go to the cinema?
B: _____, I didn't want to go again.

① Seen the film twice
② Saw the film twice
③ Not seeing the film twice
④ Having seen the film twice
⑤ Not having seen the film twice

기출응용

16

다음 중 어법상 옳은 문장의 개수는?

(a) Considered his age, he is very good at writing.
(b) Being shocking, I couldn't breathe.
(c) It being a snowy day, we had a snowball fight.
(d) The girl sat on the floor with her dog lying beside her.

① 0개 ② 1개 ③ 2개 ④ 3개 ⑤ 4개

[17-18] 다음 밑줄 친 부분이 어법상 틀린 것을 고르시오.

17

① I drove humming a song.
② Walking slowly, I thought of her.
③ Having not money, I didn't buy it.
④ Reading the newspaper, he ate breakfast.
⑤ The weather getting worse, we couldn't go on a picnic.

18

① There being no evidence, he was released.
② They sat with their eyes closed.
③ While playing football, I broke my leg.
④ Generally speaking, Japanese is easier to learn than Chinese.
⑤ Judged from his height, he can't ride this roller coaster.

19

다음 대화 중 자연스럽지 않은 것은?

① A: Why didn't you come to the party?
   B: Our dog being sick, we stayed at home.
② A: What are you going to do tomorrow?
   B: After going shopping, I'm going to go to a movie.
③ A: How long will you be in Hong Kong?
   B: Roughly speaking, I'll be there for a week.
④ A: Look at her! She is doing so great!
   B: Yes. Practicing hard, she is performing perfectly.
⑤ A: Why did he say he didn't break the desk?
   B: Afraid of being scolded, he lied.

고난도

20

다음 중 어법상 옳은 것을 모두 고르면? (3개)

① I had dinner with the candles burned.
② Not knowing where to go, we stopped.
③ My son having passed the exam, I was very happy.
④ Taken everything into consideration, he was wrong.
⑤ Having been advised by him, she won't make any mistakes.

서술형 따라잡기

01
다음 밑줄 친 부분을 분사구문으로 바꾸어 쓰시오.

(1) <u>When she was alone</u>, she finally opened the box.

→ _____, she finally opened the box.

(2) <u>Because there is no subway station</u>, I'll take a bus.

→ _____,

I'll take a bus.

02
주어진 말을 이용하여 우리말과 뜻이 같도록 문장을 완성하시오.

잠을 잘 못 잤기 때문에 나는 피곤하다.
(sleep well)

→ _____ _____ _____ _____,

I feel tired.

03
다음 그림을 보고, 주어진 말을 이용하여 문장을 완성하시오.

(1) He listened to music _____ _____

_____ _____. (eyes, close)

(2) She sat on the sofa _____ _____

_____ _____. (arms, fold)

04
다음 두 문장을 한 문장으로 만들 때, 빈칸에 알맞은 말을 쓰시오.

He fell from the tree. He is in the hospital.

→ _____ _____ _____ _____

_____, he is in the hospital.

05
다음 표를 보고, 분사구문을 이용하여 문장을 완성하시오.

Yesterday	Today
I finished writing my essay.	I can hand it in.
Henry came back from the trip.	I can play baseball with him.

(1) _____,

I can hand it in.

(2) _____,

I can play baseball with him.

고난도
06
다음 Heather의 일기를 읽고, 틀린 부분을 모두 찾아 바르게 고쳐 쓰시오. (3군데)

June 3rd, 2019
Walked on the street, I dropped my smartphone. Worried, I picked it up. It was broken. Buying it just a few months ago, I was upset. Moreover, having not enough time, I couldn't go to the service center. It was a bad day.

핵심 포인트 정리하기

1 여러 가지 분사구문

- 분사구문의 부정: 〈① _____ + 분사〉
- 완료 분사구문: 부사절의 시제가 주절의 시제보다 앞서는 경우에 사용

  〈② _____ + _____〉의 형태
- 수동형 분사구문에서 ③ _____ 생략 가능

2 독립분사구문

- 부사절의 주어가 주절의 주어와 다른 경우, 분사구문을 만들 때 부사절의 주어를 생략하지 않고 분사 앞에 남겨두는 것
- 비인칭 독립분사구문
  - Strictly speaking '엄밀히 말해서'
  - ④ _____ '~로 판단하건대'
  - Considering '~을 고려하면'
  - ⑤ _____ '일반적으로 말해서'
  - Speaking of ~ '~ 이야기가 나왔으니 말인데'

   부사절의 주어가 주절의 주어와 다르면 생략할 수 없다는 것 기억하기!

3 with + (대)명사 + 분사

- 〈with + (대)명사 + ⑥ _____〉: '~가 …한 채로' / (대)명사와 분사가 능동의 관계
- 〈with + (대)명사 + ⑦ _____〉: '~가 …된 채로' / (대)명사와 분사가 수동의 관계

   (대)명사와 분사와의 관계가 능동인지 수동인지 따져본 뒤에 문제 풀기!

문제로 개념 다지기

밑줄 친 부분이 어법상 맞으면 O, 틀리면 X 표시하고 바르게 고치시오.

1 <u>Don't knowing</u> what to do, he stared at his watch.

2 <u>Having the flight been delayed</u>, we arrived late.

3 <u>Having failing</u> the exam several times, I don't want to take it again.

4 <u>Not having finished</u> his work, he is worried.

5 <u>Disappointing</u> at the results, she did nothing for a few days.

6 <u>My sister calling me</u>, I ran toward her.

7 <u>Judged from</u> his tone of voice, his apology was not sincere.

8 She took a bow <u>with the crowd cheered</u>.

CHAPTER 06

시제

Have you ever **seen** this musical before?   [현재완료]

I realized I **had** not **turned** off the light.   [과거완료]

현재완료와 과거완료

완료형은 어느 한 시점에 시작되어 또 다른 시점까지 영향을 미치는 일을 서로 연관 지어 나타낸 것입니다. 과거에 일어난 일이 현재까지 영향을 미치는 경우에는 현재완료를, 과거의 한 시점을 기준으로 그 이전에 일어난 일이 과거까지 영향을 미치는 경우에는 과거완료를 씁니다. 현재완료나 과거완료에서 동작이 진행 중임을 강조할 때는 완료 진행형을 쓴다는 것을 기억해두세요.

현재완료의 계속 / 경험 용법

- 현재완료는 〈have[has]+v-ed〉의 형태로 과거에 일어난 일이 현재까지 영향을 미칠 때 사용한다.
- 계속을 나타내는 현재완료: 과거부터 현재까지 계속된 일을 나타낼 때 사용하며 '(계속) ~해 왔다'의 의미이다.
  I **have lived** in this house since I was born.
  He **has used** this cell phone for five years.
- 경험을 나타내는 현재완료: 과거에서 현재까지 있었던 경험을 나타낼 때 사용하며 '~한 적이 있다'의 의미이다.
  I **have bought** lots of things on the Internet before.
  They **have** never **eaten** fish and chips in England.

★ PLUS TIP   계속을 나타내는 현재완료는 주로 since, for, how long 등과, 경험을 나타내는 현재완료는 ever, never, before, often, … times 등과 함께 쓴다.

A 다음 (   ) 안에서 알맞은 말을 고르시오.

1 I (have never driven / have never driving) such a big truck before.

2 He (is taking / has taken) taekwondo lessons for the last three years.

3 Thousands of people (visited / have visited) this place since last year.

4 She (sees / has seen) this movie three times.

B 다음 우리말과 같은 뜻이 되도록 (   ) 안의 말을 이용하여 문장을 완성하시오.

1 일주일 동안 계속 비가 왔다. (rain)
It _____ _____ for a week.

2 나는 전에 길에서 그를 만난 적이 있다. (meet)
I _____ _____ _____ before on the street.

3 나는 우리가 처음 만났을 때부터 너를 사랑했다. (love)
I _____ _____ _____ since we first met.

4 너는 복권에 당첨된 적이 있니? (win)
_____ _____ ever _____ the lottery?

C 다음 문장을 현재완료의 용법에 유의하여 우리말로 해석하시오.

1 Cindy has been sick for two weeks.

_____

2 Have you ever ridden a roller coaster before?

_____

3 I have danced ballet since I was seven years old.

_____

현재완료의 완료 / 결과 용법

- 완료를 나타내는 현재완료: 과거에 시작된 일이 (가까운) 현재에 완료되었음을 나타낼 때 사용하며 '벌써/이미/막 ~했다'의 의미이다.

Jimmy and Kate's wedding **has** just **started**.

They **haven't decided** on the price of the product yet.

- 결과를 나타내는 현재완료: 과거의 일로 인해 현재에 어떠한 결과가 생겼음을 나타낼 때 사용하며 '~해 버렸다'의 의미이다.

Dylan **has left** for Brazil with his family.

She **has lost** her purse somewhere.

★ PLUS TIP 완료를 나타내는 현재완료는 주로 부사 just, yet, already 등과 함께 쓴다.

★ 내신만점 TIP when과 특정 과거 시점을 나타내는 말(yesterday, ago, last 등)은 현재완료와 함께 쓰지 않음에 유의하자.

A 다음 두 문장이 같은 뜻이 되도록 문장을 완성하시오.

1 He went to Sydney last year, and he is in Korea now.

→ He _____ Sydney.

2 Amy lost her striped umbrella, so she doesn't have it now.

→ Amy _____ her striped umbrella.

3 I'm going out to eat, but I didn't decide where to go.

→ I _____ where to go to eat yet.

B 다음 우리말과 같은 뜻이 되도록 ( ) 안의 말을 이용하여 문장을 완성하시오.

1 그녀는 아직 그에게 그녀의 답변을 보내지 않았다. (send)

She _____ _____ her response to him yet.

2 그 퍼레이드는 막 끝났다. (end)

The parade _____ _____ _____.

3 아니요, 괜찮습니다. 저는 충분히 먹었습니다. (have)

No, thank you. I _____ _____ enough.

4 Tom은 벌써 공항에 도착했다. (arrive)

Tom _____ _____ _____ at the airport.

5 그는 자신의 여자친구를 위해 비싼 반지를 사 버렸다. (buy)

He _____ _____ an expensive ring for his girlfriend.

6 Joe의 요리 실력은 지난달 이후로 크게 향상되었다. (improve)

Joe's cooking ability _____ _____ greatly since last month.

현재완료 진행형

■ 현재완료 진행형은 〈have[has]+been+v-ing〉의 형태로 과거에 시작된 일이 현재에도 계속 진행 중임을 나타낼 때 사용한다.
I **have been taking** piano lessons for a month.
He **has been talking** on the phone for two hours.

A 다음 주어진 문장과 같은 뜻이 되도록 문장을 완성하시오.

1 I began to clean the house one hour ago. I'm still cleaning it.
→ I _____ for one hour.

2 The telephone began to ring a few minutes ago. It is still ringing.
→ The telephone _____ for a few minutes.

3 Last Friday, Erica came to my house. She is still staying here.
→ Erica _____ at my house since last Friday.

4 He started his homework this morning. He is still doing his homework.
→ He _____ since this morning.

5 Brad left two hours ago. He is still driving.
→ Brad _____ for two hours.

B 다음 우리말과 같은 뜻이 되도록 ( ) 안의 말을 이용하여 문장을 완성하시오.

1 당신은 여기서 얼마나 오랫동안 일해왔습니까? (work)
How long _____ you _____ _____ here?

2 나는 지난 3일 동안 이 에세이를 써 오고 있다. (write)
I _____ _____ _____ this essay for the last three days.

3 그는 몇 시간째 축구에 대해서 이야기하고 있다. (talk)
He _____ _____ _____ about soccer for hours.

4 2시간째 걷고 있어서 나는 지금 매우 피곤하다. (walk)
I _____ _____ _____ for two hours, so I'm very tired now.

5 Dick은 한국에서 5년째 영어를 가르치고 있다. (teach)
Dick _____ _____ _____ _____ in Korea for five years.

6 그녀는 여기에 도착한 이후로 계속 그를 기다리고 있다. (wait for)
She _____ _____ _____ _____ him since she arrived here.

과거완료의 계속 / 경험 용법

- 과거완료는 〈had+v-ed〉의 형태로 과거의 어느 시점을 기준으로 그 이전에 일어난 일이 과거까지 영향을 미칠 때 쓴다.
- 계속을 나타내는 과거완료: 과거 이전부터 과거의 어느 시점까지 계속된 일을 나타낼 때 사용한다.
  I **had known** Kevin for a year when he told me that he liked me.
  David **had been** an announcer before he became an actor.
- 경험을 나타내는 과거완료: 과거 이전부터 과거의 어느 시점까지 있었던 경험을 나타낼 때 사용한다.
  I **had** never **tasted** a durian before I visited the Philippines.
  Had you ever **met** Jacob before last Friday?

A 다음 ( ) 안에서 알맞은 말을 고르시오.

1 Renee (has tried / had tried) scuba diving recently.

2 He (has been / had been) in Paris before he came to Italy.

3 I (have never read / had never read) the novel series until he recommended it.

4 I (have known / had known) her for many years when she became a lawyer.

5 A: Is she your science teacher?
B: Yes. She (has taught / had taught) me since I was a freshman.

6 (Has Sarah won / Had Sarah won) a piano competition before you knew her?

B 다음 우리말과 같은 뜻이 되도록 ( ) 안의 말을 이용하여 문장을 완성하시오.

1 오디션 전에 그녀는 그 노래를 여러 번 연습했었다. (practice)
She _____ _____ the song many times before her audition.

2 Mike는 그때까지 어떤 전자책도 읽어 본 적이 없었다. (never, read)
Mike _____ _____ _____ any e-books until then.

3 그때까지 우리 부모님은 남미에 가 본 적이 없으셨다. (never, be)
My parents _____ _____ _____ to South America until then.

4 이전에 그를 TV에서 본 적이 있었기 때문에 나는 그를 바로 알아보았다. (see)
Because I _____ _____ him on TV before, I recognized him at once.

5 내가 병원에 입원한 Julie에게 갔을 때, 그녀는 지난 가을 이래로 계속 아팠던 상태였다. (be)
When I visited Julie in the hospital, she _____ _____ ill since last fall.

6 Jerry는 교내 밴드부에 가입하기 전에는 친구들이 거의 없었다. (have, few)
Jerry _____ _____ _____ _____ before he joined the school band.

■ 완료를 나타내는 과거완료: 과거 이전에 시작된 일이 과거의 어느 시점에 막 완료되었음을 나타낼 때 사용한다.
The movie **had started** when I reached the cinema.
They **had finished** eating when I entered the restaurant.
■ 결과를 나타내는 과거완료: 과거 이전에 일어난 일로 인해 과거에 어떠한 결과가 생겼음을 나타낼 때 사용한다.
When she arrived at the bus stop, she found she **had lost** her wallet.
When I went to pick her up, she **had** already **gone** home.

★ **PLUS TIP** 과거보다 훨씬 이전에 일어난 일을 나타내는 경우에 대과거(had+v-ed)를 쓴다. 단, before, after 등의 접속사와 함께 쓰여 시간의 전후 관계가 분명한 경우에는 과거 이전에 일어난 일이라도 과거시제를 쓸 수 있다.
Mary returned to her job *after* she **had recovered[recovered]** from her illness.

A 다음 ( ) 안에서 알맞은 말을 고르시오.

1 The first train (has left / had left) when she arrived at the station.

2 My sister (has been / was) upset with me since Tuesday.

3 I couldn't see clearly because I (have broken / had broken) my glasses.

4 Mr. Kim (has quit / quit) the job one year before he started his own business.

5 He (has already cleaned / had already cleaned) his room when his parents came home.

B 다음 우리말과 같은 뜻이 되도록 ( ) 안의 말을 배열하여 문장을 완성하시오.

1 그는 한 달 전에 다리를 다쳐서 어제 축구를 할 수 없었다.
(he, hurt, leg, had, a month, his, before)
_____, so he couldn't play soccer yesterday.

2 버스에 올라탔을 때, 나는 집에 가방을 두고 왔다는 것을 알았다.
(I, at home, bag, had, my, left)
When I got on the bus, I found _____.

3 그 남자가 연주를 마쳤을 때, 조명이 나갔다.
(finished, the man, had, playing, when)
_____, the lights went out.

4 그가 그곳에 도착했을 때 Ann은 이미 떠나고 없었다. (left, had, Ann, already)
_____ when he got there.

5 내가 음식점에 들어갔을 땐, 그녀는 이미 그녀의 음식을 주문해 두었었다.
(already, her, had, food, ordered, she)
When I entered the restaurant, _____.

과거완료 진행형

- 과거완료 진행형은 〈had+been+v-ing〉의 형태로 과거의 어느 시점 이전에 시작된 일이 과거에도 진행 중임을 나타낼 때 사용한다.

  He **had been preparing** dinner for an hour when I entered the kitchen.

  I **had been studying** Spanish for a year before I went on a trip to Mexico.

A 다음 밑줄 친 부분을 과거완료 진행형으로 바꾸어 쓰시오.

1 It <u>rained</u> before I came here.

2 I <u>watched</u> a TV show before you called me.

3 He <u>played</u> the piano for 45 minutes.

4 She <u>read</u> the newspaper for half an hour when the doorbell rang.

5 I <u>chatted</u> on my smartphone all afternoon, so my dad told me to go play outside.

B 다음 우리말과 같은 뜻이 되도록 ( ) 안의 말을 이용하여 문장을 완성하시오.

1 내가 토론토에 도착했을 때, 3일째 눈이 내리던 중이었다. (snow)
It _____ _____ _____ for three days when I arrived in Toronto.

2 Kelly는 한 번도 외국에 가본 적이 없다. (be)
Kelly _____ _____ _____ to a foreign country.

3 그 부부는 여름휴가로 발리에 가고 없었다. (go)
The couple _____ _____ to Bali for their summer vacation.

4 그가 마침내 무대에 올랐을 때, 사람들은 10분 넘게 그의 이름을 외치던 중이었다. (shout)
When he finally got on stage, people _____ _____ _____ his name for over ten minutes.

5 Sam은 이틀을 걷고 나서, 사막에서 오아시스를 발견했다. (walk)
After Sam _____ _____ _____ for two days, he found an oasis in the desert.

6 기차가 마침내 도착했을 때, 사람들은 몇 시간째 그것을 기다리던 중이었다. (wait)
People _____ _____ _____ for the train for hours when it finally arrived.

7 선생님이 그녀의 이름을 불렀을 때, Sue는 그녀의 자리에서 자던 중이었다. (sleep)
Sue _____ _____ _____ at her desk when her teacher called her name.

[01-03] 다음 빈칸에 알맞은 말을 고르시오.

01

> I _____ to Japan twice since last year.

① have been   ② went   ③ have being
④ had gone   ⑤ was

02

> I _____ the Internet when he came in.

① surf
② have surfed
③ had been surfing
④ have been surfing
⑤ am surfing

03

> A: How long have you lived here?
> B: I _____ here for ten years.

① had lived
② have lived
③ had living
④ was living
⑤ have living

[04-06] 다음 빈칸에 공통으로 들어갈 말을 고르시오.

04

> • I have had a cat _____ I was a kid.
> • He has been playing badminton _____ 2015.

① for   ② in   ③ since
④ before   ⑤ when

05

> • He realized that she _____ sick for three days.
> • I _____ to Europe three times by the time I graduated from middle school.

① had
② was
③ have been
④ had been
⑤ having been

06

> • We _____ Hong Kong twice before we decided to move there.
> • Hundreds of people _____ this restaurant before it closed.

① visit
② had visited
③ will visit
④ have visited
⑤ have been visiting

[07-08] 빈칸에 들어갈 말이 순서대로 알맞게 짝지어진 것을 고르시오.

07

> A: How long have you _____ here?
> B: _____ here for two years.

① work – I'm working
② worked – I was working
③ been worked – I've worked
④ been working – I'm working
⑤ been working – I've been working

08

When I _____ the door, he _____ the computer game for three hours.

① opened – plays
② opened – is playing
③ had opened – was playing
④ opened – had been playing
⑤ was opening – had been played

기출응용

09

다음 중 빈칸에 들어갈 말로 알맞지 <u>않은</u> 것은?

- I ___①___ to the festival before.
- Nancy has been ___②___ with her friend at a café.
- How long have you ___③___ TV?
- When I arrived at the concert hall, the show ___④___ .
- He ___⑤___ at this company since 2016.

① have never been ② talking
③ watching ④ had already begun
⑤ has worked

[10-12] 다음 밑줄 친 부분의 쓰임이 나머지와 <u>다른</u> 것을 고르시오.

10

① She <u>has seen</u> a musical recently.
② He <u>has loved</u> that song since he first heard it.
③ They <u>have helped</u> poor children for a year.
④ I <u>have been</u> in the hospital since last month.
⑤ I <u>have used</u> this smartphone since I bought it.

11

① I <u>have already had</u> dinner.
② He <u>has gone</u> to Croatia.
③ I <u>haven't decided</u> where to go.
④ He <u>hasn't finished</u> his lesson yet.
⑤ Your favorite show <u>has just ended</u>.

12

① Jenny <u>had never been</u> to a zoo.
② <u>Had you talked</u> to James before you graduated?
③ I <u>hadn't ridden</u> a horse before I became ten.
④ The train <u>had already left</u> when I arrived at the station.
⑤ Because I <u>had visited</u> New York several times, I was familiar with the city.

13

다음 두 문장을 한 문장으로 만든 것으로 알맞은 것은?

The boys fell asleep an hour ago.
They are still sleeping now.

① The boys slept for an hour.
② The boys had slept for an hour.
③ The boys have been slept for an hour.
④ The boys had been sleeping for an hour.
⑤ The boys have been sleeping for an hour.

[14-15] 다음 우리말을 영어로 바르게 옮긴 것을 고르시오.

14

내가 도착했을 때 대회는 막 시작했었다.

① The contest had just begun when I arrived.
② The contest began when I was arriving.
③ The contest began when I have arrived.
④ The contest was beginning when I arrived.
⑤ The contest has just begun when I arrived.

15

> 그는 두 시간째 연설하고 있는 중이다.

① He gave a speech for two hours.
② He was giving a speech for two hours.
③ He had given a speech for two hours.
④ He had been giving a speech for two hours.
⑤ He has been giving a speech for two hours.

16

빈칸에 들어갈 말이 나머지와 다른 것은?

① I _____ to the dentist a week earlier.
② He _____ cooking in the kitchen when I called.
③ I _____ living in Spain for five years before I met her.
④ I knew the place because I _____ there before we went.
⑤ I'm in the hotel now. I _____ here since yesterday.

[17–18] 다음 밑줄 친 부분이 어법상 틀린 것을 고르시오.

17

① He has moved to Africa.
② I haven't talked to her since last year.
③ How long have you been waiting?
④ He hasn't had his dinner when I visited his house.
⑤ She had worked as a nurse before she moved here.

18

① He has been washing the dishes.
② I have taken a picture with that actor.
③ He had been standing in front of the garage for an hour when I arrived.
④ James has studied English since kindergarten.
⑤ I stopped by her house after I have finished the work.

19

다음 대화 중 자연스럽지 않은 것은?

① A: Why don't you eat something?
   B: I've already had lunch.
② A: How long have you been married?
   B: We've been married for five years.
③ A: What has he been doing?
   B: He has cooked for his wife before.
④ A: When did you lose your phone?
   B: I lost it when I was on the bus.
⑤ A: When did you start playing tennis?
   B: Last month. I'd never played tennis until then.

고난도

20

다음 중 어법상 옳은 문장의 개수는?

(a) Ian has never met Daisy yesterday.
(b) Bob has been cleaning the house since this morning.
(c) I prepared to go to school after I had had breakfast.
(d) Kathy had been writing a novel until she got sick.

① 0개   ② 1개   ③ 2개   ④ 3개   ⑤ 4개

서술형 따라잡기

01
다음 두 문장을 완료형을 이용하여 한 문장으로 만들 때, 빈칸에 알맞은 말을 쓰시오.

(1) Jack went to his hometown.
   And he is still there.
   → Jack _____ _____ to his hometown.

(2) My mother was coughing a lot a week ago.
   She is still coughing a lot.
   → My mother _____ _____ _____
   a lot for a week.

02
주어진 말을 알맞게 배열하여 우리말과 뜻이 같도록 문장을 완성하시오.

(1) 너는 그 책 읽는 것을 끝냈니?
   (reading, finished, the, have, book, you)
   → _____

(2) 그녀는 12살 때까지 수영을 해 본 적이 없었다.
   (twelve, swum, until, she, had, was, she, never)
   → _____

03
다음 그림을 보고, 주어진 말을 이용하여 문장을 완성하시오.

one year ago   three days ago
now   yesterday

(1) The girl _____ _____ _____ the
   violin for a year as a hobby. (play)

(2) It _____ _____ _____ for three
   days when I got there yesterday. (rain)

04
주어진 말을 이용하여 대화를 완성하시오.

A: _____ _____ _____ you
   _____ Jessie? (know)
B: I've known her for about two years.

05
다음 야구 경기 기록표를 보고, 주어진 말을 이용하여 문장을 완성하시오. (단, 팀명은 복수 취급할 것)

Day	Game	Final Score
Wed.	Bears vs. Tigers	0 – 3
Thu.	Bears vs. Tigers	7 – 4
Fri. (Today)	Bears vs. Lions	2 – 1

(1) The Bears _____ _____ _____
   _____ _____ every day since
   Wednesday. (have, a baseball game)

(2) The Bears _____ _____ their last two
   games. (win)

고난도

06
다음 대화를 읽고, 틀린 부분을 모두 찾아 바르게 고쳐 쓰시오. (3군데)

A: Have you lived in an English-speaking
   country before?
B: No, I had never been to one. Why?
A: I have heard you speaking perfect
   English yesterday. How did you learn?
B: I watched English TV shows since I was
   five.

핵심 포인트 정리하기

1 현재완료

- 형태: ⟨① _____ + _____⟩
- 과거에 일어난 일이 현재까지 영향을 미칠 때 사용

 when과 특정 과거 시점을 나타내는 말은 현재완료와 함께 쓰지 않는다는 것 기억하기!

2 과거완료

- 형태: ⟨② _____ + _____⟩
- 과거의 어느 시점을 기준으로 그 이전에 일어난 일이 과거까지 영향을 미칠 때 사용

3 완료형의 용법

용법	의미	현재완료	과거완료
계속	'(계속) ~해 왔다'	과거부터 현재까지 계속되어 온 상태나 동작	과거 이전부터 과거의 어느 시점까지 계속된 일
경험	③ '_____'	과거에서 현재까지 있었던 경험	과거 이전부터 과거의 어느 시점까지 있었던 경험
완료	④ '_____'	과거에 시작된 일이 현재에 완료됨	과거 이전에 시작된 일이 과거의 어느 시점에 막 완료됨
결과	'~해 버렸다'	과거의 일로 인해 현재에 어떠한 결과가 발생함	과거 이전에 일어난 일로 인해 과거에 어떠한 결과가 발생함

* 대과거(had+v-ed): 과거에 일어난 일보다 훨씬 이전에 있었던 일을 나타낼 경우에 씀

 완료형의 용법 구분하기!

4 현재완료 진행형과 과거완료 진행형

- 현재완료 진행형: ⟨⑤ _____ + _____ + _____⟩
  과거에 시작된 일이 현재에도 진행 중임을 나타냄
- 과거완료 진행형: ⟨⑥ _____ + _____ + _____⟩
  과거의 어느 시점 이전에 시작된 일이 과거에도 진행 중임을 나타냄

문제로 개념 다지기

밑줄 친 부분이 어법상 맞으면 O, 틀리면 X 표시하고 바르게 고치시오.

1 We <u>have gone</u> to the White House before.

2 I <u>had not seen</u> Mickey since he left here four years ago.

3 Ray looks tired. He <u>has been working</u> overtime this month.

4 She <u>had broken</u> her legs during the vacation, so she didn't attend any P.E. classes.

5 When Ellen called him, Billy <u>is just finished</u> his homework.

food truck

CHAPTER 07

수동태

개념 쏙쏙

He **is giving** <u>my sister</u> <u>a piano lesson</u>.
　　　　　　간접목적어　　　직접목적어
→ <u>My sister</u> **is being given** a piano lesson by him.
→ <u>A piano lesson</u> **is being given** *to* my sister by him.　　　　**[4형식 문장의 수동태]**

She **made** us stand in the corner.
　　　　　　목적격 보어
→ We **were made** <u>to stand</u> in the corner by her.　　　　**[5형식 문장의 수동태]**

수동태

주어가 행위의 영향을 받거나 당하는 상황일 때 수동태를 사용합니다. 4형식 문장을 수동태로 만들 때는 일반적으로 간접목적어나 직접목적어를 주어로 나타낼 수 있습니다. 5형식 문장을 수동태로 만들 때는 동사에 따라 목적격 보어가 그대로 쓰이기도 하고 to부정사 또는 현재분사로 바뀌기도 한다는 점을 기억해 두세요.

수동태의 의미

- 수동태: 〈be동사+v-ed(+by 행위자)〉의 형태로, 주어가 행위의 영향을 받거나 당할 때 사용하며 '~가 …되다[받다]'라고 해석한다.

A lot of people all over the world drink milk. (능동태)

→ Milk **is drunk by** a lot of people all over the world. (수동태)

- 행위자가 일반인이거나 불특정 다수일 때, 혹은 너무 분명하거나 중요하지 않을 때 행위자(by+목적격)를 생략하기도 한다.

Spanish **is spoken** in Mexico and Argentina.

- 과거시제: 〈be동사의 과거형[was/were]+v-ed〉　　This song **was written** by Bruno Mars.
- 미래시제: 〈will+be+v-ed〉　　　　　　　　　　A live concert **will be given** by the group.

A 다음 두 문장이 같은 뜻이 되도록 문장을 완성하시오.

1 His friends didn't call him last night.

→ He _____ last night.

2 They will open the Blue House to the public this weekend.

→ The Blue House _____ this weekend.

3 I baked the chocolate chip cookies in the oven.

→ The chocolate chip cookies _____ by me.

4 The company offers free Wi-Fi to all employees.

→ Free Wi-Fi _____ by the company.

5 People usually use this cell phone as a camera.

→ This cell phone _____ .

B 다음 우리말과 같은 뜻이 되도록 ( ) 안의 말을 이용하여 문장을 완성하시오.

1 기다려 주세요. 당신의 음식이 곧 제공될 것입니다. (serve)

Please wait. Your food _____ _____ _____ soon.

2 이 그림은 그 박물관이 소유하고 있나요? (own)

_____ this painting _____ by the museum?

3 그의 상처는 간호사에 의해 닦일 것이다. (clean)

His wound _____ _____ _____ by the nurse.

4 그 피자는 당신에게 배달될 것이다. (deliver)

The pizza _____ _____ _____ to you.

5 작년에 그 공장에 의해 많은 양의 종이가 생산되었다. (produce)

A lot of paper _____ _____ by the factory last year.

수동태의 형태

- 완료형: ⟨have[has/had]+been+v-ed⟩
  The car **has been parked** in front of the shop for days.
- 진행형: ⟨be동사+being+v-ed⟩
  The rumor **is being spread**.
- 조동사의 수동태: ⟨조동사+be+v-ed⟩
  This pasta dish **can be made** quickly.

★ PLUS TIP 미래시제, 완료형, 조동사 수동태의 부정형은 조동사에 not을 붙여 나타낸다.
These shoes **will not[won't] be sold** anymore.
That computer **has not[hasn't] been used** for a long time.
That mistake **should not[shouldn't] be made** again.

A 다음 밑줄 친 부분을 어법에 맞게 고쳐 쓰시오.

1 My sister is been examining by a doctor right now.

2 These earphones have used for three years by Nancy.

3 This exercise should been repeated five times a day.

B 다음 문장을 수동태로 바꾸어 쓰시오.

1 The school may accept our proposal.

→ _____

2 We must not forget his birthday again.

→ _____

3 The kids were building sand castles on the beach.

→ _____

C 다음 우리말과 같은 뜻이 되도록 ( ) 안의 말을 이용하여 문장을 완성하시오.

1 그것은 차게 먹을 수 있다. (can, eat)
It _____ _____ _____ cold.

2 그녀는 수년간 아이처럼 취급당해 왔다. (treat)
She _____ _____ _____ like a child for years.

3 Paul은 경찰관에 의해 사실대로 말할 것을 요구받는 중이다. (ask)
Paul _____ _____ _____ to tell the truth by the police.

4 그의 차는 정비사에게 옮겨져야 한다. (should, take)
His car _____ _____ _____ to a mechanic.

4형식 문장의 수동태

- 4형식 문장은 간접목적어와 직접목적어를 각각 주어로 한 두 개의 수동태 문장을 만들 수 있다.
- 직접목적어가 수동태 문장의 주어가 되면 간접목적어 앞에 to나 for와 같은 전치사를 쓴다. 대부분의 동사는 간접목적어 앞에 to를 쓰지만 buy, make, get 등의 동사는 for를 쓴다.

My uncle gave me some advice.
　　　　　　　간접목적어　직접목적어

→ I **was given** some advice by my uncle.

→ Some advice **was given** *to* me by my uncle.

★ PLUS TIP buy, make, get과 같은 동사는 수동태의 주어로 간접목적어를 거의 쓰지 않는다.

A　다음 문장을 두 가지 형태의 수동태로 바꾸어 쓰시오.

1　Mrs. Park gave us an impressive lesson in Korean history class.

→ We _____ .

→ An impressive lesson _____ .

2　The man told the children an interesting story.

→ The children _____ .

→ An interesting story _____ .

3　My secretary handed me my travel schedule.

→ I _____ .

→ My travel schedule _____ .

B　다음 우리말과 같은 뜻이 되도록 (　) 안의 말을 이용하여 문장을 완성하시오.

1　그 재미있는 영상들은 Jerry에 의해 그녀에게 보내졌다. (send)

Those funny video clips _____ _____ _____ _____ by Jerry.

2　그 라자냐는 그를 위해 만들어졌다. (make)

The lasagna _____ _____ _____ .

3　내 오래된 사진들이 Mark에게 보여졌다. (show)

My old photos _____ _____ _____ _____ .

4　이 목걸이는 내 남자친구에 의해 나에게 주어졌다. (give)

This necklace _____ _____ _____ _____ by my boyfriend.

5　새 신발 한 켤레는 Julie를 위해 Helen에 의해 구매되었다. (buy)

A pair of new shoes _____ _____ _____ _____ by Helen.

5형식 문장의 수동태 I

- 5형식 문장을 수동태로 바꿀 경우, 능동태 문장의 목적어를 주어로 하고 동사는 〈be+v-ed〉 형태로 바꾼다.
  목적격 보어로 쓰인 명사, 형용사, to부정사, 분사는 동사 뒤에 그대로 둔다.
  They painted the wall *blue*.
  → The wall **was painted** *blue* by them.
  My mom told me *to stay calm*.
  → I **was told** *to stay calm* by my mom.

A 다음 문장을 수동태로 바꾸어 쓰시오.

1 Everyone considers the boy clever.

→ _____

2 The zookeeper kept the baby tigers warm.

→ _____

3 Serena found him to be satisfied with the results.

→ _____

4 They asked the man to empty all the boxes.

→ _____

5 The teacher told us not to make noise during the test.

→ _____

B 다음 우리말과 같은 뜻이 되도록 ( ) 안의 말을 이용하여 능동태 문장을 완성한 후, 이를 수동태 문장으로 바꾸어 쓰시오.

1 사람들은 그를 전문가로 여겼다. (consider, an expert)
People _____.

→ _____

2 부모님은 내가 여행 가는 것을 허락하셨다. (allow, travel)
My parents _____.

→ _____

3 그녀는 내게 택시를 타라고 조언해 주었다. (advise, take a taxi)
She _____.

→ _____

4 그 아이들은 내게 무서운 이야기를 해 달라고 부탁했다. (ask, a scary story)
The children _____.

→ _____

Point 05 — 5형식 문장의 수동태 II

- 사역동사 make의 목적격 보어로 쓰인 원형부정사는 수동태 문장에서 to부정사 형태로 바뀐다.
  He **made** me *read* it out loud.
  → I **was made** *to read* it out loud by him.
- 지각동사의 목적격 보어로 쓰인 원형부정사는 수동태 문장에서 to부정사로 바뀐다. 지각동사의 목적격 보어가
  현재분사인 경우에는 그대로 둔다.
  I **heard** him *shout[shouting]* in the kitchen.
  → He **was heard** *to shout[shouting]* in the kitchen.

A 다음 밑줄 친 부분을 어법에 맞게 고쳐 쓰시오.

1 They were <u>made wear</u> school uniforms.

2 He was <u>heard to whispering</u>, "Let's go now."

3 The woman was <u>saw jogging</u> in the park.

4 A strange man <u>was seen enter</u> the bank by the guard.

B 다음 문장을 수동태로 바꾸어 쓰시오.

1 She saw the couple holding hands.

→ _____

2 My mom always makes me clean my room.

→ _____

3 A reporter saw the people cheer for the baseball team.

→ _____

C 다음 우리말과 같은 뜻이 되도록 ( ) 안의 말을 이용하여 문장을 완성하시오.

1 그는 방과 후에 남게 되었다. (make, stay)

_____ _____ _____ _____ _____ after school.

2 그들이 새 대통령에 대해 이야기하고 있는 것이 들렸다. (heard, talk)

_____ _____ _____ _____ about the new president.

3 그녀가 큰 가방 하나를 집으로 옮기는 것이 보였다. (see, carry)

_____ _____ _____ _____ _____ a big bag into her house.

4 아기가 방에서 울고 있는 것이 들렸다. (heard, cry)

The baby _____ _____ _____ in the room.

주의해야 하는 수동태 I − by 이외의 전치사를 쓰는 수동태

- 수동태 문장에서 행위자는 〈by+목적격〉으로 나타내는 것이 일반적이지만, by 이외의 전치사가 쓰이는 경우도 많다.
  - be worried about: ~에 대해 걱정하다
  - be covered with[in]: ~로 덮여 있다
  - be filled with: ~로 가득 차다
  - be crowded with: ~로 붐비다
  - be interested in: ~에 관심이 있다

  - be satisfied with: ~에 만족하다
  - be surprised at: ~에 놀라다
  - be pleased with: ~로 즐거워하다
  - be made of[from]: ~로 만들어지다(물리[화학]적 변화)
  - be known to: ~에게 알려지다

  The basket **is filled with** red apples.　　I **was surprised at** the news.

A 다음 우리말과 같은 뜻이 되도록 위의 표현들을 이용하여 문장을 완성하시오.

1 나는 Jamie의 병이 걱정된다.

I _____ _____ _____ Jamie's illness.

2 그녀는 끔찍한 광경에 놀랐다.

She _____ _____ _____ the terrible sight.

3 그의 선행은 모든 사람에게 알려졌다.

His good deeds _____ _____ _____ everyone.

4 그 공연장은 수천 명의 팬들로 붐볐다.

The concert hall _____ _____ _____ thousands of fans.

5 교실은 학생들로 가득 차 있다.

The classroom _____ _____ _____ students.

B 자연스러운 대화가 되도록 〈보기〉에서 알맞은 말을 골라 빈칸에 적절한 형태로 써넣으시오.
(단, 한 번씩만 사용할 것)

〈보기〉	make	interest	cover	satisfy

1 A: How's your new laptop?

B: It has a lot of useful functions. I _____ _____ _____ it.

2 A: This lunchbox is light, so it is easy to carry.

B: Yes, that's because it _____ _____ _____ plastic.

3 A: When did you make this snowman?

B: I made it this morning. Our front yard _____ _____ _____ snow.

4 A: I've heard Sue joined your winter sports club.

B: That's right. She is _____ _____ learning how to snowboard.

주의해야 하는 수동태 II – 동사구의 수동태

■ 동사구의 수동태: 동사구를 하나의 동사처럼 취급하여 동사만 〈be+v-ed〉의 형태로 바꾸고, 동사구에 포함된 부사나 전치사 등은 그대로 쓴다.

The man **swept away** the leaves on the street.
→ The leaves on the street **were swept away** by the man.
Someone will **carry out** the plan soon.
→ The plan will **be carried out** soon.

★ 내신만점 TIP ▶ 목적어가 필요 없는 동사와 상태나 소유를 나타내는 동사 have, resemble, fit, lack, suit 등은 수동태로 쓰지 않음에 유의하자.
The car accident **happened**(→ ~~was happened~~) on the crosswalk.

A 다음 문장에서 동사구에 ( ) 표시를 한 후, 수동태 문장으로 바꾸어 쓰시오.

1 My father turned off the light in my room.
→ The light in my room _____.

2 Mr. Kim found out the truth.
→ The truth _____.

3 Many people look up to Rebecca's parents.
→ Rebecca's parents _____.

B 다음 우리말과 같은 뜻이 되도록 ( ) 안의 말을 배열하여 문장을 완성하시오.

1 나는 우리 할머니와 많이 닮았다. (resemble, my, I, closely, grandmother)
_____

2 그 보고서는 오늘 아침에 제출되었다. (handed in, the report, this morning, was)
_____

3 Beyonce의 콘서트는 하루 만에 매진되었다.
(a day, was, in, sold out, Beyonce's concert)
_____

C 다음 문장을 수동태 문장으로 바꾸어 쓰시오.

1 Kelly took care of the baby.
→ _____

2 The principal called off the school trip to Taiwan.
→ _____

3 The kids laugh at his strange hat all the time.
→ _____

that절을 목적어로 하는 문장의 수동태

■ 문장의 동사가 say, believe, think, consider, report 등인 경우, ⟨It is + v-ed that …⟩ 형태의 수동태 문장을 만들 수 있다. that절의 주어를 수동태 문장의 주어로 할 수도 있는데, 이때 that절의 동사는 to부정사로 바뀐다.

People say that <u>eating too much sugar</u> is dangerous for your health.
→ **It is said that** <u>eating too much sugar</u> is dangerous for your health.
→ <u>Eating too much sugar</u> **is said *to be*** dangerous for your health.

A 다음 두 문장이 같은 뜻이 되도록 문장을 완성하시오.

1 It is thought that artists are very sensitive.
  → Artists _____.

2 It is believed that blood type determines personality.
  → Blood type _____.

3 It is reported that doing aerobics is effective for losing weight.
  → Doing aerobics _____.

B 다음 문장을 It으로 시작하는 수동태 문장으로 바꾸어 쓰시오.

1 People think that Mr. Kang is humorous.
  → It _____.

2 They report that flowers will begin to bloom earlier than last year.
  → It _____.

3 People say that he won the medal to please his sick mother.
  → It _____.

C 다음 우리말과 같은 뜻이 되도록 ( ) 안의 말을 이용하여 문장을 완성하시오.

1 음악은 정서 발달에 도움이 된다고들 말한다. (say, help)
  Music _____ _____ _____ _____ emotional development.

2 아침 식사를 하는 것이 두뇌에 좋다고들 믿는다. (believe)
  _____ _____ _____ _____ having breakfast is good for your brain.

3 10분 동안의 낮잠이 에너지 수치를 높여준다고 보도되었다. (report, increase)
  Taking a nap for ten minutes _____ _____ _____ _____ energy levels.

내신대비 TEST

[01-03] 다음 우리말과 같은 뜻이 되도록 빈칸에 알맞은 말을 고르시오.

01

> 그 상자는 지금 막 치워졌다.
> The box has just _____ removed.

① been ② being ③ was
④ had ⑤ is

02

> 그 문은 그에 의해 수리될 것이다.
> The door will _____ by him.

① repair ② is repaired
③ be repairing ④ be repaired
⑤ have repaired

03

> 그 침대는 담요로 덮여 있었다.
> The bed was covered _____ a blanket.

① at ② with ③ to
④ of ⑤ on

04
다음 문장을 수동태로 바르게 바꾼 것을 모두 고르면? (2개)

> They say that stress causes headaches.

① Stress is said causing headaches.
② Stress is said to cause headaches.
③ It is said that stress causes headaches.
④ It is said that stress caused headaches.
⑤ It is said that stress to cause headaches.

[05-07] 빈칸에 들어갈 말이 순서대로 알맞게 짝지어진 것을 고르시오.

05

> • This slide show will _____ by Mark.
> • The package _____ me yesterday.

① present – was delivering
② present – has been delivered
③ be presented – delivered to
④ be presented – was delivered to
⑤ be presenting – was delivered

06

> • I'm afraid of _____ by my mom.
> • The coat _____ me well.

① scolding – suits
② am scolding – is suited
③ being scolded – suits
④ being scolded – is suited
⑤ was scolded – suits

07

> • I love _____ by others.
> • He _____ to score the first goal of this game.

① be respecting – expects
② be respected – is expecting
③ being respecting – is expected
④ being respected – is expected
⑤ being respected – is be expected

[08-09] 다음 문장을 수동태로 바꿀 때 빈칸에 알맞은 말을 고르시오.

08

They found him to be depressed.
→ He _____ by them.

① was found be depressed
② was find to be depressed
③ was found to be depressed
④ was found be depressing
⑤ was found to be depressing

09

People saw Jim jogging with his dog in the park.
→ Jim _____ with his dog in the park.

① is seen jog　　　　② is seen to jog
③ was seen jog　　　④ was seen jogging
⑤ had been seeing jogging

[10-11] 다음 밑줄 친 부분이 어법상 틀린 것을 고르시오.

10

① He was surprised at the news.
② I was sent an email by a friend.
③ The question hasn't been solved yet.
④ A bridge is being built over the river.
⑤ Beans are reporting to prevent cancer.

11

① This work can be finished tonight.
② The food is being preparing now.
③ They were asked to respond to the survey.
④ Susan is interested in cooking.
⑤ Many books have been written about the Korean War.

[12-13] 다음 중 어법상 틀린 것을 고르시오.

12

① I was taught English by Mr. Brown.
② The house was sold yesterday.
③ Stars can see at night here by tourists.
④ They were told to rewrite their essay.
⑤ The problem will be explained to those students.

13

① She is considered to be kind.
② He was made eat vegetables.
③ This room should be cleaned by six.
④ The old man was run over by a truck.
⑤ The man is satisfied with his new car.

기출응용
14

다음 문장을 지시대로 바르게 바꾸지 않은 것은?

① She is called the queen of jazz. (과거시제)
　→ She was called the queen of jazz.
② The gift is delivered by that postman. (완료형)
　→ The gift has been delivered by that postman.
③ Free drinks are offered for only one hour. (미래시제)
　→ Free drinks will offered for only one hour.
④ This machine is repaired by her. (진행형)
　→ This machine is being repaired by her.
⑤ These coupons are used by students. (조동사 can 이용)
　→ These coupons can be used by students.

15
다음 문장을 수동태로 바르게 바꾸지 <u>않은</u> 것은?

① Everybody knew the secret.
  → The secret was known to everybody.
② He advised me to apologize to her.
  → I was advised to apologize to her by him.
③ People think that he is a fast runner.
  → It is thought that he is a fast runner.
④ They believe that Angela studies hard.
  → Angela is believed study hard.
⑤ She should do the laundry by this evening.
  → The laundry should be done by this evening by her.

16
(A), (B), (C)의 괄호 안에서 알맞은 것끼리 바르게 짝지어진 것은?

(A) He was chosen [design / to design] the coat.
(B) Your soup [is heating / is being heated] in the pot.
(C) He is pleased [with / on] my present.

	(A)	(B)	(C)
①	design	⋯⋯ is heating	⋯⋯ with
②	design	⋯⋯ is heating	⋯⋯ on
③	design	⋯⋯ is being heated	⋯⋯ on
④	to design	⋯⋯ is being heated	⋯⋯ on
⑤	to design	⋯⋯ is being heated	⋯⋯ with

고난도

17
다음 중 어법상 옳은 것을 모두 고르면? (3개)

① This bread has just been cut.
② Jessica was elected president.
③ My mother is resembled by me.
④ The boy was told helping his brother.
⑤ She likes being visited by her friends.

기출응용

18
다음 중 어느 빈칸에도 들어갈 수 <u>없는</u> 것은?

(a) The bottle is filled _____ milk.
(b) This wine is made _____ green grapes.
(c) She is worried _____ tomorrow's weather.
(d) My uncle was interested _____ rock music.

① at   ② with   ③ from
④ in   ⑤ about

19
다음 밑줄 친 부분을 바르게 고치지 <u>않은</u> 것은?

① The air conditioner <u>turned off</u> by her.
            → was turned off
② Kids were <u>made focus on</u> the class by the teacher.   → made focusing on
③ Eating well every day is thought <u>be important</u>.
            → to be important
④ The kitten <u>is being taken care</u> by my sister.
            → is being taken care of
⑤ People were heard <u>complain</u> about the play.
            → complaining

20
빈칸에 들어갈 말이 나머지와 <u>다른</u> 것은?

① The speech was given _____ the president.
② The machine was invented _____ the scientist.
③ The music was played _____ a famous pianist.
④ The principal was visited _____ some students.
⑤ The room was crowded _____ photographers.

서술형 따라잡기

01
다음 문장을 수동태로 바꾸어 쓰시오.

(1) My mom bought me this eco bag.

→ This eco bag _____.

(2) He will fix your bicycle by tomorrow.

→ Your bicycle _____.

02
다음 우리말과 같은 뜻이 되도록 **틀린** 부분을 바르게 고쳐 문장으로 쓰시오.

(1) 짐은 배로 보내져야 한다.

Luggage should send to the ship.

→ _____

(2) 당신의 코트는 지금 세탁 중이다.

Your coat is washing now.

→ _____

03
다음 그림을 보고, 주어진 말을 이용하여 수동태 문장을 만드시오.

John   Holly

(1) _____ (7단어)

(the house, paint)

(2) _____ (9단어)

(the bookshelf, will, fill, books)

04
주어진 말을 이용하여 우리말과 뜻이 같도록 문장을 완성하시오.

그녀는 그 친절한 승객들에게 도움을 받았다.
(help out)

→ _____ _____ _____ _____ by
the friendly passengers.

05
다음 학생신문이 보도한 내용을 읽고, 문장을 완성하시오.

The school newspaper reports that …
(1) The tennis club is looking for a new member.
(2) The school cafeteria is preparing a special lunch today.
(3) A pop singer is coming to our school festival.

(1) The tennis club is reported _____

_____.

(2) The school cafeteria _____

_____.

(3) It is reported _____

_____.

고난도

06
다음 Judy가 SNS에 올린 글을 읽고, **틀린** 부분을 모두 찾아 바르게 고쳐 쓰시오. (3군데)

I have just been arrived here for a speech contest. I practiced really hard, and I was told deliver my speech with confidence. But I'm still worried by making a mistake.

핵심 포인트 정리하기

1 수동태의 의미와 형태

■ 주어가 행위의 영향을 받거나 당할 때 사용하는 표현

- 기본형: 〈① _____ + _____ (+by 행위자)〉
- 과거시제: 〈② _____ + _____〉
- 미래시제: 〈③ _____ + _____ + _____〉
- 완료형: 〈have[has/had] + ④ _____ + v-ed〉
- 진행형: 〈be동사 + ⑤ _____ + v-ed〉
- 조동사의 수동태: 〈조동사 + ⑥ _____ + v-ed〉

2 4형식 / 5형식 문장의 수동태

■ 4형식 문장의 수동태: 간접목적어와 직접목적어 각각을 주어로 한 두 개의 수동태 문장 가능

- 직접목적어가 수동태의 주어일 때 간접목적어 앞에 전치사를 씀
  (대부분의 동사: ⑦ _____ / buy, make, get 등의 동사: for)

■ 5형식 문장의 수동태

- 대부분의 동사는 수동태로 바뀌어도 목적격 보어의 형태가 변하지 않음
- 사역동사 make의 목적격 보어인 원형부정사는 수동태에서 ⑧ _____로 바뀜
- 지각동사의 목적격 보어로 쓰인 원형부정사는 수동태에서 ⑨ _____로 바뀜
  지각동사의 목적격 보어가 현재분사인 경우에는 그대로 유지

 사역동사나 지각동사가 쓰인 5형식 문장의 수동태에서 목적격 보어의 형태 알아두기!

3 주의해야 하는 수동태

by 이외의 전치사를 쓰는 경우	be filled with '~로 가득 차다' / ⑩ _____ '~에 만족하다' 등
동사구의 수동태	동사구 전체를 하나의 동사처럼 취급
수동태로 쓸 수 없는 동사	목적어가 필요 없거나, 상태나 소유를 나타내는 동사
that절을 목적어로 하는 수동태 (say, believe 등의 동사)	〈It is + v-ed that + 주어 + 동사〉 *that절의 주어를 수동태의 주어로 할 경우, that절의 동사는 ⑪ _____로 바뀜

 by 이외의 전치사를 쓰는 수동태 표현과, 수동태로 쓸 수 없는 동사 기억하기!

문제로 개념 다지기

밑줄 친 부분이 어법상 맞으면 O, 틀리면 X 표시하고 바르게 고치시오.

1 Dogs were heard <u>bark</u> all night long.

2 A cake <u>is been made</u> in the kitchen now.

3 Those animals should be <u>taken by experts care of</u>.

4 Hey, look out the window! Everything <u>is covered with</u> snow.

5 Between the tests, students will <u>be giving</u> 10 minutes to rest.

6 A broken mirror is said <u>that means</u> bad luck.

food truck

CHAPTER 08

조동사

개념 쏙쏙

I **would rather** see a doctor than take some medicine.
Nick **used to** eat ice cream before meals.
He **may have wanted** to talk with us.

조동사

조동사는 일반동사나 be동사 앞에 쓰여 능력, 추측, 허가, 의무 등의 의미를 더해주는 말입니다.
주어의 수나 인칭, 시제에 따라 변하지 않고 뒤에 반드시 동사원형을 씁니다. <조동사+have+v-ed>의
형태로 지난 일에 대한 추측, 의심, 후회, 유감을 나타낼 수도 있습니다.

- can의 의미
  ① 능력(~할 수 있다 = be able to): I **can** make a speech in front of a large audience.
  ② 가능성(~일 수도 있다): The weather **can** quickly change.
  ③ 허가 및 요청(~해도 된다): **Can** I get some information about the project?
  ③ 강한 의문(과연 ~일까?): **Can** it be true?
  ④ 부정적 추측(~일 리가 없다): You saw a dragon? That **cannot[can't]** be possible.
- can의 의문형은 〈Can+주어+동사원형 ~?〉, 부정형은 cannot 혹은 can't로 쓴다.

 내신만점 TIP   조동사는 두 개 이상 연달아 쓸 수 없으므로 can이 다른 조동사와 함께 올 경우에는 be able to를 사용한다는 것을 알아두자.
I **will be able to** go skating tomorrow.

A   다음 두 문장이 같은 뜻이 되도록 문장을 완성하시오.

1 He can use this fax machine.
→ He _____ _____ _____ _____ this fax machine.

2 We are not able to find a solution.
→ We _____ _____ a solution.

3 My brother can fix his car by himself.
→ My brother _____ _____ _____ _____ his car by himself.

B   다음 문장에서 틀린 부분을 어법에 맞게 고쳐 쓰시오.

1 He can changes his mind later.

2 She hasn't been able move the sofa.

3 I will can show you the way to the airport.

C   다음 우리말과 같은 뜻이 되도록 can과 ( ) 안의 말을 이용하여 문장을 완성하시오.

1 그녀는 정말로 행복할까? (happy)
_____ _____ truly _____ _____?

2 그가 지금 도서관에 있을 리가 없다. (be)
_____ _____ _____ in the library now.

3 제가 저 방에서 하루 더 묵을 수 있을까요? (stay)
_____ _____ _____ one more day in that room?

4 그는 심지어 겨울에도 바다에 뛰어들 수 있다. (dive)
_____ _____ _____ into the ocean even in winter.

may

- may의 의미
  ① 허가(~해도 된다)
  You **may** walk your dog in this park.
  May I use this copy machine? — Yes, you **may**. / No, you **may not**.
  ② 약한 추측(~일지도 모른다)
  He **may** agree with our ideas.
- may의 의문형은 〈May+주어+동사원형 ~?〉, 부정형은 may not으로 쓴다.

★ PLUS TIP 허가의 의미를 지닌 may는 같은 의미의 can보다 격식을 차린 말이며, 일상생활에서는 can을 더 많이 쓴다.

A 다음 ( ) 안의 말을 배열하여 대화를 완성하시오.

1 A: Excuse me. _____
(share, with you, may, this table, I)
B: Yes, you may. Take a seat.

2 A: I can't find my sunglasses. Have you seen them?
B: _____ (on the sofa, may, they, be)

3 A: Where are you going for your vacation?
B: I haven't decided yet. _____
(to, may, San Francisco, go, I)

4 A: What time does the party start tomorrow?
B: It starts at 6 p.m., but _____ after three.
(may, you, any time, come)

B 다음 우리말과 같은 뜻이 되도록 may와 ( ) 안의 말을 이용하여 문장을 완성하시오.

1 제가 당신에게 따뜻한 마실 것 좀 드릴까요? (offer)
____ ____ ____ ____ something hot to drink?

2 Mike가 집들이에 올지도 모른다. (come)
____ ____ ____ to the housewarming party.

3 그녀는 지금 집에서 쉬는 중일지도 모른다. (rest)
____ ____ ____ ____ at home now.

4 당신은 이 건물에서 담배를 피우면 안 됩니다. (smoke)
____ ____ ____ ____ in this building.

5 질문이 하나도 없으시면 떠나셔도 됩니다. (leave)
If you don't have any questions, you ____ ____.

Point 03   must

- must의 의미

① 필요 · 의무(~해야 한다) = have[has] to

All the students in our school **must[have to]** wear uniforms.

* 과거의 필요 · 의무는 had to, 미래의 필요 · 의무는 will have to로 나타낸다.

② 강한 추측(~임이 틀림없다)

He **must** be very tired after work.

★ 내신만점 *TIP*
- must와 have to는 같은 의미지만 각각의 부정형은 전혀 다른 의미를 나타내므로 주의하자.
  must not[mustn't]: ~하면 안 된다(금지) / don't have to: ~할 필요가 없다(불필요)
- 강한 추측을 나타내는 must(~임이 틀림없다)의 부정은 cannot[can't](~일 리가 없다)이라는 것을 기억하자.

A 다음 두 문장이 같은 뜻이 되도록 문장을 완성하시오.

1 I must clean my room every Saturday.

→ _____ every Saturday.

2 He has to wake up early tomorrow morning.

→ He _____ tomorrow morning.

B 다음 우리말과 같은 뜻이 되도록 ( ) 안의 말을 이용하여 문장을 완성하시오.

1 그 목걸이는 품절된 것이 틀림없다. (sold out)

The necklace _____ _____ _____ _____ .

2 신호등이 파란불에서 노란불로 바뀌면 속도를 낮춰야 한다. (slow down)

You _____ _____ _____ when the green light changes to yellow.

3 나는 방과 후에 조부모님 댁을 방문해야 했다. (visit)

I _____ _____ _____ my grandparents' house after school.

C 다음 우리말과 같은 뜻이 되도록 할 때, 틀린 부분을 어법에 맞게 고쳐 쓰시오.

1 그가 여기에 Jane과 함께 있을 리가 없다.

He must not be here with Jane.

2 내 개는 너를 무서워하는 것이 틀림없다.

My dog may be scared of you.

3 Jimmy는 설거지를 할 필요가 없다.

Jimmy must not wash the dishes.

4 너는 TV를 보면서 먹으면 안 된다.

You don't have to eat while watching TV.

have to

- have to(~해야 한다): 필요 · 의무를 나타내며 조동사 must와 쓰임이 유사하다.
  You **have to[must]** follow the school rules.
  I **had to** stay up late to prepare for the exam.
  I **will have to** stay at my uncle's house during this summer vacation.
- have to의 부정형: don't have to(~할 필요가 없다) = don't need to, need not
  You **don't have[need] to** wait for me.
  → You **need not** wait for me.

A 다음 밑줄 친 부분을 어법에 맞게 고쳐 쓰시오.

1 I <u>must</u> tell her the truth last night.

2 It's getting dark. We <u>had to</u> go home now.

3 You <u>don't need</u> buy all the books on the list.

4 He will <u>must</u> exercise to keep in shape.

B 다음 빈칸에 must와 have to 중 알맞은 말을 쓰시오. (단, must와 have to를 모두 쓸 수 있는 경우에는 must를 쓸 것)

1 We _____ run to catch the bus.

2 I _____ leave in a few minutes.

3 You don't _____ do it right away.

4 She will _____ work overtime tomorrow.

C 다음 우리말과 같은 뜻이 되도록 ( ) 안의 말을 이용하여 문장을 완성하시오.

1 그는 어제 비행기를 타야 했다. (take a plane)
   He _____ _____ _____ _____ _____ yesterday.

2 그녀는 너무 걱정할 필요가 없다. (worry)
   She _____ _____ _____ _____ too much.

3 Tom은 매달 집세를 지불해야 한다. (pay rent)
   Tom _____ _____ _____ _____ every month.

4 그 시험에 실패하면, 너는 그것을 다시 봐야 할 것이다. (take)
   If you fail the exam, you _____ _____ _____ _____ it again.

5 너는 오늘 아침에 화분에 물을 줄 필요가 없었다. (water)
   You _____ _____ _____ _____ the plants this morning.

should / ought to

- should / ought to((마땅히) ~해야 한다): 당연한 의무나 충고·조언을 나타낸다.
  You **should[ought to]** listen to your parents.
- should의 부정형은 should not(shouldn't), ought to의 부정형은 ought not to로 쓴다.
  You **should not[shouldn't]** speak loudly in the library.
  You **ought not to** tell the secret to anybody.

★ PLUS TIP must와 have to는 상황이나 규칙에 의해 어쩔 수 없이 해야 하는 일에 쓰는 반면, should와 ought to는 반드시 할 필요는 없지만 사회적 관습이나 윤리에 비추어 옳다고 생각되는 일에 쓴다.

A 다음 문장을 부정문으로 바꾸어 쓰시오.

1 He ought to wear a suit.

→ _____

2 We should close the store before midnight.

→ _____

3 Jamie ought to focus on her role.

→ _____

4 You should take notes during the interview.

→ _____

B 다음 우리말과 같은 뜻이 되도록 should 또는 ought to와 ( ) 안의 말을 이용하여 문장을 완성하시오.

1 너는 그 프로젝트를 열심히 해야 한다. (work hard)

_____ _____ _____ _____ on the project.

2 네가 그녀에게 사과해야 할 한 가지 이유가 있다. (apologize)
There is one reason why you _____ _____ to her.

3 그녀는 선생님의 조언을 따라야 한다. (follow)

_____ _____ _____ _____ the teacher's advice.

4 너는 시간을 낭비하면 안 된다. (waste)

_____ _____ _____ your time.

5 우리는 친구들에게 거짓말을 하면 안 된다. (tell)

_____ _____ _____ _____ lies to our friends.

6 James는 내일 시험을 위해 잠을 충분히 자야 한다. (get enough sleep)
James _____ _____ _____ _____ for the exam tomorrow.

had better / would rather

- had better(~하는 게 좋겠다): 상대방이나 자신에게 하는 강한 충고나 권고를 나타낸다. 축약형은 'd better, 부정형은 had better not으로 쓴다.
  You **had better** leave now, or you'll miss the bus.
- would rather((차라리) ~하는 편이 낫다): 선택의 상황에서 선호하는 것을 나타낸다. 축약형은 'd rather, 부정형은 would rather not으로 쓴다.
  I **would rather** go to sleep. This movie is too boring.
- would rather A than B(B하느니 차라리 A하겠다)
  I **would rather** play soccer **than** watch TV.

★ **PLUS TIP** ▶ had better는 경고나 위협의 의미로 들릴 수 있기 때문에, 호의의 뜻으로 충고를 할 때는 should를 쓰는 것이 바람직하다.

A 다음 우리말과 같은 뜻이 되도록 할 때, <u>틀린</u> 부분을 어법에 맞게 고쳐 쓰시오.

1 너는 지금 자는 게 좋겠어.
  You would rather go to bed now.

2 우리는 내일 하이킹을 가지 않는 편이 낫겠다.
  We would not rather go hiking tomorrow.

3 그녀는 시험에서 부정행위를 하지 않는 게 좋겠다.
  She had better cheat on her test.

4 나는 집에 있느니 차라리 도서관에 가겠다.
  I would better go to the library than stay at home.

B 다음 우리말과 같은 뜻이 되도록 (   ) 안의 말을 이용하여 문장을 완성하시오.

1 너는 조심해서 운전을 하는 게 좋겠어. (drive)
  You _____ _____ _____ carefully.

2 나는 학교에 걸어가느니 차라리 자전거를 타고 가겠다. (ride one's bike)
  I _____ _____ _____ _____ _____ than walk to school.

3 너는 네 선생님께 무례하게 굴지 않는 게 좋을 거야. (be rude)
  You'd _____ _____ _____ _____ to your teacher.

4 우리는 저 슈퍼마켓에 다시 가지 않는 편이 낫겠다. (go)
  We'd _____ _____ _____ to that supermarket again.

5 너는 서두르는 게 좋겠다, 그러지 않으면 수업에 늦을 것이다. (hurry up)
  You _____ _____ _____ _____, or you'll be late for class.

6 나는 시원한 음료수를 마시느니 차라리 샤워를 하겠다. (take a shower)
  I'd _____ _____ _____ _____ _____ have a cool drink.

used to / would

- used to(~하곤 했다, ~이었다): 과거의 습관이나 상태를 나타낸다.

  I **used to** play at this playground when I was a boy. (과거의 습관)

  My favorite bookstore **used to** be here. (과거의 상태)

- would의 의미

  ① 과거의 습관(~하곤 했다): He **would** take me to the baseball stadium on Sundays.

  ② 정중한 부탁(~해 주시겠습니까?): **Would** you send me a copy of the report?

  ③ 권유(~하시겠습니까?): **Would** you like to have more tea?

★ PLUS TIP   used to와 would 모두 과거의 습관을 나타낼 수 있다. 그러나 과거의 상태를 나타낼 때는 would를 쓸 수 없다.
There **used to**[~~would~~] be a drugstore on the corner.

A   다음 우리말과 같은 뜻이 되도록 할 때, <u>틀린</u> 부분을 어법에 맞게 고쳐 쓰시오.

1   Harry는 어렸을 때 사랑스러웠었다.
Harry would be lovely when he was little.

2   내 여동생은 어디든 나를 따라오곤 했다.
My younger sister should follow me everywhere.

3   그녀는 남자친구가 있었지만 지금은 혼자이다.
She would have a boyfriend, but now she is single.

4   우리는 일요일마다 저 교회에 가곤 했다.
We would rather go to that church every Sunday.

B   다음 우리말과 같은 뜻이 되도록 (   ) 안의 말을 이용하여 문장을 완성하시오.

1   Susan은 머리가 매우 길었다. (have)
Susan _____ _____ _____ very long hair.

2   그는 매일 저녁 강아지와 산책하곤 했다. (take a walk)
He _____ _____ _____ _____ with his puppy every evening.

3   언덕 위에 세 그루의 나무가 있었는데, 더는 없다. (be)
There _____ _____ _____ three trees on the hill, but there are not anymore.

4   우리 아버지는 한 달에 한 번 낚시하러 가시곤 했다. (go fishing)
My father _____ _____ _____ _____ once a month.

5   이 치마 한 번 입어 보시겠어요? (try on)
_____ _____ _____ _____ _____ _____ this skirt?

6   나는 어렸을 때 손톱을 물어뜯곤 했다. (bite)
When I was young, I _____ _____ _____ my nails.

〈조동사＋have＋v-ed〉

- 〈must＋have＋v-ed〉 (~이었음이 틀림없다): 과거의 일에 대한 강한 추측을 나타낸다.
  He doesn't want to have dinner. He **must have eaten** too much for lunch.
- 〈can't＋have＋v-ed〉 (~이었을 리가 없다): 과거의 일에 대한 강한 의심을 나타낸다.
  She **can't have jumped** that high.
- 〈should＋have＋v-ed〉 (~했어야 했다): 과거의 일에 대한 후회나 유감을 나타낸다.
  I **should have gone** to Bill's birthday party. (Bill의 생일 파티에 가지 못했음)
- 〈may[might]＋have＋v-ed〉 (~했을지도 모른다): 과거의 일에 대한 약한 추측을 나타낸다.
  He **may[might] have met** her before.

A 다음 우리말과 같은 뜻이 되도록 할 때, <u>틀린</u> 부분을 어법에 맞게 고쳐 쓰시오.

1 그녀가 헬스장에 있었을 리가 없다.
She can't have be in the gym.

2 그녀는 이미 집에 갔을지도 모른다.
She may go home already.

3 그 아이가 그것을 말했을 리가 없다.
The child can't say it.

4 그는 오늘 아침에 신문을 읽은 것이 틀림없다.
He must had read the newspaper this morning.

5 너는 아버지 말을 들었어야 했다.
You should had listen to your father.

B 다음 우리말과 같은 뜻이 되도록 (   ) 안의 말을 이용하여 문장을 완성하시오.

1 David가 일등상을 탔을 리가 없다. (win)
David ＿＿＿＿＿ ＿＿＿＿＿ ＿＿＿＿＿ first prize.

2 그녀는 이미 소문을 들은 것이 틀림없다. (hear)
She ＿＿＿＿＿ ＿＿＿＿＿ ＿＿＿＿＿ the rumors already.

3 Owen은 서울행 비행기를 놓친 것이 틀림없다. (miss)
Owen ＿＿＿＿＿ ＿＿＿＿＿ ＿＿＿＿＿ the plane to Seoul.

4 너는 유학을 가지 말았어야 했다. (study)
You ＿＿＿＿＿ ＿＿＿＿＿ ＿＿＿＿＿ ＿＿＿＿＿ abroad.

5 Jake는 세 시간 전에 호텔에서 체크인을 했을지도 모른다. (check in)
Jake ＿＿＿＿＿ ＿＿＿＿＿ ＿＿＿＿＿ ＿＿＿＿＿ at the hotel three hours ago.

내신대비 TEST

[01-03] 다음 우리말과 같은 뜻이 되도록 빈칸에 알맞은 말을 고르시오.

01

> 이상하게 들릴지도 모르지만, 그 이야기는 사실이다.
> It _____ sound strange, but the story is true.

① can't ② ought to
③ is able to ④ may
⑤ has to

02

> 너는 신발을 벗을 필요가 없다.
> You _____ take off your shoes.

① should not ② don't have to
③ are not able to ④ ought not to
⑤ must not

03

> 너는 나가지 않는 게 좋겠어. 감기에 걸렸잖니.
> You _____ go out. You have a cold.

① would not ② don't have to
③ need not ④ had better not
⑤ may not

[04-06] 다음 두 문장이 같은 뜻이 되도록 빈칸에 알맞은 말을 고르시오.

04

> This watch _____ be very expensive.
> → I'm sure this watch is very expensive.

① must ② cannot ③ can
④ may ⑤ would rather

05

> I _____ my teacher the truth.
> → I feel sorry I didn't tell my teacher the truth.

① would tell ② may have told
③ must have told ④ can't have told
⑤ should have told

06

> She _____ visit my house often.
> → She often visited my house before, but she doesn't anymore.

① has to ② should
③ must have ④ would
⑤ ought to

기출응용
07
다음 대화의 빈칸에 알맞은 말은?

> A: Where's Ellie? Is she late today?
> B: I think so. She _____ overslept this morning.

① may have ② should have
③ can't have ④ ought not to
⑤ had better not

08

> • I _____ skip lunch than eat a sandwich.
> • I saw him in the library five minutes ago, so he _____ be in the shopping mall.

① should – had better not
② was able to – don't have to
③ would rather – cannot
④ had better – need not
⑤ ought to – don't have to

09

> • You can use my camera. You _____ buy one.
> • He didn't even send me a message. He _____ my birthday.

① would not – should have forgotten
② don't have to – should have forgotten
③ may not – must forget
④ must not – had better forget
⑤ don't have to – must have forgotten

[10-11] 다음 빈칸에 공통으로 들어갈 말을 고르시오.

10

> • I _____ have gone camping with my family.
> • You _____ get under a table when an earthquake occurs.

① should   ② have to
③ had better   ④ can
⑤ used to

11

> • Alan said that he _____ move to another school next month.
> • I _____ rather rent a car than take the bus.

① could   ② may
③ would   ④ ought to
⑤ can't

12

다음 우리말을 영어로 바르게 옮긴 것은?

> 당신은 내 이름을 불렀어야 했다.

① You ought to call my name.
② You would call my name.
③ You must have called my name.
④ You may have called my name.
⑤ You should have called my name.

[13-14] 다음 밑줄 친 부분의 의미가 나머지와 다른 것을 고르시오.

13

① May I see your smartphone?
② The rumor may not be true.
③ You may sleep here if you want.
④ You may look around, but do not touch anything.
⑤ You may not borrow books if you don't have an ID card.

14

① My teacher must like yellow.
② He must be happy to have won the race.
③ She must bring my bag by tomorrow.
④ Mike must have taken cooking lessons.
⑤ He must have shown my picture to Tom.

15

다음 우리말을 영어로 옮긴 것 중 잘못된 것은?

① 그녀는 과연 그와 함께 있어 행복할까?

Can she be happy with him?

② 그가 런던에 있을 리가 없다.

He may not be in London.

③ 너는 새 자전거를 살 필요가 없다.

You don't have to buy a new bicycle.

④ 그 수업은 지루했음이 틀림없다.

The class must have been boring.

⑤ 당신은 휴대전화의 전원을 꺼야 합니다.

You should turn off your cell phone.

16

다음 중 빈칸에 들어갈 말로 알맞지 않은 것은?

- She fell asleep at her desk. She ___①___ have been tired from working.
- I ___②___ work at a convenience store, but I don't anymore.
- We don't ___③___ hurry. We have enough time.
- You ___④___ stop cheating, or you will be punished.
- He ___⑤___ meet his deadline this time. This is his last chance.

① can't   ② used to

③ need to   ④ had better

⑤ ought to

[17–18] 다음 중 어법상 틀린 것을 고르시오.

17

① You should say it clearly and loudly.

② I will be able to drive my father's car.

③ You have to start working early today.

④ They may have wanted to see our garden.

⑤ She must wait for him for an hour yesterday.

18

① You must sit here when you eat.

② I would rather eat chicken than pork.

③ You'd better to use a tool to open it.

④ He can't have done such a bad thing.

⑤ My grandmother used to tell me interesting stories.

고난도

19

다음 대화 중 자연스럽지 않은 것은?

① A: Do they have to go to the airport?

B: No, they need not go there.

② A: May I eat a piece of cake for dessert?

B: That's not good for your health. You should have some fruit.

③ A: Look at that huge swimming pool!

B: Yes, I would swim there when I was young.

④ A: Can he get an A in math?

B: No, he can't have gotten such a good grade.

⑤ A: James is angry because you were late.

B: Oh, no. I should have gotten up earlier.

고난도

20

다음 중 어법상 옳은 것을 모두 고르면? (2개)

① I would rather to teach her French.

② I had to sing the song for the class.

③ You ought to not copy my report.

④ When he was young, he would be careless.

⑤ He must have spent a lot of money on the car.

01

다음 우리말과 뜻이 같도록 조동사와 주어진 말을 이용하여 문장을 완성하시오.

(1) 저 건물은 예전에 경찰서였었다. (be)

→ That building _____ _____

_____ a police station.

(2) 나는 어제 내 여동생을 돌봐야 했다. (look after)

→ I _____ _____ _____ _____

my sister yesterday.

02

다음 문장을 지시대로 바꾸어 쓰시오.

(1) He can come back to Seoul.

→ _____

(미래시제)

(2) I would rather join the debate club.

→ _____

(부정문)

03

주어진 말을 이용하여 대화를 완성하시오.

(1) A: Did you do well on your exam?

B: No, I failed the exam again. I _____

_____ _____ harder yesterday.

(2) A: I think Jack cleaned his room this morning.

B: No, he _____ _____ _____

his room. He went to summer camp yesterday. (clean)

04

다음 그림을 보고, 조동사와 주어진 말을 이용하여 문장을 완성하시오.

past   past

now   now

(1) She _____ _____ _____ _____

_____. (have curly hair)

(2) He _____ _____ _____ _____

_____ to work. (drive a car)

05

다음 표를 보고, 〈보기〉와 같이 충고하는 글을 완성하시오.

Nina	She doesn't read her history book.
Nick	He eats too much junk food.
Julie	She doesn't help her mom prepare dinner.

〈보기〉 Nina had better read her history book.

(1) Nick had better _____.

(2) Julie had better _____.

고난도

06

다음 대화를 읽고, 틀린 부분을 모두 찾아 바르게 고쳐 쓰시오. (2군데)

A: You are going hiking, aren't you? If you are, you had not better go today.

B: Why not?

A: It rained heavily last night. The trail must be very slippery.

B: Oh, I must have checked the weather forecast before I made plans.

핵심 포인트 정리하기

1 조동사

can	'~할 수 있다', '~일 수도 있다', '~해도 된다', '과연 ~일까?', '~일 리가 없다'
①_____	'~해도 된다', '~일지도 모른다'
must	'~해야 한다' (= have[has] to), '~임이 틀림없다' 부정형 〈must not(mustn't) '~하면 안 된다'〉, 〈cannot(can't) '~일 리가 없다'〉
have to	'~해야 한다' (미래 〈will have to〉, 부정형 〈don't have to '~할 필요가 없다'〉)
should / ②_____	'(마땅히) ~해야 한다' (부정형 〈should not[shouldn't]〉 / 〈③_____〉)
had better	'~하는 게 좋겠다' (축약형 'd better, 부정형 〈had better not〉)
would rather	'(차라리) ~하는 편이 낫다' (축약형 'd rather, 부정형 〈④_____〉)
⑤_____	(과거의 습관·상태) '~하곤 했다', '~이었다'
would	(과거의 습관) '~하곤 했다', '~해 주시겠습니까?', '~하시겠습니까?'

꼭! 조동사 뒤에는 동사원형이 오며, 조동사를 연달아 쓸 수 없다는 점 기억하기!
조동사의 서로 다른 의미와 부정형 알아두기!

2 〈조동사＋have＋v-ed〉

- 〈must + have + v-ed〉 '~이었음이 틀림없다'
- 〈⑥_____ + have + v-ed〉 '~이었을 리가 없다'
- 〈⑦_____ + have + v-ed〉 '~했어야 했다'
- 〈may[might] + have + v-ed〉 '~했을지도 모른다'

꼭! 〈조동사 + have + v-ed〉의 의미 반드시 구분하기!

문제로 개념 다지기

밑줄 친 부분이 어법상 맞으면 O, 틀리면 X 표시하고 바르게 고치시오.

1 너는 다음 달 학교 축제에 참여해야 할 것이다.

You will <u>should</u> participate in the school festival next month.

2 너는 식사 전에 간식을 먹지 말아야 한다.

You <u>ought to not</u> have snacks before meals.

3 예전에는 이 근처에 유명한 초콜릿 가게가 있었다.

There <u>would</u> be a famous chocolate store around here.

4 우리는 집을 떠나기 전에 비행 일정을 확인했어야 했다.

We <u>should have checked</u> the flight schedule before leaving home.

5 Alex가 어제 저녁을 걸렀을 리가 없다.

Alex <u>may not have skipped</u> dinner yesterday.

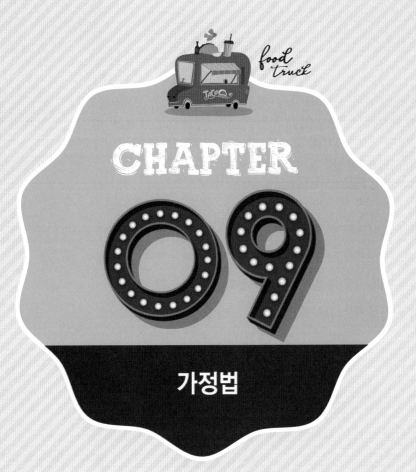

CHAPTER 09

가정법

If I **had studied** hard, I **could solve** this math problem now. [혼합 가정법]
[가정법 과거완료]　　　　[가정법 과거]

I **wish** she **would** start the concert. [I wish+가정법 과거]

He smiled **as if** he **knew** everything. [as if+가정법 과거]

가정법

사실과 반대되거나 실현 가능성이 희박한 일을 가정할 때 가정법을 씁니다. 현재에 대한 가정이면
가정법 과거 〈If+주어+동사의 과거형 ~, 주어+조동사의 과거형+동사원형 …〉을, 과거에 대한
가정이면 가정법 과거완료 〈If+주어+had v-ed ~, 주어+조동사의 과거형+have v-ed …〉를 씁니다.
이 밖에 〈혼합 가정법〉, 〈I wish+가정법〉, 〈as if+가정법〉, 〈Without[But for] ~+가정법〉 등이
있다는 것도 함께 알아 두세요.

가정법 과거 / 과거완료

- 가정법 과거: 현재 사실과 반대되거나 실현 가능성이 희박한 일을 가정할 때 사용하며 '만약 ~하면 …할 텐데'로 해석한다.
  - 형태: 〈If+주어+동사의 과거형 ~, 주어+조동사의 과거형+동사원형 …〉
    If you **lived** here, I **could see** you every day.
- 가정법 과거완료: 과거 사실과 반대되는 상황을 가정할 때 사용하며, '만약 ~했다면 …했을 텐데'로 해석한다.
  - 형태: 〈If+주어+had v-ed ~, 주어+조동사의 과거형+have v-ed …〉
    If I **had left** earlier, I **would** not **have missed** the plane.

★ PLUS TIP 가정법 과거 문장에서 if절의 동사가 be동사일 경우에는 주어의 인칭과 수에 상관없이 were를 쓰는 것이 원칙이다.

A 다음 우리말과 같은 뜻이 되도록 ( ) 안의 말을 이용하여 문장을 완성하시오.

1 비가 오고 있지 않다면, 우리는 야구를 할 수 있을 텐데. (rain, play)
If it _____ _____ _____, we _____ _____ baseball.

2 내가 네 충고를 따랐다면, 나는 같은 실수를 하지 않았을 텐데. (follow, make)
If I _____ _____ your advice, I _____ _____ _____
_____ the same mistake.

3 내가 남자친구가 있다면, 나는 그와 함께 놀이공원에 갈 텐데. (have, go)
If I _____ _____ _____, I _____ _____ to an amusement
park with him.

4 네가 숙제를 했었다면, 너는 꾸중을 듣지 않았을 텐데. (do, scold)
If you _____ _____ your homework, you _____ _____
_____ _____ _____.

5 내가 그 이메일을 읽었다면, 나는 일정 변경에 대해 알았을 텐데. (read, know)
If I _____ _____ the email, I _____ _____ _____ about
the schedule changes.

B 다음 문장을 지시대로 바꾸어 쓰시오.

1 He doesn't have a key, so he can't open the locker. (가정법 과거)
→ _____

2 I have a milk allergy, so I can't drink milk. (가정법 과거)
→ _____

3 As I was not there, I couldn't see the accident. (가정법 과거완료)
→ _____

혼합 가정법

■ 혼합 가정법: 과거에 실현되지 못한 일이 현재까지 영향을 미치는 상황을 가정할 때 사용하며, '(과거에) 만약
~했다면 (지금) …할 텐데'로 해석한다.
- 형태: 〈If+주어+had v-ed ~, 주어+조동사의 과거형+동사원형 …〉
If it **had** not **rained** last night, the road **would** not **be** wet now.

A 다음 우리말과 같은 뜻이 되도록 (   ) 안의 말을 이용하여 문장을 완성하시오.

1 내가 차를 가져왔다면, 너를 집에 태워다 줄 수 있을 텐데. (bring, drive)
If I _____ _____ my car, I _____ _____ you home.

2 형이 내 노트북을 가져가지 않았다면, 나는 컴퓨터 게임을 할 수 있을 텐데. (take, play)
If my brother _____ _____ _____ my laptop, I _____
_____ computer games.

3 그녀가 비싼 구두를 사지 않았다면, 지금 충분한 돈을 가지고 있을 텐데. (buy, have)
If she _____ _____ _____ the expensive shoes, she _____
_____ enough money now.

4 네가 약을 먹었다면, 좀 나을 텐데. (take, feel)
If you _____ _____ the medicine, you _____ _____ better.

5 내가 어젯밤에 공부를 더 했다면, 이 문제들에 답할 수 있을 텐데. (study, answer)
If I _____ _____ more last night, I _____ _____ these
questions.

6 네가 나를 위해 빵을 좀 남겼다면, 나는 지금 배고프지 않을 텐데. (leave, be)
If you _____ _____ some bread for me, I _____ _____
_____ hungry now.

B 다음 문장을 혼합 가정법 문장으로 바꾸어 쓰시오.

1 He broke my printer, so I can't use it now.
→ _____

2 She lost her wallet, so she can't lend me money.
→ _____

3 He didn't clean the room, so it doesn't look tidy.
→ _____

I wish＋가정법 과거

- 〈I wish＋가정법 과거〉는 현재는 이루기 어려운 소망을 나타낼 때 사용하며, '~라면 좋을 텐데'로 해석한다.
  - 형태: 〈I wish＋주어＋동사의 과거형〉
  - **I wish** I **were** a millionaire. (→ I'm sorry (that) I am not a millionaire.)
  - **I wish** I **could go** to New York. (→ I'm sorry (that) I can't go to New York.)

A 다음 두 문장이 같은 뜻이 되도록 문장을 완성하시오.

1 I'm sorry that I can't go to space.
→ I wish _____.

2 I'm sorry that I am not good at singing.
→ I wish _____.

3 I'm sorry that you are not here with me.
→ I wish _____.

4 I'm sorry that I don't have an umbrella.
→ I wish _____.

5 I'm sorry that I don't live near the subway station.
→ I wish _____.

6 I'm sorry that I can't give you good advice.
→ I wish _____.

B 다음 우리말과 같은 뜻이 되도록 ( ) 안의 말을 이용하여 문장을 완성하시오.

1 내가 그의 이름을 알면 좋을 텐데. (know, name)
I wish _____ _____ _____ _____.

2 그 회의가 연기되면 좋을 텐데. (the meeting, postpone)
I wish _____ _____ _____.

3 내가 내 부모님과 함께 살면 좋을 텐데. (live, parents)
I wish _____ _____ _____ _____.

4 내가 스포츠카를 운전하면 좋을 텐데. (drive, a sports car)
I wish _____ _____ _____ _____.

5 여름 방학이 더 길면 좋을 텐데. (the summer vacation, longer)
I wish _____ _____ _____ _____.

I wish+가정법 과거완료

■ 〈I wish+가정법 과거완료〉는 과거에 이루지 못한 일에 대한 소망이나 아쉬움을 나타낼 때 사용하며, '~했더라면 좋을 텐데'로 해석한다.
- 형태: 〈I wish+주어+had v-ed〉
  I wish I had bought the bag. (→ I'm sorry (that) I didn't buy the bag.)
  I wish I had learned how to ski. (→ I'm sorry (that) I didn't learn how to ski.)

A 다음 ( ) 안에서 알맞은 말을 고르시오.

1 A: Jenny became a famous actress.
   B: Yeah. I wish we (got / had gotten) her autograph before.

2 A: Where were you yesterday?
   B: We were at a party. I wish you (were / had been) there, too.

3 A: Why don't we go to see *Avengers* today?
   B: I'm sorry, but I'm too young. I wish I (were / had been) old enough to see it.

B 다음 두 문장이 같은 뜻이 되도록 문장을 완성하시오.

1 I'm sorry he didn't listen to the doctor's advice.
   → I wish _____ .

2 I'm sorry my mother didn't buy me a new jacket.
   → I wish _____ .

3 I'm sorry my school canceled its plan to build a gym.
   → I wish _____ .

C 다음 우리말과 같은 뜻이 되도록 ( ) 안의 말을 이용하여 문장을 완성하시오.

1 그녀가 우리와 함께 쇼핑을 갔더라면 좋을 텐데. (go shopping)
   I wish _____ _____ _____ with us.

2 내가 그 병원에 예약을 했더라면 좋을 텐데. (make a reservation)
   I wish _____ _____ _____ _____ _____ at the hospital.

3 내가 그에게 그 소설의 결말을 말하지 않았더라면 좋을 텐데. (tell)
   I wish _____ _____ _____ _____ the ending of
   the novel.

as if+가정법 과거

■ 〈as if+가정법 과거〉는 주절의 시제와 같은 시점의 상황을 반대로 가정할 때 사용한다. 해석은 '마치 ~인 것처럼'으로 한다.
- 형태: 〈as if+주어+동사의 과거형〉
  You sound **as if** you **were** happy. (→ In fact, you are not happy.)
  She acts **as if** she **were** a teacher. (→ In fact, she is not a teacher.)

A 다음 〈보기〉와 같이 주어진 문장을 as if를 이용한 가정법 문장으로 바꾸어 쓰시오.

〈보기〉 In fact, James is not the class president.
→ James behaves as if he were the class president.

1 In fact, it isn't Christmas.
→ I feel as if _____.

2 In fact, she isn't angry.
→ She looks as if _____.

3 In fact, he doesn't know my brother.
→ He talks as if _____.

4 In fact, he isn't a doctor.
→ He acts as if _____.

5 In fact, I'm not a child.
→ My mother treats me as if _____.

B 다음 우리말과 같은 뜻이 되도록 ( ) 안의 말을 이용하여 문장을 완성하시오.

1 나는 마치 그게 내 잘못인 것처럼 느껴졌다. (be, fault)
I felt _____ _____ _____ _____ _____.

2 그녀는 마치 그녀가 모델인 것처럼 서 있다. (be, model)
She stands _____.

3 Jerry는 마치 이 집을 소유한 것처럼 행동한다. (own, house)
Jerry acts _____.

4 그는 마치 모든 것을 아는 것처럼 행동한다. (know, everything)
He behaves _____ _____ _____ _____.

5 그들은 마치 그들이 운동 선수들인 것처럼 연습한다. (be, athlete)
They practice _____ _____ _____ _____.

as if + 가정법 과거완료

- 〈as if+가정법 과거완료〉는 주절의 시제보다 앞선 시점의 상황을 반대로 가정할 때 사용한다. 해석은 '마치 ～였던 것처럼'으로 한다.
  - 형태: 〈as if+주어+had v-ed〉
    You look **as if** you **had won** the race. (→ In fact, you didn't win the race.)
    Mary talked **as if** she **had known** the news. (→ In fact, Mary had not known the news.)

A 다음 〈보기〉와 같이 주어진 문장을 as if를 이용한 가정법 문장으로 바꾸어 쓰시오.

> 〈보기〉 In fact, he was not popular with girls.
> → He talks as if he had been popular with girls.

1 In fact, Jason didn't see me.
→ Jason talks as if _____.

2 In fact, Mike wasn't in a fight.
→ Mike looks as if _____.

3 In fact, he was not in New York.
→ He talks as if _____.

4 In fact, she had liked my present.
→ She acted as if _____.

5 In fact, Tom hadn't paid for your lunch.
→ Tom talked as if _____.

B 다음 우리말과 같은 뜻이 되도록 〈보기〉에서 알맞은 말을 골라 가정법 문장을 완성하시오.

> 〈보기〉 win   visit   live   cry

1 그는 마치 울고 있었던 것처럼 보인다.
He looks _____.

2 그녀는 마치 중국에 살았던 것처럼 말했다.
She talked _____.

3 Christina는 마치 파리를 방문했던 것처럼 말한다.
Christina talks _____.

4 Danny는 마치 그가 그 경기를 이겼던 것처럼 말했다.
Danny talked _____.

Without[But for] ~+가정법 과거

- 현재 있는 것이 없다고 가정할 때 〈Without[But for] ~+가정법 과거〉의 형태로 쓰며, '(만약) ~이 없다면' 으로 해석한다.
  Without your help, I **would be** in trouble.
  But for his laptop, I **could not write** my report.
- 〈Without[But for] ~+가정법 과거〉에서 Without과 But for는 If it were not for ~로 바꾸어 쓸 수 있다.
  Without[But for] the manual, I would have problems.
  → **If it were not for** the manual, I would have problems.

A 다음 우리말과 같은 뜻이 되도록 문장을 완성하시오.

1 공기가 없다면, 우리는 숨을 쉴 수 없을 것이다.
_____ _____, we could not breathe.

2 그 버스가 없다면, 나는 학교에 걸어가야 할 것이다.
_____ _____ _____, I would have to walk to school.

3 너의 농담들이 없다면, 나는 내 일을 즐길 수 없을 것이다.
_____ _____ _____ _____, I could not enjoy my job.

B 다음 두 문장이 같은 뜻이 되도록 if를 이용하여 바꾸어 쓰시오.

1 But for the map application, I could not find my way around the city.
→ _____

2 Without my alarm clock, I could not wake up early in the morning.
→ _____

3 Without the Internet, we could not get information quickly.
→ _____

C 다음 우리말과 같은 뜻이 되도록 ( ) 안의 말을 배열하여 문장을 완성하시오.

1 물이 없다면, 아무도 살아남을 수 없을 것이다.
(water, for, no one, if, were, survive, it, could, not)

_____

2 Betty가 없다면, 우리는 축구 경기를 이길 수 없을 것이다.
(Betty, we, not, our soccer games, win, could, without)

_____

Point 08 Without[But for] ～+가정법 과거완료

- 과거에 있었던 것이 없었다고 가정할 때 〈Without[But for] ～+가정법 과거완료〉의 형태로 쓰며, '(만약) ～이 없었더라면'으로 해석한다.

  Without her care, the men **would have died**.

  But for him, we **would have missed** a good chance.

- 〈Without[But for] ～+가정법 과거완료〉에서 Without이나 But for는 If it had not been for ～로 바꾸어 쓸 수 있다.

  Without[But for] her mother's support, she would not have become an athlete.

  → **If it had not been for** her mother's support, she would not have become an athlete.

★ 내신만점 *TIP* 〈Without[But for] ～〉 가정법 과거와 가정법 과거완료를 구분할 때는 주절의 시제를 확인하자.

A 다음 우리말과 같은 뜻이 되도록 ( ) 안의 말을 이용하여 문장을 완성하시오.

1 네가 없었더라면, 나는 이 프로젝트를 끝내지 못했을 것이다. (finish)

Without you, I would _____ _____ _____ _____ _____.

2 그의 조언이 없었더라면, 나는 그것을 시도하지 않았을 것이다. (try)

But for his advice, I would _____ _____ _____ _____.

3 손전등이 없었더라면, 우리는 길을 잃었을 것이다. (get lost)

Without the flashlight, we would _____ _____ _____.

B 다음 두 문장이 같은 뜻이 되도록 if를 이용하여 바꾸어 쓰시오.

1 Without your reminder, I could not have remembered his birthday.

→ _____

2 But for Jamie, I would not have enjoyed going to school.

→ _____

C 다음 우리말과 같은 뜻이 되도록 ( ) 안의 말을 배열하여 문장을 완성하시오.

1 개인 트레이너가 없었더라면, 나는 살을 뺄 수 없었을 것이다.

(I, without, couldn't, a personal trainer, weight, lost, have)

_____

2 너의 도움이 없었더라면, 나는 시험에 떨어졌을지도 모른다.

(I, help, the exam, have, might, failed, but, your, for)

_____

[01-03] 다음 빈칸에 알맞은 말을 고르시오.

01

> If she _____ my friend, I would be very happy.

① be   ② am   ③ were
④ is   ⑤ have been

02

> If he _____ a little faster, he would have broken the world record.

① runs   ② had run   ③ ran
④ has run   ⑤ would run

03

> She acts as if she _____ his wife.

① is   ② were   ③ be
④ has been   ⑤ would be

[04-05] 다음 문장을 가정법 문장으로 바꿀 때, 빈칸에 들어갈 말로 알맞은 것을 고르시오.

04

> In fact, she didn't get good grades.
> → She talks as if she _____ good grades.

① gets   ② got   ③ has gotten
④ had gotten   ⑤ would get

05

> I'm sorry that I can't remember his face.
> → I wish I _____ his face.

① can remember   ② can't remember
③ could remember   ④ couldn't remember
⑤ could have remembered

[06-08] 다음 우리말과 같은 뜻이 되도록 빈칸에 알맞은 말을 고르시오.

06

> 우리가 10시에 떠났더라면, 점심시간에 맞춰 도착했을 텐데.
> If we had left at 10, we _____ in time for lunch.

① arrive   ② had arrived
③ would arrive   ④ will have arrived
⑤ would have arrived

07

> 그가 지난주에 다치지 않았더라면, 그는 오늘 현장 학습을 갈 텐데.
> If he _____ last week, he would go on a field trip today.

① gotten injured
② didn't get injured
③ have not gotten injured
④ not had gotten injured
⑤ had not gotten injured

08

이 단어들을 외우지 않아도 된다면 좋을 텐데.
I wish I _____ these words.

① do not memorize
② had not had to memorize
③ don't have to memorize
④ didn't have to memorize
⑤ could not have to memorize

11

다음 빈칸에 공통으로 들어갈 말은?

• He didn't know her then, but he talks as if he _____ familiar with her.
• If they _____ angry at me, they would not have come today.

① are   ② were   ③ has been
④ had been   ⑤ would have been

[09-10] 빈칸에 들어갈 말이 순서대로 알맞게 짝지어진 것을 고르시오.

09

• Jason likes pizza, but he talks as if he _____ it.
• If you had studied hard, you _____ well on the exam now.

① likes – did
② liked – can do
③ didn't like – could do
④ doesn't like – could have done
⑤ had not liked – had done

기출응용

12

다음 밑줄 친 부분과 바꾸어 쓸 수 있는 것은?

Without our coach's advice, we could not have scored a goal.

① If it were for our coach's advice
② If it were not for our coach's advice
③ If it had been for our coach's advice
④ If it had not been for our coach's advice
⑤ If it had been our coach's advice

10

• I wish I _____ more free time now.
• If I _____ how to swim, I would have joined you.

① had – had known
② have – knew
③ have had – would know
④ will have – have known
⑤ would have – would have known

[13-14] 다음 대화의 빈칸에 알맞은 말을 고르시오.

13

A: He didn't visit India with us last year.
B: That's right. But _____.

① he talks as if he visits India with us last year
② he talks as if he has visited India with us last year
③ he talks as if he had visited India with us last year
④ he talks as if he will visit India with us last year
⑤ he talks as if he will have visited India with us last year

14

A: I heard you were late for the interview.
B: Yeah. I wish _____.

① I don't miss the subway
② I didn't miss the subway
③ I haven't missed the subway
④ I hadn't missed the subway
⑤ I couldn't have missed the subway

[15-16] 다음 우리말을 영어로 바르게 옮긴 것을 고르시오.

15

내가 저녁을 먹었더라면 지금 배고프지 않을 텐데.

① If I had dinner, I wouldn't be hungry now.
② If I didn't have dinner, I am not hungry now.
③ If I had had dinner, I wouldn't be hungry now.
④ If I had had dinner, I wouldn't have been hungry now.
⑤ If I had dinner, I wouldn't have been hungry now.

16

Ann은 그에 대해 전부 아는 것처럼 행동한다.

① Ann acts as if she knows all about him.
② Ann acts as if she knew all about him.
③ Ann acts as if she has known all about him.
④ Ann acts as if she had known all about him.
⑤ Ann acts as if she will know all about him.

17

다음 밑줄 친 부분의 쓰임이 올바른 것은?

① She sounded as if she has been upset.
② If he hurried, he can see her.
③ I wish I bought some shoes yesterday.
④ If there were a bus stop, we will take a bus.
⑤ But for your help, we could not have arrived there on time.

[18-19] 다음 중 어법상 틀린 것을 고르시오.

18

① I wish he would come to the party.
② She talks as if she were older than me.
③ If I were you, I would buy this jacket.
④ If it had not been so hot, I would go hiking last Sunday.
⑤ Without your idea, I could not have gotten ready for his birthday party.

19

① If I were not sick, I would go to school.
② I wish I could speak Chinese like him.
③ What would happen if I pushed the button?
④ If I had seen her message, I would have replied.
⑤ If I had enough money, I could have bought you a car.

고난도
20

다음 중 어법상 옳은 것을 모두 고르면? (3개)

① They looked as if they had seen a ghost.
② Would you mind if I borrowed your bike?
③ I wish I had gone camping with you.
④ If I knew the truth, I would have called her.
⑤ But for their complaints, we didn't know the situation.

서술형 따라잡기

01

주어진 말을 이용하여 우리말과 뜻이 같도록 문장을 완성하시오.

(1) 그가 제때 회복되었더라면, 그는 우리와 농구를 했을 텐데. (play basketball)

→ If he had recovered in time, he _____ _____ _____ _____ with us.

(2) 어머니의 도움이 없었더라면, 나는 대학을 졸업할 수 없었을 것이다. (graduate)

→ Without my mother's help, I _____ _____ _____ _____ from college.

02

다음 그림을 보고, 주어진 말과 가정법을 이용하여 문장을 완성하시오.

(kite, fly)　　　　(umbrella, get wet)

(1) If I _____ _____ _____, I would _____ it with my friends.

(2) If I _____ _____ _____ _____, I would _____ _____.

03

다음 두 문장이 같은 뜻이 되도록 빈칸에 알맞은 말을 쓰시오.

If it had not been for this boat, I would have died at sea.

→ _____, I would have died at sea.

04

주어진 말을 알맞게 배열하여 우리말과 뜻이 같도록 문장을 완성하시오.

Lucy는 마치 아무 일도 일어나지 않았던 것처럼 행동했다.

(acted, happened, Lucy, if, had, nothing, as)

→ _____

05

주어진 말을 이용하여 대화를 완성하시오.

(1) A: Did you go to see the movie?
B: No, I didn't. If I _____ _____ my essay, I _____ _____ _____ to see it. (finish, will, go)

(2) A: Did you use the coupon that I gave you?
B: Yes. If _____ _____ _____ _____ _____ the coupon, I _____ _____ _____ a lot of money on these sneakers. (be, will, spend)

고난도

06

다음 조건에 맞게 우리말을 영어로 옮겨 쓰시오.

〈조건〉 1. 가정법 구문을 이용할 것
　　　　2. 표현 fix, close the window를 이용할 것

(1) 그들이 내 스마트폰을 고쳤다면 좋을 텐데.
→ _____ (7단어)

(2) 우리가 창문을 닫았더라면 우리는 지금 춥지 않을 텐데.
→ _____
_____ (12단어)

핵심 포인트 정리하기

1 가정법 과거 / 과거완료 & 혼합 가정법

- 가정법 과거: 현재 사실과 반대되거나 실현 가능성이 희박한 일을 가정 ('만약 ~하면 …할 텐데')

  〈If + 주어 + ① _____ ~, 주어 + ② _____ + _____ …〉

- 가정법 과거완료: 과거 사실과 반대되는 상황을 가정 ('만약 ~했다면 …했을 텐데')

  〈If + 주어 + ③ _____ ~, 주어 + ④ _____ + _____〉

- 혼합 가정법: 과거에 실현되지 못한 일이 현재까지 영향을 미치는 상황을 가정 ('만약 ~했다면 …할 텐데')

  〈If + 주어 + ⑤ _____ ~, 주어 + ⑥ _____ + _____〉

 가정법 과거, 과거완료, 혼합 가정법에서 if절과 주절의 시제에 유의하기!

2 다양한 가정법

	가정법 과거	가정법 과거완료
I wish	현재는 이루기 어려운 소망 표현 '~라면 좋을 텐데'	과거에 이루지 못한 일에 대한 소망이나 아쉬움 표현 ⑦ '_____'
⑧ _____	주절과 같은 시점의 상황을 반대로 가정 '마치 ~인 것처럼'	주절의 시제보다 앞선 시점의 상황을 반대로 가정 '마치 ~였던 것처럼'
⑨ _____ [But for]	현재 있는 것이 없다고 가정 '(만약) ~이 없다면' (→ If it were not for ~)	과거에 있었던 것이 없었다고 가정 '(만약) ~이 없었더라면' (→ If it had not been for ~)

 〈I wish〉, 〈as if〉, 〈Without[But for]〉의 가정법 과거와 가정법 과거완료 형태 및 의미 구분하기!

문제로 개념 다지기

밑줄 친 부분이 어법상 맞으면 O, 틀리면 X 표시하고 바르게 고치시오.

1 그녀가 사과를 충분히 많이 가지고 있다면, 그녀는 애플파이를 구울 수 있을 텐데.

  If she had enough apples, she could <u>bake</u> an apple pie.

2 네 전화가 없었더라면, 나는 학교에 지각했을 것이다.

  If it were not for your call, I would have been late for school.

3 아빠가 매일 아침 나를 학교까지 차로 데려다주시면 좋을 텐데.

  I wish my dad <u>drives</u> me to school every morning.

4 그는 마치 경기에 이미 졌던 것처럼 뛰었다.

  He played as if he <u>has already lost</u> the game.

5 그의 노력이 없었더라면, 우리는 가게를 열지 못했을 것이다.

  Without his efforts, we <u>could not open</u> the shop.

food truck

CHAPTER 10

접속사

개념 쏙쏙

As soon as the bell rang, he ran out of the classroom.   [종속 접속사]

Both pizza **and** spaghetti sound delicious.   [상관 접속사]

Do it right away, **or** you'll miss your chance.   [명령문 + or]

접속사

단어와 단어, 구와 구, 절과 절을 연결해 주는 접속사에는 문법적으로 대등한 말을 연결하는 등위 접속사와 시간, 이유, 조건, 양보 등을 나타내는 종속 접속사, 두 개 이상의 단어가 짝을 이루어 쓰이는 상관 접속사가 있습니다. 명령문 뒤에 접속사 and와 or가 오면 어떤 의미가 되는지도 알아 두어야 합니다.

시간, 이유를 나타내는 종속 접속사 I – when/while/as/since

- when: '~할 때'
  He was popular **when** he was a student.
- while: '~하는 동안'
  I drank milk **while** I was reading the newspaper.
- as: 1) '~하고 있을 때' 2) '~함에 따라' 3) '~ 때문에'
  As she was walking down the street, she saw Tim. (~하고 있을 때)
  As time went by, the city changed a lot. (~함에 따라)
  As she had a headache, she took the medicine. (~ 때문에)
- since: 1) '~ 이래로' 2) '~ 때문에'
  I've been thinking about you **since** I met you. (~ 이래로)
  Since he was tired, he didn't feel like going out. (~ 때문에)

★ PLUS TIP   while은 '~이지만', '~인 데 반하여'라는 뜻으로도 사용된다.
While I understand your situation, I can't help you.

A 다음 우리말과 같은 뜻이 되도록 〈보기〉에서 알맞은 말을 골라 빈칸에 쓰시오.

〈보기〉	while	as	since	when

1 내가 너를 마지막으로 본 지 오래되었다.
It's been a long time _____ I saw you last.

2 나는 열차를 기다리는 동안 잡지를 읽었다.
I read a magazine _____ I was waiting for the train.

3 유가가 인상됨에 따라, 사람들은 기분이 상했다.
_____ oil prices increased, people became upset.

4 내가 13살 때, 우리 가족은 세계 여행을 했다.
_____ I was 13 years old, my family traveled around the world.

B 다음 우리말과 같은 뜻이 되도록 ( ) 안의 말을 이용하여 문장을 완성하시오.

1 네가 샤워하고 있는 동안 Chris가 전화했었다. (take a shower)
Chris called _____ _____ _____ _____ _____.

2 그는 더 높이 올라감에 따라 무서워졌다. (go up higher)
_____ _____ _____ _____ _____, he became scared.

3 우리는 그녀가 미국으로 이주한 이래로 서로 보지 못했다. (move to)
We haven't seen each other _____ _____ _____ _____
America.

시간, 이유를 나타내는 종속 접속사 II – until[till]/every time/ as soon as

- until[till]: '~할 때까지'
  He stood in front of the door **until** she came out.
- every time: '~할 때마다'(= whenever / each time)
  Every time I see you, I feel happy.
- as soon as: '~하자마자'(= on[upon] v-ing)
  As soon as he finished breakfast, he ran out.
  → **On[Upon] finishing** breakfast, he ran out.

★ 내신만점 *TIP*　시간의 부사절에서는 미래의 일도 현재시제로 나타낸다는 것을 기억하자.
We'll hand out gifts to the children when the event **ends**.

A 다음 두 문장이 같은 뜻이 되도록 문장을 완성하시오.

1 She left for Paris five years ago.
→ Five years have passed _____ she left for Paris.

2 Whenever I ask him a question, he answers kindly.
→ _____ _____ I ask him a question, he answers kindly.

3 We stopped talking when the teacher arrived.
→ We talked _____ the teacher arrived.

4 On entering the house, he called my name.
→ _____ _____ _____ he entered the house, he called my name.

B 다음 우리말과 같은 뜻이 되도록 (　) 안의 말을 이용하여 문장을 완성하시오.

1 나는 눕자마자 잠들었다. (lie down)
_____ _____ _____, I fell asleep.

2 나는 알람 시계가 울릴 때까지 잤다. (go off)
I slept _____ the alarm clock _____ _____.

3 그는 도서관에 갈 때마다 그녀를 본다. (go)
_____ _____ _____ _____ to the library, he sees her.

4 우리는 배달원이 올 때까지 집에 있을 것이다. (the delivery man, come)
We'll stay at home _____ _____ _____ _____ _____.

5 내가 우산을 가져갈 때마다 비는 오지 않는다. (take, an umbrella)
_____ _____ _____ _____ _____, it doesn't rain.

6 그녀는 버스에서 내리자마자 넘어졌다. (get off)
_____ _____ _____ she _____ _____ the bus, she fell down.

조건을 나타내는 종속 접속사 − if / unless

- if: '만약 ~라면[한다면]'

  If you come tomorrow, I'll make dinner.
- unless: '~하지 않으면'(= if ~ not)

  Unless you leave now, you'll be late.

  → **If** you do**n't** leave now, you'll be late.

★ PLUS TIP

- 조건의 부사절에서는 미래의 일도 현재시제로 나타낸다.
- if[whether]는 '~인지 (아닌지)'라는 뜻으로 명사절을 이끌기도 하는데, 이때 if절에는 미래시제가 올 수 있다.

  I don't know **if** he **will** come tomorrow.

A 다음 두 문장이 같은 뜻이 되도록 If나 Unless를 이용하여 문장을 완성하시오.

1 If I don't write it down, I'll forget about it.

→ _____

2 Unless you wear a coat, you'll catch a cold.

→ _____

3 If you don't have a receipt, we can't give you a refund.

→ _____

B 다음 문장이 어법상 맞으면 O, 틀리면 X 표시하고 바르게 고치시오.

1 Unless we get a ticket, we can't watch the show.

2 If Amy will arrive tomorrow morning, I will pick her up at the airport.

3 I'm not sure if he supports my idea at the next meeting.

C 다음 우리말과 같은 뜻이 되도록 ( ) 안의 말을 이용하여 문장을 완성하시오.

1 내일 비가 오지 않으면, 우리는 소풍을 갈 것이다. (rain)

_____ _____ _____ tomorrow, we'll go on a picnic.

2 그녀가 나에게 말해주면, 나는 그것을 믿을 것이다. (tell)

_____ _____ _____ me, I will believe it.

3 그는 돈이 필요하지 않으면, 나에게 절대 말을 하지 않는다. (need)

_____ _____ _____ _____, he never talks to me.

4 네가 담양을 방문한다면, 대나무를 많이 볼 수 있을 것이다. (visit)

_____ _____ _____ Damyang, you'll see a lot of bamboo.

양보를 나타내는 종속 접속사 – though/even though/even if

- though[although]: '비록 ~이지만'(even though는 though보다 양보의 의미가 강함)

  Though his English is not perfect, he keeps practicing.

  Even though he tried hard, he didn't succeed.

- even if: '만약 ~할지라도'

  Even if you help me, I can't finish it by tomorrow.

★ **PLUS TIP** even though는 사실에 대해, even if는 가상의 일을 전제로 하여 양보의 의미를 나타낸다.

We should go out **even though** it's raining.　(비가 내리고 있음 〈사실〉)

We should go out **even if** it rains.　　　(비가 내릴 수도 있음 〈가상의 일〉)

A 다음 우리말과 같은 뜻이 되도록 〈보기〉에서 알맞은 말을 골라 빈칸에 쓰시오.

〈보기〉　even though　　　even if　　　if

1 비록 나는 그녀의 이름을 잊어버렸지만 그녀의 얼굴은 확실히 기억했다.

_____ I forgot her name, I remembered her face clearly.

2 내가 만약 공짜 표를 얻게 될지라도, 나는 저 영화를 보지 않을 것이다.

I won't watch that movie _____ I get a free ticket.

3 만약 네가 그 약속을 지키지 않는다면, 나는 실망할 것이다.

_____ you don't keep the promise, I will be disappointed.

4 그는 지갑을 잃어버렸지만 그것에 대해 걱정하지 않았다.

_____ he lost his wallet, he didn't worry about it.

B 다음 우리말과 같은 뜻이 되도록 ( ) 안의 말을 배열하여 문장을 완성하시오.

1 네가 만약 바쁠지라도 아침 식사를 해야 한다. (you, even, busy, are, if)

_____, you must eat breakfast.

2 비록 그 케이크는 흉하게 보였지만 맛있었다. (though, the cake, awful, even, looked)

_____, it was delicious.

3 비록 나는 그를 좋아하지 않지만 그가 똑똑하다고 생각한다.

(don't, him, I, like, although)

_____, I think he is intelligent.

4 만약 그것이 네 잘못이었을지라도 나는 너를 비난하지 않는다.

(fault, if, it, even, was, your)

_____, I don't blame you.

- 〈so ~ that …〉: '너무 ~해서 …하다' (결과)
  It was **so** dark **that** he was a little scared.
- 〈so that ~〉: '~하기 위해서', '~할 수 있도록' (목적) (= in order that ~)
  I raised my hand **so that** she could find me.
  → I raised my hand **in order that** she could find me.

A 다음 우리말과 같은 뜻이 되도록 ( ) 안의 말을 이용하여 문장을 완성하시오.

1 너무 추워서 우리는 온종일 집에 있었다.
It was _____ _____ _____ _____ _____ at home all day long. (cold, stay)

2 나는 내년에 해외여행을 갈 수 있도록 돈을 좀 모으고 있다.
I'm saving some money _____ _____ _____ _____ _____ _____ next year. (travel abroad)

3 그가 너무 빨리 말해서 다른 사람들은 그를 이해할 수가 없었다.
He spoke _____ _____ _____ others could not _____ him. (quickly, understand)

4 제가 전화 통화를 할 수 있도록 음악 소리를 좀 줄여주세요.
Please turn down the music _____ _____ _____ _____ _____ on the phone. (talk)

B 다음 우리말과 같은 뜻이 되도록 ( ) 안의 말을 배열하여 문장을 완성하시오.

1 나는 너무 화가 나서 여기를 뛰쳐나가고 싶다.
(want, angry, run, that, so, to, out of here, I)
I feel _____.

2 그녀는 너무 배가 고파서 간식을 만들기로 결심했다.
(hungry, decided, she, so, that, some snacks, make, to)
She was _____.

3 Peter는 공부에 집중할 수 있도록 TV를 껐다.
(he, so, focus on, the TV, his studying, could, that)
Peter turned off _____.

4 우리는 미래에 더 나은 삶을 살 수 있도록 최선을 다해야 한다.
(order, have, can, that, we, a better life, in)
We should do our best _____ in the future.

상관 접속사 I – both A and B / not only A but also B

- both A and B는 'A와 B 둘 다'라는 뜻으로, 복수 취급한다.
  Both James **and** Harry *like* swimming.
- not only A but also B(≒ B as well as A)는 'A뿐만 아니라 B도'라는 뜻으로, B에 동사의 수를 일치시킨다.
  Julia is **not only** smart **but also** friendly.
  → Julia is friendly **as well as** smart.
  Not only Thomas **but also** the twins *want* to come with us.
  → The twins, **as well as** Thomas, *want* to come with us.

A 다음 주어진 문장과 같은 뜻이 되도록 문장을 완성하시오.

1 Mike reads German. And he writes it, too.
→ Mike _____ reads _____ writes German.

2 The movie was not only interesting but also sad.
→ The movie was sad _____ _____ _____ interesting.

3 You should bring your ID card. And you should bring a photo, too.
→ You should bring _____ your ID card _____ a photo.

4 He bought a DVD player as well as a television.
→ He bought _____ _____ a television _____ _____ a DVD player.

B 다음 문장에서 틀린 부분을 어법에 맞게 고쳐 쓰시오.

1 Both Alice and I was late for school.

2 Not only I but also my sister like skiing.

3 The father, as well as his children, were singing a song.

C 다음 우리말과 같은 뜻이 되도록 문장을 완성하시오.

1 나는 겨울뿐만 아니라 여름에도 그곳에 갔다.
I went there _____ _____ in winter _____ _____ in summer.

2 여행을 하기 위해서는 시간과 돈 둘 다 필요하다.
We need _____ time _____ money to travel.

3 그는 화가 났을 뿐만 아니라 그녀에게 실망하기도 했다.
He was _____ _____ angry _____ _____ disappointed with her.

4 Cindy뿐만 아니라 그녀의 부모님도 파티에 초대되었다.
Her parents, _____ _____ _____ Cindy, were invited to the party.

상관 접속사 II – either A or B / neither A nor B

- either A or B는 'A와 B 중 하나'라는 뜻이다.
  You can come **either** on Tuesday **or** Thursday.
- neither A nor B는 'A도 B도 아닌'이라는 뜻이다.
  Neither Sue **nor** Laura has called me yet.

★ 내신만점 *TIP* ⟨either A or B⟩, ⟨neither A nor B⟩는 B에 동사의 수를 일치시킴에 유의하자.

A 다음 ( ) 안에서 알맞은 말을 고르시오.

1 Neither Tina nor Tom (wear / wears) glasses.

2 Bananas are not only sweet (and / but) also healthy.

3 Either Mom or Dad (is / are) going to pick me up after school.

4 We are proud of both our service (or / and) our products.

5 She is (either / neither) in her office or in a meeting room.

B 다음 주어진 문장과 같은 뜻이 되도록 문장을 완성하시오.

1 Jake will come to help you. Or Lucy will help you.
  → _____ Jake _____ Lucy will help you.

2 I can't speak French. I can't speak Spanish, either.
  → I can speak _____ French _____ Spanish.

3 You can come with me. Or you can stay home.
  → You can _____ come with me _____ stay home.

C 다음 우리말과 같은 뜻이 되도록 ( ) 안의 말을 이용하여 문장을 완성하시오.

1 그는 담배도 피우지 않고 술도 마시지 않는다. (smoke, drink)
  He _____ _____ _____ _____.

2 그 콘서트는 재미도 없었고 성공적이지도 않았다. (exciting, successful)
  The concert was _____ _____ _____ _____.

3 우리는 버스를 타거나 걸어갈 수 있다. (take a bus, walk)
  We can _____ _____ _____ _____ _____ _____.

4 Jane은 나를 쳐다보지도, 나에게 말을 걸지도 않았다. (look at, talk to)
  Jane _____ _____ _____ _____

  _____ _____.

명령문+and / 명령문+or

- 〈명령문+and …〉는 '~해라, 그러면 …할 것이다'라는 뜻이다.
  Come early, **and** you will get the best seat.
  → If you come early, you will get the best seat.
- 〈명령문+or …〉는 '~해라, 그러지 않으면 …할 것이다'라는 뜻이다.
  Eat something, **or** you will get hungry later.
  → If you don't eat something, you will get hungry later.
  → Unless you eat something, you will get hungry later.

A 다음 빈칸에 and와 or 중 알맞은 말을 쓰시오.

1 Call him now, _____ he'll give you advice.

2 Drink a glass of water, _____ you'll be thirsty soon.

3 Bring your own cup, _____ you can save money.

4 Turn down the volume, _____ you'll wake everybody up.

B 다음 문장을 주어진 말을 이용하여 명령문으로 바꾸어 쓰시오.

1 If you come to the party, you will see him. (and)
→ _____

2 If you don't give it a try, you will regret it later. (or)
→ _____

3 If you read this article, you'll understand my point of view. (and)
→ _____

4 Unless you go to bed early, you'll wake up late tomorrow. (or)
→ _____

5 If you fasten your seat belt, you'll have a safe flight. (and)
→ _____

C 다음 문장을 밑줄 친 부분에 유의하여 우리말로 해석하시오.

1 Take this medicine, <u>and</u> you will feel better.

_____

2 Celebrate his birthday, <u>and</u> he will be happy.

_____

3 Don't eat too much, <u>or</u> you will get a stomachache.

_____

내신대비 TEST

[01-03] 다음 빈칸에 알맞은 말을 고르시오.

01

His driving skills have become better
_____ he has been practicing.

① unless ② even if ③ though
④ until ⑤ as

02

_____ he was tired, he stayed up all
night studying.

① Though ② Since ③ As
④ Even if ⑤ Unless

03

He eats _____ meat nor eggs because he
is a vegetarian.

① both ② either ③ so
④ not only ⑤ neither

[04-06] 다음 빈칸에 공통으로 들어갈 말을 고르시오.

04

• I haven't seen you _____ you moved to
  Daegu.
• He didn't come to school _____ he was
  sick.

① when ② until
③ if ④ since
⑤ though

05

• We can either eat out _____ order
  something to eat.
• Start preparing for the contest, _____
  you won't win first prize.

① and ② or
③ nor ④ as well as
⑤ but

06

• _____ I kept saying sorry, she's still
  upset at me.
• _____ he studied hard, he failed the
  test.

① When ② Since
③ Unless ④ Even though
⑤ As soon as

[07-08] 다음 주어진 문장과 같은 뜻이 되도록 할 때 빈칸에 알맞은 말을 고르시오.

07

Jordan is learning how to skate. Eric is
learning how to skate, too.
→ _____ Jordan _____ Eric are
  learning how to skate.

① Either – or ② Not – but
③ Both – and ④ Neither – nor
⑤ So – that

08

The boy winks at me whenever I see him.
→ The boy winks at me _____ I see him.

① as well as ② unless
③ while ④ every time
⑤ even if

09

다음 대화 중 자연스럽지 않은 것은?

① A: What do you want to drink?
   B: Either Coke or milk.
② A: Wow, this skirt is pretty.
   B: Buy it now, and you won't be able to find it later.
③ A: Did you enjoy the movie?
   B: No, it was neither funny nor interesting.
④ A: How was your date?
   B: It was bad. Though she was cute, she didn't seem to like me.
⑤ A: Why are you late?
   B: I woke up so late that I missed the bus.

[10-11] 빈칸에 들어갈 말이 순서대로 알맞게 짝지어진 것을 고르시오.

10

· Jimmy has neither emailed _____ called me.
· He ran as fast as possible _____ he could win the race.

① nor – so that ② or – unless
③ or – so that ④ nor – if
⑤ nor – even if

11

· _____ I look for my cap, I can't find it.
· The baby began crying _____ his mother left the room.

① While – as soon as ② While – though
③ Until – as soon as ④ Whenever – though
⑤ Whenever – as soon as

12

다음 우리말을 영어로 바르게 옮긴 것은?

비밀이 아니라면 나에게 그것에 대해 말해줘.

① If it is a secret, tell me about it.
② If not it is a secret, tell me about it.
③ Unless it is a secret, tell me about it.
④ Unless it is not a secret, tell me about it.
⑤ Even if it is not a secret, tell me about it.

[13-15] 다음 밑줄 친 부분의 쓰임이 나머지와 다른 것을 고르시오.

13

① If you visit them, they'll be glad.
② I have no idea if he will come.
③ If you need help, you can ask Alice.
④ You'll see more stars if the sky is clear.
⑤ We will go hiking if the weather is good.

14

① As it was late, we decided not to go.
② You'll understand me as time passes.
③ The roads were dangerous as it had snowed a lot.
④ As he wanted to swim, we went to the beach.
⑤ She likes going to the zoo as she loves animals.

15

① He loves cats, <u>while</u> he hates dogs.

② <u>While</u> she was cooking, the bell rang.

③ <u>While</u> he was passing by the mall, he ran into an old friend.

④ They kept silent <u>while</u> they were in the church.

⑤ Someone called for you <u>while</u> you were sleeping.

16

빈칸에 들어갈 말이 나머지와 다른 것은?

① I'm still hungry _____ I had dinner.

② He keeps studying _____ he isn't a student.

③ They have had the dog _____ they were little.

④ She doesn't speak French _____ she lived in Paris.

⑤ He didn't go to see a doctor _____ he had a headache.

고난도

17

다음 두 문장이 같은 뜻이 되도록 할 때 잘못된 것은?

① If you come here, you'll be able to relax.
   → Come here, and you'll be able to relax.

② I started jogging two years ago.
   → Two years have passed since I started jogging.

③ On getting up, he brushed his teeth.
   → As soon as he got up, he brushed his teeth.

④ Not only Ian but also Jim will vote for him.
   → Jim as well as Ian will vote for him.

⑤ Don't feed your dog too much, or he'll get fat.
   → Unless you feed your dog too much, he'll get fat.

[18-19] 다음 중 어법상 틀린 것을 고르시오.

18

① It was so cold that I almost froze.

② You can wear either a skirt or jeans.

③ Both Tim and I am soccer players.

④ He is not only a singer but also a professor.

⑤ On arriving at the airport, he exchanged some money.

19

① As soon as she saw me, she ran away.

② I've known her since she was a baby.

③ Let's go for a walk unless you're tired.

④ If you'll come over, we'll order some pizza.

⑤ Even though it was an expensive restaurant, the service was not good.

기출응용

20

다음 중 어법상 틀린 문장의 개수는?

(a) Since I met her, I haven't called her.

(b) Every time I visit him, he isn't at home.

(c) Though we are young, we have some responsibilities.

(d) Not only the children but also the teacher are laughing.

① 0개   ② 1개   ③ 2개   ④ 3개   ⑤ 4개

서술형 따라잡기

01
다음 두 문장이 같은 뜻이 되도록 빈칸에 알맞은 말을 쓰시오.

(1) As soon as he got on the bus, he saw her.

→ _____ _____ on the bus, he saw her.

(2) Whenever I call her, she's out.

→ _____ _____ I call her, she's out.

02
주어진 말을 알맞게 배열하여 우리말과 뜻이 같도록 문장을 완성하시오.

그는 소설뿐만 아니라 시도 쓴다.

(poems, as, he, novels, well, writes, as)

→ _____

03
주어진 말을 이용하여 우리말과 뜻이 같도록 문장을 완성하시오.

(1) 그는 시험에 합격할 수 있도록 많은 책을 읽었다.
(pass the test)

→ He read a lot of books _____ _____

_____ _____ _____

_____.

(2) 쇼핑 목록을 만들어라, 그러지 않으면 너는 무엇인가 살 것을 깜박할 것이다.
(forget, something)

→ Make a shopping list, _____ you'll

_____ _____ _____ _____.

04
다음 표를 보고, both와 neither를 각각 한 번씩만 사용하여 문장을 완성하시오.

Health Check List
(1) What do you eat?
☑ fruit ☑ vegetables ☐ none
(2) What kind of exercise do you do?
☐ run ☐ ride a bike ☑ none

(1) I eat _____ _____ _____ _____.

(2) I _____ _____ _____ _____

_____ _____.

05
다음 대화를 읽고, 주어진 접속사를 이용하여 한 문장으로 표현하시오.

(1) A: The TV show was very boring.
B: Yes. So Dad turned off the TV.

→ _____

(so ~ that …)

(2) A: Why is Mike boiling water?
B: He will cook some noodles.

→ _____

(so that ~)

고난도

06
다음 도서관 규칙을 읽고, 틀린 부분을 모두 찾아 바르게 고쳐 쓰시오. (3군데)

Library Rules
• Turn off your cell phone, and it will bother others.
• Unless you will return your book in a week, you will have to pay a fine.
• You are allowed to bring neither food or pets.

핵심 포인트 정리하기

1 종속 접속사

시간, 이유	when '~할 때' / while '~하는 동안' ① _____ '~하고 있을 때', '~함에 따라', '~ 때문에' ② _____ '~ 이래로', '~ 때문에' / until[till] '~할 때까지' every time '~할 때마다' / ③ _____ '~하자마자'
조건	④ _____ '만약 ~라면[한다면]' unless '~하지 않으면'
양보	though[although, even though] '비록 ~이지만' ⑤ _____ '만약 ~할지라도'
기타	결과: so ~ that … '너무 ~해서 …하다' 목적: ⑥ _____ ~ '~하기 위해서', '~할 수 있도록'

 시간이나 조건을 나타내는 부사절에서는 미래의 일도 현재시제로 나타낸다는 것 기억하기!

2 상관 접속사

⟨both A and B⟩ 'A와 B 둘 다'

⟨⑦_____⟩ (≒ B as well as A) 'A뿐만 아니라 B도'

⟨⑧_____ A or B⟩ 'A와 B 중 하나'

⟨neither A ⑨_____ B⟩ 'A도 B도 아닌'

 주어로 사용되는 상관 접속사의 수 일치에 유의하기!

3 명령문 + and / or

■ ⟨명령문 + ⑩_____⟩ '~해라, 그러면 …할 것이다'

■ ⟨명령문 + or⟩ '~해라, 그러지 않으면 …할 것이다'

문제로 개념 다지기

밑줄 친 부분이 어법상 맞으면 O, 틀리면 X 표시하고 바르게 고치시오.

1 <u>Even though</u> it was a nice watch, I didn't want to buy it.

2 You can wear either a dress <u>nor</u> a suit.

3 If I <u>won't see</u> you tomorrow, I'll call you.

4 <u>As</u> you grow older, you will learn more about patience.

5 She bought both a present <u>or</u> a birthday cake.

6 Not only he but also his mother <u>are</u> wearing sunglasses.

7 The book was <u>long so that</u> it took me several months to read it.

8 Please fasten your seat belt during takeoff, <u>and</u> you may get hurt.

주격 관계대명사

■ 주격 관계대명사: 관계사절 안에서 주어 역할을 하는 관계대명사

Eva is **a student**. + **She** likes playing tennis.

→ Eva is a student **who** likes playing tennis.

선행사	주격 관계대명사
사람	who[that]
동물, 사물	which[that]
〈사람+동물〉, 〈사람+사물〉, 최상급, 서수, -thing, the only, the very, the same, the last, all, every 등이 포함된 경우	that
X (관계대명사에 선행사가 포함되어 있는 경우)	what

★ PLUS TIP 〈주격 관계대명사+be동사+분사[형용사]〉 구문에서 '주격 관계대명사+be동사'는 흔히 생략된다.
I repaired the fence **(that was)** broken by the wind.

A 다음 문장에서 <u>틀린</u> 부분을 어법에 맞게 고쳐 쓰시오.

1 Which I want is your love.

2 Do you have a bag what is striped?

3 She is the person which helped me on the subway!

4 Look at the boy and the dog who are playing over there.

5 I'm looking for a blue shirt what goes well with white jeans.

B 다음 두 문장을 관계대명사를 이용하여 한 문장으로 만드시오.

1 Bring me the pencil case. It is on my desk.

→ _____

2 I saw a girl. She was crying in the street.

→ _____

3 She gave me a tiny doll. It was made of paper.

→ _____

4 Lily introduced me to a boy. He was wearing glasses.

→ _____

5 Logan has two cats and a dog. They are friendly.

→ _____

6 I have a comic book. It is very popular with teenagers.

→ _____

CHAPTER

관계사 I

What I really want to do is get some sleep for a few minutes.
→ The thing which[that]

She recommended a restaurant **where** I could have a party.

관계사

관계사에는 〈접속사+대명사〉 역할을 하는 관계대명사와 〈접속사+부사(구)〉 역할을 하는 관계부사가 있습니다. 관계사절은 앞의 명사(선행사)를 꾸며주는 형용사 역할을 합니다. 관계대명사는 관계사절 안에서의 역할에 따라 주격, 소유격, 목적격으로 나뉘고, 관계부사는 선행사(시간, 장소, 이유, 방법)에 따라 달라집니다.

소유격 관계대명사

- 소유격 관계대명사: 관계대명사가 수식하는 명사의 소유격 역할을 하는 관계대명사

I'm looking for **a boy**. + **His** name is Brian.

→ I'm looking for a boy **whose** name is Brian.

선행사	소유격 관계대명사
사람	whose
동물, 사물	whose[of which]

* 선행사가 동물·사물인 경우 of which를 쓸 수 있지만, 주로 whose를 쓴다.

A 다음 두 문장을 관계대명사를 이용하여 한 문장으로 만드시오.

1 Have you seen a book? Its cover is red.

→ _____

2 I chose a puppy. Its ears were white.

→ _____

3 He met a woman. Her husband is a pianist.

→ _____

4 She knows a man. His family lives in Sweden.

→ _____

B 다음 우리말과 같은 뜻이 되도록 ( ) 안의 말을 배열하여 문장을 완성하시오.

1 너는 리본이 분홍색인 모자를 가지고 있니?
(ribbon, you, do, a hat, is, whose, have, pink)

_____

2 그녀는 직업이 과학을 가르치는 것인 친구 한 명이 있다.
(a friend, teaching, has, is, whose, she, job, science)

_____

3 신 씨는 부인이 제작자인 코미디언이다.
(is, wife, a producer, a comedian, Mr. Shin, whose, is)

_____

4 그는 이름이 나와 같은 한 여자아이에 대해 이야기했다.
(the same, he, is, a girl, as mine, whose, talked about, name)

_____

목적격 관계대명사

■ 목적격 관계대명사: 관계사절 안에서 목적어 역할을 하는 관계대명사

This is **the car**. + A lot of people like **it** because it has a nice design.

→ This is the car **which[that]** a lot of people like because it has a nice design.

선행사	목적격 관계대명사
사람	who(m)[that]
동물, 사물	which[that]
〈사람+동물〉, 〈사람+사물〉, 최상급, 서수, -thing, the only, the very, the same, the last, all, every 등이 포함된 경우	that
X (관계대명사에 선행사가 포함되어 있는 경우)	what

★ PLUS TIP 목적격 관계대명사는 생략하는 경우가 많으며, 특히 구어체에서 목적격 관계대명사 whom은 who로 많이 쓴다.
단, 전치사의 목적어로 전치사 바로 뒤에 이어질 때는 whom을 쓴다.

A 다음 두 문장을 관계대명사를 이용하여 한 문장으로 만드시오.

1 You will like the movie. I saw it yesterday.

→ _____

2 This is the girl. I like her the most of all my friends.

→ _____

3 I ate lunch with the boy. You introduced me to him the other day.

→ _____

4 When can you give me the money? You borrowed it last week.

→ _____

B 다음 우리말과 같은 뜻이 되도록 ( ) 안의 말을 배열하여 문장을 완성하시오.

1 여기에 네가 찾고 있었던 열쇠가 있다. (you, looking for, the key, is, which, were, here)

_____

2 나는 도서관에서 일하는 친절한 한 여자를 안다.
(know, works, a friendly woman, who, at, I, the library)

_____

3 네가 만든 샌드위치들은 맛있었다. (made, which, the sandwiches, delicious, were, you)

_____

4 네가 가장 좋아하는 컴퓨터 게임의 이름이 무엇이니?
(the computer game, the name, like, that, you, what, of, is, the most)

_____

관계대명사 what

■ 관계대명사 what은 선행사를 포함한 관계대명사로 '~하는 것'으로 해석한다. the thing(s) which[that]로
바꾸어 쓸 수 있으며, what이 이끄는 명사절은 단수 취급한다.
What scared me was a big dog.
→ **The thing which[that]** scared me was a big dog.
This is **what** you talked about yesterday.
→ This is **the thing which[that]** you talked about yesterday.

★ **내신만점 TIP** 의문사 what과 관계대명사 what의 쓰임을 구분하자.
He asked me **what** I did in my free time. 〈의문사 what – '무엇'의 의미〉
That's exactly **what** I want to know. 〈관계대명사 what – '~하는 것'의 의미〉

A 다음 빈칸에 알맞은 관계대명사를 쓰시오.

1 _____ gives me energy is her support.

2 The man _____ owns this car is my father.

3 Thank you for _____ you offered us for free.

4 The hair dryer _____ I bought isn't working now.

5 They took away _____ the boy was carrying.

B 다음 문장이 어법상 맞으면 O, 틀리면 X 표시하고 바르게 고치시오.

1 What I ate for dinner were a doughnut.

2 Did you understand the teacher said?

3 I'm interested in that you are looking at now.

4 What I need is to take a walk to get some fresh air.

5 I am sorry for the trouble what I caused yesterday.

C 다음 우리말과 같은 뜻이 되도록 ( ) 안의 말을 이용하여 문장을 완성하시오.

1 네가 말한 것은 틀렸다. (say)
_____ _____ _____ is wrong.

2 나는 그가 내게 한 짓을 믿을 수가 없다. (do)
I can't believe _____ _____ _____ to me.

3 액션 영화는 그녀가 즐겨 보는 것이다. (enjoy, watch)
Action movies are _____ _____ _____ _____.

4 이 청바지는 내가 입고 싶은 것이다. (want, wear)
These jeans are _____ _____ _____ _____.

주로 관계대명사 that을 쓰는 경우

- 관계대명사 that은 관계대명사 whose와 what을 제외한 모든 관계대명사 대신 쓸 수 있다.
  특히 다음의 경우에는 주로 관계대명사 that을 쓴다.
  - 선행사가 〈사람+사물〉, 〈사람+동물〉인 경우
    She writes about *the people and things* **that** she is interested in.
  - something, anything 등이 선행사인 경우
    He gave me *something* **that** I could eat.
  - 선행사에 최상급, 서수, the only, the very, the same, the last, all, every 등이 포함된 경우
    You were *the first person* **that** visited my restaurant.

 접속사 that과 관계대명사 that을 구분하여 알아두자.
I learned **that** Mr. Song would be my new homeroom teacher. 〈접속사 that+완전한 절〉
Mr. Song is the best teacher **that** I've ever met. 〈관계대명사 that+불완전한 절〉

A 다음 빈칸에 알맞은 관계대명사를 쓰시오.

1 I received an invitation letter _____ envelope was blue.

2 She wrote something _____ I could hardly understand.

3 You are the only student _____ can win this contest.

B 다음 두 문장을 관계대명사를 이용하여 한 문장으로 만드시오.

1 I want to buy something. I can wear it to the party.
→ _____

2 This is the only article. I read it last month.
→ _____

3 Did you see the old man and the cat? They were sitting on the bench.
→ _____

C 다음 우리말과 같은 뜻이 되도록 (   ) 안의 말을 이용하여 문장을 완성하시오.

1 그것이 내가 가지고 있는 가장 심각한 문제이다. (serious, problem)
It is _____ _____ _____ _____ I have.

2 그녀는 금메달을 딴 첫 번째 여자였다. (win)
She was _____ _____ _____ _____ _____ a gold medal.

3 나는 칼로리가 낮은 무언가를 주문하고 싶다. (be low)
I'd like to order _____ _____ _____ _____ in calories.

관계부사 when / where

- 관계부사 when: 선행사가 시간이나 때(the day, the time, the year 등)를 나타내는 경우에 쓴다.
  I remember **the day**. + You first said my name **on that day**.
  → I remember *the day* **when(= on which)** you first said my name.
- 관계부사 where: 선행사가 장소(the place, the country, the house 등)를 나타내는 경우에 쓴다.
  This is **the restaurant**. + I met my boyfriend **at this restaurant**.
  → This is *the restaurant* **where(= at which)** I met my boyfriend.

★ PLUS TIP   관계부사는 〈전치사+관계대명사〉로 바꿔 쓸 수 있다.

A 다음 빈칸에 알맞은 관계부사를 쓰시오.

1 There was a time _____ people couldn't vote.

2 Sometimes I miss the town _____ I used to live.

3 I'll never forget the day _____ we became friends.

4 The year _____ my little brother was born was 2014.

5 This is the house _____ Picasso painted his last picture.

B 다음 두 문장을 관계부사를 이용하여 한 문장으로 만드시오.

1 The day was the happiest day of my life. My midterms ended on that day.
→ _____

2 He showed me the place. He had hidden there for an hour.
→ _____

3 They found a wounded dolphin in the area. People were swimming there.
→ _____

C 다음 우리말과 같은 뜻이 되도록 ( ) 안의 말을 배열하여 문장을 완성하시오.

1 그의 여동생이 공부하는 교실은 책으로 가득 차 있다.
(where, studies, the classroom, full of, his sister, books, is)

_____

2 나는 우리 가족이 제주도로 여행을 갔던 때가 그립다.
(my family, when, I, the time, traveled to, miss, Jeju Island)

_____

- 관계부사 why: 선행사가 이유(the reason)를 나타내는 경우에 쓴다.

  I know **the reason**. + My friend recommended this movie to me **for that reason**.

  → I know *the reason* **why** my friend recommended this movie to me.

- 관계부사 how: 선행사가 방법(the way)을 나타내는 경우에 쓴다. 단, 선행사 the way와 관계부사 how는 함께 쓰지 않는다.

  He told me **the way**. + He proposed to Linda **in that way**.

  → He told me **how** he proposed to Linda.
              (= the way)

A 다음 빈칸에 알맞은 말을 쓰시오.

1 That's _____ _____ why I changed my mind.

2 The reason _____ he called me is clear.

3 I learned _____ Japanese letters are pronounced.

4 I want to change _____ _____ we do business.

5 I know the reason _____ she didn't turn in her homework.

6 The man told me _____ this copy machine works.

7 Chris doesn't know _____ _____ why he was scolded.

B 다음 두 문장을 관계부사를 이용하여 한 문장으로 만드시오.

1 We talked about the way. He shoots a basketball in that way.

  → We talked about _____.

2 Bill told me the reason. He was moving to another town for that reason.

  → Bill told me the reason _____.

3 She showed me the way. She cooks such delicious ramen in that way.

  → She showed me _____.

4 I don't like the way. The waiters at this restaurant act in that way.

  → I don't like _____.

5 Cindy wanted to know the reason. Her boyfriend didn't call her for that reason.

  → Cindy wanted to know the reason _____.

6 My mother told me the reason. I need to live with my grandparents for that reason.

  → My mother told me the reason _____.

관계부사와 선행사의 생략

- 선행사가 the time, the place, the reason 등 일반적인 명사이면 선행사와 관계부사 중 하나를 생략하는 경우가 많은데, 보통 선행사를 생략한다.
  This is **(the place) where** I want to take pictures.
  He told me **(the reason) why** Helen was angry with me.
- 선행사 the way와 관계부사 how는 함께 쓰지 않으므로 둘 중 하나는 반드시 생략한다.
  I wanted to learn ~~the ways~~ **how** Indians lived in their villages.
  He was curious about **the way** ~~how~~ the earth was created.

A 다음 밑줄 친 부분을 생략할 수 있으면 O, 생략할 수 없으면 X 표시하시오.

1 This is the place where Mozart lived in his twenties.

2 That's the reason why Jeremy ran out of the house.

3 He showed me the way he finishes his homework so quickly.

4 Nobody knows the reason why this couple had a fight last night.

5 I remember the days when we would play with sand.

B 다음 우리말과 같은 뜻이 되도록 ( ) 안의 말을 배열하여 문장을 완성하시오.

1 여기가 내 친구가 일하는 곳이다. (works, friend, is, my, where, this)

_____

2 내가 이 대학에 입학한 몇 가지 이유들이 있다.
(entered, why, are, this college, reasons, several, there, I)

_____

3 나는 Jim이 세계 선수권 대회에서 우승했던 때를 절대 잊지 않을 것이다.
(forget, Jim, the world championship, will, when, never, won, I)

_____

4 나는 우리가 점심을 먹곤 했던 식당에서 Megan을 보았다.
(eat, saw, lunch, I, used to, where, Megan, at the restaurant, we)

_____

5 우리는 그녀가 그녀의 시험을 위해 공부한 방법에 대해 이야기했다.
(her exams, talked about, for, she, we, how, studied)

_____

Chapter 11

내신대비 TEST

[01-03] 다음 빈칸에 알맞은 말을 고르시오.

01

> She didn't like _____ I made for her birthday.

① what   ② it   ③ whose
④ whom   ⑤ which

02

> The street _____ I was walking on was very slippery.

① what   ② who   ③ which
④ whose   ⑤ where

03

> This is the city _____ the 2018 Winter Olympics took place.

① which   ② what   ③ when
④ why   ⑤ where

기출응용
04

다음 빈칸에 들어갈 말로 적절하지 <u>않은</u> 것은?

> I still remember _____ when I first saw you.

① the moment   ② the day
③ the season   ④ the town
⑤ the year

[05-07] 다음 빈칸에 공통으로 들어갈 말을 고르시오.

05

> • She was the first president _____ visited that country.
> • I know everyone _____ is waiting in line.

① whom   ② that   ③ which
④ when   ⑤ why

06

> • The man told me _____ he knew about this animal.
> • I know _____ you bought at the market.

① which   ② that   ③ who
④ whom   ⑤ what

07

> • We should hire the person _____ is right for the job.
> • My brother gave me a laptop _____ he never used.

① who   ② which   ③ what
④ that   ⑤ whose

08

다음 밑줄 친 부분에서 생략된 말로 알맞은 것은?

> <u>The woman reading</u> a magazine on a rocking chair is my sister.

① that is   ② who are
③ which is   ④ what is
⑤ which are

09

- This is _____ I had gotten straight A's.
- My sister knew the reason _____ my father came home so early today.

① how – which
② the way – whom
③ how – why
④ what – why
⑤ why – when

10

- Try to remember the evening _____ you danced with him.
- After school, Liz reviews _____ she learned.

① where – what
② when – where
③ what – when
④ when – what
⑤ what – which

11

빈칸에 들어갈 말이 나머지와 다른 것은?

① He always does something _____ bothers me.
② You will never believe _____ I heard.
③ He couldn't think of anything _____ is exciting.
④ Sally was the first woman _____ joined this club.
⑤ I think Dr. Shin is the funniest man _____ I've ever met.

12

다음 중 밑줄 친 부분을 생략할 수 없는 것은?

① I don't like the man that I work with.
② The boy who offered me a seat was very kind.
③ She was waiting for the bus that I used to take.
④ We play soccer on days when we don't go to school.
⑤ The driver who is sitting in the car will take you to the airport.

기출응용
13

다음 중 빈칸에 'what'이 들어갈 수 있는 문장의 개수는?

(a) Be happy with _____ you have.
(b) She has earphones _____ are not working.
(c) Listening is the only thing _____ I can do for you.
(d) _____ I saw last night in my dreams was dinosaurs.

① 0개 ② 1개 ③ 2개 ④ 3개 ⑤ 4개

[14-15] 다음 중 어법상 틀린 것을 고르시오.

14

① What I want to eat is chicken curry.
② I live in a house that has no garden.
③ Tell me the way how you invited her.
④ The man who is wearing a hat is my dad.
⑤ This is the place where I feel at home.

15

① Look at the wooden chair that has red legs.

② I live in a small village that has no theater.

③ This is the bag which I have been looking for.

④ This is the longest bridge that I have ever seen.

⑤ I work with Sam of which brother is a drummer.

[16-17] 다음 밑줄 친 부분의 쓰임이 나머지와 다른 것을 고르시오.

16

① She hasn't decided <u>where</u> to put her bed.

② I have been to the place <u>where</u> Van Gogh is buried.

③ My grandma still misses the place <u>where</u> she was born.

④ He visited the town <u>where</u> he went to school.

⑤ This is the playground <u>where</u> we used to play hide-and-seek.

17

① I'll go to the city <u>that</u> he recommended.

② I can't understand all the words <u>that</u> he is saying.

③ They saw two men and a lion <u>that</u> lived together.

④ She told the doctor <u>that</u> she had eye trouble.

⑤ This is the very novel <u>that</u> has sold over 1 million copies.

18

(A), (B), (C)의 괄호 안에서 알맞은 것끼리 바르게 짝지어진 것은?

> (A) Have you found the wallet [that / what] you lost?
> (B) I will buy Tom [who / what] he wants.
> (C) This is a park [which / where] people can relax and enjoy nature.

	(A)		(B)		(C)
①	that	⋯⋯	who	⋯⋯	which
②	that	⋯⋯	what	⋯⋯	which
③	that	⋯⋯	what	⋯⋯	where
④	what	⋯⋯	who	⋯⋯	where
⑤	what	⋯⋯	what	⋯⋯	where

고난도

19

다음 중 어법상 옳은 것을 모두 고르면? (3개)

① The printer was broken is now fixed.

② He is the only friend that I can talk to.

③ There's another reason why he got angry.

④ May is a month when many couples get married.

⑤ I like the lady that black hair comes down to her shoulders.

고난도

20

다음 글의 밑줄 친 부분 중 어법상 틀린 것은?

> Today was the day ① <u>when</u> my friend Yumi moved to Canada. She was a friend ② <u>who</u> I could tell my secrets. She did everything ③ <u>which</u> she could do for me. I will never forget ④ <u>what</u> we did and ⑤ <u>where</u> we went together.

01

다음 두 문장을 관계사를 이용하여 한 문장으로 바꾸어 쓰시오.

(1) I won't forget the day.

   I won the speech contest on that day.

   → I won't forget the day _____ _____

   _____ _____ _____ _____.

(2) I taught a girl.

   Her father was a famous lawyer.

   → I taught a girl _____ _____

   _____ _____ _____ _____.

02

주어진 말을 알맞게 배열하여 우리말과 뜻이 같도록 문장을 완성하시오.

(1) 나는 집이 해안에 있는 친척이 한 명 있다.

   (whose, a relative, house, on the coast, have, is, I)

   → _____

(2) 나는 그가 일하는 은행을 방문했다.

   (I, where, the bank, he, visited, works)

   → _____

03

다음 그림을 보고, 주어진 말과 관계사를 이용하여 문장을 완성하시오.

(1) There is a girl _____ _____ _____

   _____. (gloves)

(2) There is a doghouse _____ _____

   _____ _____. (sleep)

04

주어진 관계사를 이용하여 우리말과 뜻이 같도록 문장을 완성하시오.

(1) 그가 내게 준 것은 목걸이였다. (what)

   → _____ _____ _____ _____

   was a necklace.

(2) 나는 그가 결석한 이유를 안다. (why)

   → _____ _____ _____ _____

   _____ he was absent.

05

다음 표를 보고, 〈보기〉의 관계사를 이용하여 문장을 완성하시오.

Ryu Hyun Jin (Baseball player)
Birth: 1987 in Incheon
Height: 190 cm   * Won 14 games in 2014

〈보기〉 when   where   whose

(1) Incheon is the city _____

   _____.

(2) Ryu is a baseball player _____

   _____ 190 cm.

(3) 2014 was the year _____

   _____.

06

다음 대화를 읽고, 틀린 부분을 모두 찾아 바르게 고쳐 쓰시오. (2군데)

A: I took this picture at the beach last summer.

B: Did you go scuba diving?

A: Yes, that is the reason how I went to that beach.

B: How was it?

A: It was fantastic. It was the very thing which I wanted to try.

핵심 포인트 정리하기

1 관계대명사

선행사	주격 관계대명사	소유격 관계대명사	목적격 관계대명사
사람	who[that]	① _____	who(m)[that]
동물, 사물	② _____	whose[of which]	which[that]
〈사람+동물〉, 〈사람+사물〉, 최상급, 서수, -thing, the only, the very, the same, the last, all, every 등 포함	③ _____	–	that
X(관계대명사에 선행사 포함)	④ _____ (→ the thing(s) which[that])	–	what (→ the thing(s) which[that])

 관계대명사 what은 선행사를 취하지 않는다는 것 기억하기!
관계대명사를 생략할 수 있는 경우 잊지 말기!
접속사 that과 관계대명사 that의 쓰임 구분하기!
의문사(who, what 등)와 관계대명사(who, what 등)의 쓰임 구분하기!

2 관계부사

- 선행사가 시간이나 때를 나타낼 때: ⑤ _____
- 선행사가 장소를 나타낼 때: ⑥ _____
- 선행사가 이유를 나타낼 때: ⑦ _____
- 선행사가 방법을 나타낼 때: how (단, 선행사 the way와 관계부사 how 중 하나는 반드시 생략)

관계대명사 뒤에는 불완전한 절, 관계부사 뒤에는 완전한 절이 온다는 것 기억하기!

문제로 개념 다지기

밑줄 친 부분이 어법상 맞으면 O, 틀리면 X 표시하고 바르게 고치시오.

1 Do you remember the girl <u>which</u> I used to tell you about?

2 He is the very man <u>what</u> gave me some useful advice.

3 I met someone <u>whose</u> mother owns a private jet.

4 We'd like to live in a place <u>when</u> there is a beautiful view.

5 I've been to a resort <u>that</u> is very popular.

6 I really don't like <u>the way how</u> she talks to me.

food truck

CHAPTER 12

관계사 II

개념 쏙쏙

Whoever is interested in movies will like this festival.
(= Anyone who)

Whenever I'm late for school, I meet my teacher in front of the school.
(= At any time when)

Brian visited Italy, **where** his father first met his mother 15 years ago.
　　　　　　　(= and there)

복합관계사

복합관계사에는 〈관계대명사+ever〉의 형태로 선행사를 포함하는 복합관계대명사와
〈관계부사+ever〉의 형태인 복합관계부사가 있습니다. 복합관계대명사는 문맥에 따라 명사절
이나 양보의 부사절을 이끌고, 복합관계부사는 시간·장소·방법의 부사절이나 양보의 부사절을
이끕니다.

관계사의 계속적 용법

선행사에 대한 부가적인 정보를 제공할 때 관계사 앞에 쉼표(,)를 써서 나타냅니다.

Point 01

복합관계대명사 whoever

- 복합관계대명사는 〈관계대명사+ever〉의 형태로 선행사를 포함하는 관계대명사이다. 문맥에 따라 명사절이나 양보의 부사절을 이끈다.
- whoever는 사람을 선행사로 하는 복합관계대명사이다.

복합관계대명사	명사절(~든지)	양보의 부사절(~라도)
whoever	~하는 사람은 누구든지 (= anyone who)	누가[누구를] ~하더라도 (= no matter who)

★ PLUS TIP   원칙적으로 목적격 복합관계대명사는 whomever이지만 현대 영어에서는 잘 쓰지 않는다.

A 다음 두 문장이 같은 뜻이 되도록 문장을 완성하시오.

1 Anyone who breaks the law will be punished.
→ _____ breaks the law will be punished.

2 Whoever she meets becomes her friend.
→ _____ _____ she meets becomes her friend.

3 No matter who is responsible for this, that person should apologize to me.
→ _____ is responsible for this, that person should apologize to me.

B 다음 우리말과 같은 뜻이 되도록 복합관계대명사와 ( ) 안의 말을 이용하여 문장을 완성하시오.

1 먼저 그것을 발견하는 사람은 누구든지 그것을 가질 수 있다. (find)
_____ _____ _____ first can have it.

2 나는 상을 받는 사람이 누구든지 축하해줄 것이다. (win a prize)
I will congratulate _____ _____ _____ _____ .

3 그 퍼즐을 푸는 사람은 누구든지 세계를 놀라게 할 것이다. (solve, puzzle)
_____ _____ _____ will surprise the world.

4 이 우산을 원하는 사람은 누구든지 그것을 가져갈 수 있다. (want, umbrella)
_____ _____ _____ _____ may take it.

5 누가 그 사고를 목격했더라도, 그 사람은 도움을 주려고 노력했을 것이다. (see, accident)
_____ _____ _____ _____ _____ ,
the person would have tried to be helpful.

6 일찍 오는 사람은 누구든지 좋은 자리를 얻을 것이다. (come, get a good seat)
_____ _____ _____ will _____ _____ _____
_____ .

복합관계대명사 whichever / whatever

■ whichever와 whatever는 사물을 선행사로 하는 복합관계대명사이다.

복합관계대명사	명사절(~든지)	양보의 부사절(~라도)
whichever	~하는 것은 어느 것이든지 (= anything which)	어느 것을[이] ~하더라도 (= no matter which)
whatever	~하는 것은 무엇이든지 (= anything that)	무엇을[이] ~하더라도 (= no matter what)

A 다음 두 문장의 뜻이 같도록 빈칸에 알맞은 말을 쓰시오.

1 No matter what you say, I can't believe you.
→ _____ you say, I can't believe you.

2 Anyone who joins our website will get a coupon.
→ _____ joins our website will get a coupon.

3 No matter what she does, she always complains.
→ _____ she does, she always complains.

4 Whichever you choose, you will be satisfied.
→ _____ _____ _____ you choose, you will be satisfied.

B 다음 우리말과 같은 뜻이 되도록 복합관계대명사와 ( ) 안의 말을 이용하여 문장을 완성하시오.

1 네가 원하는 것이 어느 것이든지 골라보아라. (want)
Just pick _____ _____ _____.

2 무슨 일이 일어나더라도 나는 포기하지 않을 것이다. (happen)
_____ _____ _____ _____, I won't give up.

3 네가 무엇을 하더라도, 내가 네 편이 되어줄 것이다. (do)
I'll be on your side _____ _____ _____.

4 그가 요리하는 것은 무엇이든지 맛있다. (cook)
_____ _____ _____ is delicious.

5 나는 네가 요청하는 것은 어느 것이든지 너에게 빌려줄 것이다. (ask for)
I'll lend you _____ _____ _____ _____.

6 너는 이 가게에서 네가 필요한 것은 무엇이든지 살 수 있다. (need)
You can buy _____ _____ _____ in this shop.

복합관계부사 whenever / wherever / however

- 복합관계부사는 〈관계부사+ever〉의 형태로 선행사를 포함하는 관계부사이다. 문맥에 따라 시간·장소·방법의 부사절이나 양보의 부사절을 이끈다.

복합관계부사	시간·장소·방법의 부사절(~든지, ~나)	양보의 부사절(~라도)
whenever	~할 때는 언제나 (= at any time when)	언제 ~하더라도 (= no matter when)
wherever	~하는 곳은 어디든지 (= at[in/to] any place where)	어디서 ~하더라도 (= no matter where)
however	~하는 어떤 방법으로든지 (= in whatever way that)	아무리 ~하더라도 (= no matter how)

A 다음 빈칸에 알맞은 복합관계부사를 쓰시오.

1 _____ often I say that to my husband, he doesn't listen.

2 People want more money, _____ rich they are.

3 _____ you're ready, let me know.

4 I see Richard _____ I take this bus after school.

5 _____ you travel, you can find this doughnut shop.

6 I draw pictures _____ I have free time.

7 _____ my boyfriend is, I think of him.

B 다음 두 문장이 같은 뜻이 되도록 문장을 완성하시오.

1 At any time when you have a question, call me.

→ _____ you have a question, call me.

2 No matter where you go, I'll follow you.

→ _____ you go, I'll follow you.

3 However angry you are, you should have patience.

→ _____ _____ _____ angry you are, you should have patience.

C 다음 우리말과 같은 뜻이 되도록 복합관계부사와 ( ) 안의 말을 이용하여 문장을 완성하시오.

1 그들은 만날 때면 언제나 싸운다. (meet)

_____ _____ _____, they fight.

2 그녀가 아무리 높이 뛰어도 꼭대기 선반에 손이 닿지 않았다. (jump)

_____ _____ _____ _____, she couldn't reach the top shelf.

관계사의 계속적 용법 Ⅰ

- 관계사의 계속적 용법은 관계사 앞에 쉼표(,)를 쓰고, 선행사에 대한 부가적인 정보를 제공하는 것이다. 관계대명사 who와 which, 관계부사 when과 where를 계속적 용법으로 쓸 수 있다.

I talked to Mike, **who** is a TV producer. (계속적 용법)
           (= and he)
cf. I talked to a man **who** is a TV producer. (한정적 용법)

 ★ 내신만점 *TIP*
- 계속적 용법으로 쓰인 관계대명사는 생략할 수 없다는 것을 기억하자.
- 관계대명사 that은 계속적 용법으로 쓸 수 없음을 알아두자.
  I bought new pajamas, **which** my puppy tore up.
  (→ I bought new pajamas, **that** my puppy tore up. (X))

A 다음 우리말과 같은 뜻이 되도록 빈칸에 알맞은 관계사를 쓰시오.

1 Susan은 Greg과 John을 만났는데, 그들은 군인이었다.
Susan met Greg and John, _____ were soldiers.

2 그녀는 Brian에게 전화를 했으나, 그는 받지 않았다.
She called Brian, _____ didn't answer.

3 그들은 한국으로 이민을 왔는데, 그곳에서 그들의 아기가 태어났다.
They moved to Korea, _____ their baby was born.

4 나는 선물을 풀어보았는데, 그것은 내 남동생이 사준 것이었다.
I opened the present, _____ was bought by my brother.

5 그녀는 이 카페를 좋아하는데, 그곳은 초콜릿 케이크로 유명하다.
She likes this café, _____ is famous for its chocolate cakes.

6 그는 2017년에 대학을 졸업했는데, 그때 그의 여동생은 겨우 중학생이었다.
He graduated from college in 2017, _____ his sister was only in middle school.

B 밑줄 친 부분이 어법상 맞으면 O, 틀리면 X 표시하고 바르게 고치시오.

1 I went to New York, <u>when</u> I met Chris.

2 Emily, <u>can</u> speak French, works at a French restaurant.

3 Robert told me about his girlfriend, <u>that</u> is a barista.

4 Sylvia recommended the movie *Flipped*, <u>that</u> was very interesting.

5 She went to see the doctor, <u>who</u> told her to rest.

6 We stayed at the Green Hotel, <u>where</u> Thomas recommended.

관계사의 계속적 용법 II

■ 계속적 용법으로 쓰인 관계대명사는 〈접속사+대명사〉로, 관계부사는 〈접속사+부사〉로 바꿔 쓸 수 있다.

I went to the City Museum, **which** was closed.
(= but it)

They visited London, **where** they saw a musical.
(= and there)

A 다음 두 문장이 같은 뜻이 되도록 문장을 완성하시오.

1 He went to Namsan Seoul Tower, and there he ran into his friend.
→ He went to Namsan Seoul Tower, _____ he ran into his friend.

2 I fell in love with him in 2016, and at that time I was 20 years old.
→ I fell in love with him in 2016, _____ I was 20 years old.

3 I have two brothers, and they are elementary school students.
→ I have two brothers, _____ are elementary school students.

4 I made spaghetti with creamy sauce, and it was really delicious.
→ I made spaghetti with creamy sauce, _____ was really delicious.

5 We saw the big bell tower, which was made of stone.
→ We saw the big bell tower, _____ _____ was made of stone.

6 Sally enjoys reading at night, because at that time she can concentrate well.
→ Sally enjoys reading at night, _____ she can concentrate well.

B 다음 우리말과 같은 뜻이 되도록 문장을 완성하시오.

1 나는 Paul을 만났지만, 그는 나를 알아보지 못했다.
I met Paul, _____ didn't recognize me.
→ I met Paul, _____ _____ didn't recognize me.

2 나는 클래식 음악을 좋아하는데, 그것은 나를 쉽게 해주기 때문이다.
I like classical music, _____ helps me relax.
→ I like classical music, _____ _____ helps me relax.

3 그들은 여의도를 방문했는데, 거기에서 그들은 벚꽃 축제를 즐겼다.
They visited Yeouido, _____ they enjoyed the cherry blossom festival.
→ They visited Yeouido, _____ _____ they enjoyed the cherry blossom festival.

관계사의 계속적 용법 III

■ 계속적 용법으로 쓰인 관계대명사 which는 앞에 나온 구나 절을 선행사로 취할 수 있다.
She decided to marry him, **which** surprised everybody. (선행사: 앞 절 전체)
Some students *skip breakfast*, **which** is not good for their health. (선행사: skip breakfast)

A 다음 〈보기〉에서 알맞은 말을 골라 관계대명사 which를 이용하여 문장을 완성하시오. (단, 한 번씩만 사용할 것)

〈보기〉	This caused them to go the wrong way.	It was very inconvenient.
	This made it hard for her to sleep.	It was amazing.
	This meant he had to stay there.	It was very kind of him.

1 I won first prize, _____.

2 Josh lent me his notebook, _____.

3 Jake missed the last train, _____.

4 She drank three cups of coffee, _____.

5 I didn't have my cell phone with me, _____.

6 They didn't follow the map, _____.

B 다음 우리말과 같은 뜻이 되도록 관계대명사 which와 ( ) 안의 말을 이용하여 문장을 완성하시오.

1 나는 Jennifer를 만났는데, 그것은 비밀이었다. (a secret)
I met Jennifer, _____ _____ _____ _____.

2 Irene은 아프다고 말했지만, 그것은 사실이 아니었다. (true)
Irene said she was sick, _____ _____ _____ _____.

3 나는 버스를 놓쳤는데, 그것은 내가 학교에 늦게 만들었다. (make, late)
I missed the bus, _____ _____ _____ _____ for school.

4 그는 드디어 취업을 했는데, 그것은 그의 인생에서 가장 행복한 순간이었다.
(happy, moment)
He finally got a job, _____ _____ _____ _____
of his life.

5 Mary는 갑자기 그녀의 입을 다물었는데, 그것은 그녀가 화가 났다는 의미였다.
(mean, angry)
Mary suddenly closed her mouth, _____ _____ _____ _____
_____.

전치사＋관계대명사

■ 관계대명사가 전치사의 목적어인 경우, 전치사는 관계대명사 바로 앞이나 관계사절 끝에 올 수 있다. 전치사가 관계대명사 앞에 쓰인 경우에는 관계대명사를 생략할 수 없다.

This is the house **in which** the famous architect lives.
This is the house **which[that]** the famous architect lives **in**.

★ 내신만점 TIP 전치사 바로 뒤에는 관계대명사 that이나 who가 올 수 없다는 것을 잊지 말자.
This is the house **in that** the famous architect lives. (X)

A 다음 (   ) 안에서 알맞은 말을 고르시오.

1 This is the town (which / in which) I grew up.

2 Who is the girl to (that / whom) you were talking?

3 This is the shop (at which / which) I bought my new skirt.

4 They visited the park which they had had lunch (in / to).

5 He showed me the paintings (in which / in that) he was interested.

B 다음 주어진 문장과 같은 뜻이 되도록 문장을 완성하시오.

1 My birthday was the day. I took the exam on that day.
→ My birthday was the day _____ _____ I took the exam.

2 The building is under construction. He works in the building.
→ The building _____ he works _____ is under construction.

3 I asked her about the hotel. She stayed at the hotel.
→ I asked her about the hotel _____ she stayed _____ .

4 David is the classmate. I'm doing a project with him.
→ David is the classmate _____ _____ I'm doing a project.

5 This is the restaurant. We had dinner at the restaurant.
→ This is the restaurant _____ _____ we had dinner.

6 Where is the bag? I put my cell phone in the bag.
→ Where is the bag _____ _____ I put my cell phone?

7 Beijing is the city. I lived in the city when I was young.
→ Beijing is the city _____ I lived _____ when I was young.

8 Do you know the year? Korea hosted the World Cup in that year.
→ Do you know the year _____ _____ Korea hosted the World Cup?

관계대명사의 생략

- 동사나 전치사의 목적어로 사용된 목적격 관계대명사는 생략할 수 있다.

  Sally is a student **(who(m)[that])** everybody likes.

- 〈주격 관계대명사+be동사〉는 뒤에 형용사나 분사, 전치사가 이끄는 구가 오는 경우에 생략할 수 있다.

  The man **(who[that] is)** talking with her is Mark.

★ **PLUS TIP** 전치사의 목적어로 쓰인 관계대명사를 생략할 경우에는 전치사가 반드시 관계사절 끝에 와야 한다.

Jerry is the pet cat I'm taking care **of**. (O)
Jerry is the pet cat **of** I'm taking care. (X)

A 다음 문장에서 생략할 수 있는 부분을 찾아 ( ) 표시하고, 생략해서 쓰시오.

1 This is the book that I was looking for.

→ _____

2 This is a TV set which was made in Indonesia.

→ _____

3 The girl who is listening to music is my girlfriend.

→ _____

B 다음 문장에서 생략된 부분을 찾아 V 표시하고 쓰시오.

1 He is the man I told you about the other day.

2 The boy playing the guitar now is my brother.

3 Susan is the girl Mike fell in love with.

4 I didn't bring the notebook I borrowed.

5 Do you know the woman sitting in front of Ray over there?

6 This is the free gift given to customers now.

C 다음 우리말과 같은 뜻이 되도록 ( ) 안의 말을 알맞게 배열하여 문장을 완성하시오.

1 안경을 쓰고 있는 남자가 Joe이다. (glasses, is, the man, Joe, wearing)

_____

2 이것은 고야가 그린 그림이다. (Goya, this, a picture, painted, is)

_____

3 그는 내가 존경하는 과학자이다. (a scientist, is, he, look up to, I)

_____

내신대비 TEST

[01-03] 다음 빈칸에 알맞은 말을 고르시오.

01

_____ you call me, I'll answer.

① Whoever   ② Whomever
③ Whenever   ④ Whichever
⑤ However

02

This is the bookstore _____ I bought my favorite novel.

① which   ② that   ③ what
④ in which   ⑤ in that

03

Stephen Hawking, _____ was a great scientist, died in 2018.

① who   ② whom   ③ that
④ which   ⑤ what

04
다음 밑줄 친 부분과 바꿔 쓸 수 있는 것은?

I went hiking with an Austrian couple, <u>who</u> wanted to learn Korean.

① and he   ② but they
③ and they   ④ and it
⑤ but he

[05-07] 빈칸에 들어갈 말이 순서대로 알맞게 짝지어진 것을 고르시오.

05

• _____ you go in Spain, you can see beautiful buildings.
• _____ you choose, I'll accept your decision.

① Whatever – Whichever
② Whatever – Whenever
③ Wherever – Whichever
④ Wherever – Wherever
⑤ Whichever – However

06

• We had lunch at Café Prince, _____ is owned by my friend.
• Jeonju is the city _____ I grew up.

① that – which   ② which – that
③ that – in which   ④ what – in that
⑤ which – in which

07

• I'll give this free ticket to the music festival to _____ wants it.
• He told me a big lie, _____ was very disappointing.

① whoever – which   ② who – that
③ whom – which   ④ whoever – that
⑤ whoever – what

08

다음 대화 중 자연스럽지 <u>않은</u> 것은?

① A: You can have whatever you like.
   B: Thank you very much.
② A: Joe, who lives next door, is very kind.
   B: I really want to meet him.
③ A: However hard I study, I can't pass the exam.
   B: Cheer up! You can do it.
④ A: Wherever you go, I'll be with you.
   B: Sorry, I've been there before.
⑤ A: Let me know whenever you are in trouble.
   B: Thank you. I will.

[09-10] 다음 빈칸에 공통으로 들어갈 말을 고르시오.

09

- Brandon didn't even say hello to me,
_____ was very rude.
- I ate today's special, _____ Kate recommended.

① what
② who
③ that
④ which
⑤ when

10

- _____ hungry I am, I can't eat a whole pizza.
- _____ smart she is, she won't be able to guess the answer.

① Whenever
② However
③ Wherever
④ Whoever
⑤ Whichever

11

다음 중 밑줄 친 부분을 생략할 수 <u>없는</u> 것은?

① Here's the scarf <u>which</u> you were looking for.
② He likes the people <u>that</u> he works with.
③ She is the person <u>whom</u> I want to hire.
④ There are a lot of people <u>who are</u> standing in line.
⑤ This is the palace in <u>which</u> the king lived.

12

다음 빈칸에 들어갈 수 <u>없는</u> 말은?

A: Was Antonio Vivaldi born in Italy?
B: Yes. _____

① Italy is the country he was born in.
② Italy is the country which he was born.
③ Italy is the country where he was born.
④ Italy is the country that he was born in.
⑤ Italy is the country in which he was born.

〔기출응용〕

[13-14] 다음 빈칸에 들어갈 말로 적절한 것을 모두 고르시오. (2개)

13

_____ I say, just believe me.

① Whoever
② Whatever
③ Anything that
④ No matter what
⑤ No matter who

14

The airplane _____ taking off right now is going to Moscow.

① which
② that
③ which is
④ what is
⑤ X (없음)

15

① <u>Whatever happens</u>, don't worry.
② This is the store <u>that I worked in</u>.
③ Have a seat <u>wherever you like</u>.
④ This is Sarah, <u>that I told you about</u>.
⑤ You can visit me <u>whatever day you want</u>.

16

① <u>However much it costs</u>, I'll buy it.
② <u>Whoever calls for me</u>, tell them I'm out.
③ He is the man <u>with whom they traveled</u>.
④ I couldn't meet him, <u>which was a pity</u>.
⑤ Do you know <u>the girl is standing</u> near the window?

17

다음 빈칸에 들어갈 말이 같은 것끼리 짝지어진 것은?

(a) _____ fast I drive, I won't make it on time.
(b) _____ she winks at the baby, he laughs.
(c) _____ hot it is, he won't turn on the air conditioner.
(d) _____ participates in the survey will be given a small reward.

① (a), (b)   ② (a), (c)
③ (b), (c)   ④ (b), (d)
⑤ (c), (d)

18

빈칸에 들어갈 말이 나머지와 <u>다른</u> 것은?

① This is the shop at _____ I bought this ring.
② This is the street on _____ he had an accident.
③ You can choose _____ you want.
④ I ate at Burger Palace, _____ Tom mentioned before.
⑤ He invented the machine, _____ is now very popular.

고난도
19

다음 우리말을 영어로 바르게 옮긴 것을 모두 고르면? (3개)

> 그는 의지할 수 있는 사람을 필요로 한다.

① He needs someone he can depend on.
② He needs someone on he can depend.
③ He needs someone on whom he can depend.
④ He needs someone who he can depend on.
⑤ He needs someone on who he can depend.

고난도
20

다음 중 어법상 <u>틀린</u> 문장의 개수는?

(a) She wore her blue dress, that was beautiful.
(b) You can come whatever it is convenient.
(c) I will not forget the resort which we stayed.
(d) Spring is the season we can see tulips in.

① 0개   ② 1개   ③ 2개   ④ 3개   ⑤ 4개

01

다음 두 문장이 같은 뜻이 되도록 빈칸에 알맞은 말을 쓰시오.

(1) No matter who arrives last, that person should close the door.

→ _____ _____ _____, that person should close the door.

(2) The movie was filmed in the town that I live in.

→ The movie was filmed in the town _____ _____ I live.

02

다음 우리말과 뜻이 같도록 관계사와 주어진 말을 이용하여 문장을 완성하시오.

(1) 네가 어디서 일하더라도, 항상 최선을 다해라. (work)

→ _____ _____ _____, always do your best.

(2) 이 박물관을 방문하는 사람은 누구든지 음성 가이드를 무료로 이용할 수 있다. (visit)

→ _____ _____ _____ _____ can use the audio guide for free.

03

다음 문장을 〈보기〉와 같이 바꿔 쓰시오.

〈보기〉

Even if it is very hard, he won't stop running.
→ However hard it is, he won't stop running.

(1) Even if it is very cold, they will go fishing.

→ _____

(2) Even if you arrive early, you cannot enter the room until 10.

→ _____

04

주어진 말을 알맞게 배열하여 우리말과 뜻이 같도록 문장을 완성하시오.

이곳은 내가 머리를 자른 미용실이다.
(cut, in, hair, got, I, which, my)

→ This is the beauty shop _____

_____.

05

다음 포스터를 보고, 관계사를 이용하여 문장을 완성하시오.

Autumn Music Festival

*The festival that music fans have been waiting for!

(1) October 3, a national holiday

(2) Free lunch for anyone who has a ticket

(1) The music festival will be held on October 3,

_____.

(2) Lunch will be provided to _____

_____.

고난도

06

다음 조건에 맞게 우리말을 영어로 옮겨 쓰시오.

〈조건〉 1. 관계사를 이용할 것
        2. 표현 say, agree with, the department store, be on sale을 이용할 것

(1) 그가 무엇을 말하더라도, 나는 그에게 동의하지 않는다.

→ _____ (8단어)

(2) 나는 백화점에 갔는데, 그곳에서 장난감들이 할인판매 중이었다.

→ _____ (11단어)

SELF NOTE

핵심 포인트 정리하기

1 복합관계대명사 & 복합관계부사

복합관계대명사: 〈관계대명사+ever〉		복합관계부사: 〈관계부사+ever〉	
① _____	'~하는 사람은 누구든지' (= anyone who) '누가[누구를] ~하더라도' (= no matter who)	④ _____	'~할 때는 언제나' (= at any time when) '언제 ~하더라도' (= no matter when)
② _____	'~하는 것은 어느 것이든지' (= anything which) '어느 것을[이] ~하더라도' (= no matter which)	⑤ _____	'~하는 곳은 어디든지' (= at[in/to] any place where) '어디서 ~하더라도' (= no matter where)
③ _____	'~하는 것은 무엇이든지' (= anything that) '무엇을[이] ~하더라도' (= no matter what)	⑥ _____	'~하는 어떤 방법으로든지' (= in whatever way that) '아무리 ~하더라도' (= no matter how)

2 관계사의 계속적 용법

- 관계사 앞에 쉼표(,)를 쓰고, 선행사에 대한 부가적인 정보를 제공
- 관계대명사 ⑦ _____, _____ 와 관계부사 ⑧ _____, _____ 를 계속적 용법으로 쓸 수 있음
- 관계대명사는 〈접속사+대명사〉, 관계부사는 〈접속사+부사〉로 바꾸어 쓸 수 있음
- 계속적 용법의 관계대명사 which는 앞서 나온 구나 절을 선행사로 취할 수 있음

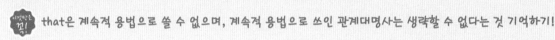

꼭! that은 계속적 용법으로 쓸 수 없으며, 계속적 용법으로 쓰인 관계대명사는 생략할 수 없다는 것 기억하기!

3 〈전치사+관계대명사〉 / 관계대명사의 생략

- 전치사는 관계대명사 바로 앞(관계대명사 생략 불가능) 또는 관계사절 끝(관계대명사 생략 가능)에 올 수 있음
- 목적격 관계대명사나 〈⑨ _____ + _____〉는 생략 가능

꼭! 전치사 바로 뒤에 관계대명사 that이나 who가 올 수 없다는 것 알아두기!

문제로 개념 다지기

밑줄 친 부분이 어법상 맞으면 O, 틀리면 X 표시하고 바르게 고치시오.

1 Anyone who has a receipt can exchange the items they bought.
   → <u>Whoever</u> has a receipt can exchange the items they bought.

2 The weather was terrible, <u>that</u> caused the flight to be delayed.

3 Lena and Noah first met last Christmas, <u>when</u> they were introduced by Carl.

4 Here is the paper on <u>that</u> you should write down your answers.

5 My parents sold a house <u>located</u> in the countryside.

CHAPTER 13

비교 구문

These pants are **three times as expensive as** mine.

The more I meet James, **the more** I like him.

Mina is **the best** researcher in the lab.

→ **No** researcher in the lab is **better than** Mina.

→ **No** researcher in the lab is **as good as** Mina.

비교 구문

비교 구문이란 둘 이상의 사람이나 사물의 성질·상태를 비교하는 것으로, 형용사나 부사의 형태를
그대로 사용하거나 변형하여 원급, 비교급, 최상급으로 표현하는 구문을 말합니다. 원급과 비교급을
이용하여 최상급의 의미를 나타낼 수도 있습니다.

as+원급+as

- 원급 비교는 〈as+형용사/부사의 원급+as〉의 형태로 '～만큼 …한[하게]'라는 뜻을 나타낸다.
  This film camera is **as expensive as** the digital one.
- 〈not as[so]+형용사/부사의 원급+as〉는 '～만큼 …하지 않은[않게]'라는 뜻이다.
  Plays are **not as[so] popular as** movies.

A 다음 우리말과 같은 뜻이 되도록 ( ) 안의 말을 이용하여 문장을 완성하시오.

1 그는 Edward만큼 부유하다. (rich)
He is _____ _____ _____ Edward.

2 Beth는 Kelly만큼 재미있다. (funny)
Beth is _____ _____ _____ Kelly.

3 Robert는 그의 아버지만큼 키가 크지 않다. (tall)
Robert is _____ _____ _____ _____ his father.

4 수학은 네가 생각하는 것만큼 어렵지 않다. (difficult)
Math _____ _____ _____ _____ _____ you think.

5 그녀는 내가 가지고 있는 것만큼 많은 만화책을 가지고 있다. (comic books)
She has _____ _____ _____ _____ _____ I have.

B 다음 우리말과 같은 뜻이 되도록 〈보기〉에서 알맞은 말을 골라 빈칸에 적절한 형태로 써넣으시오.

〈보기〉 comfortable	fast	good	large	old	smart

1 내 자전거는 그의 것만큼 좋다.
My bicycle is _____ _____ _____ his.

2 Samantha는 보이는 것만큼 나이가 많지 않다.
Samantha is _____ _____ _____ _____ she looks.

3 그의 방은 내 방만큼 크다.
His room is _____ _____ _____ mine.

4 그녀는 Mike만큼 수영을 빠르게 한다.
She swims _____ _____ _____ Mike.

5 의자는 소파만큼 편안하지 않다.
Chairs are _____ _____ _____ _____ sofas.

6 그는 그의 형만큼 똑똑하지 않다.
He is _____ _____ _____ _____ his brother.

비교급과 최상급 만드는 방법

■ 형용사나 부사의 비교급은 보통 단어에 -(e)r 또는 more를 붙이고, 최상급은 -(e)st 또는 most를 붙여 나타낸다.

대부분의 단어	+-(e)r / -(e)st	hard – harder – hardest large – larger – largest
〈단모음+단자음〉으로 끝나는 단어	자음을 한 번 더 쓰고 +-er / -est	hot – hotter – hottest big – bigger – biggest
-y로 끝나는 단어	y를 i로 바꾸고 +-er / -est	pretty – prettier – prettiest easy – easier – easiest
-ful, -ous, -ing, -ive 등으로 끝나는 단어	단어의 앞에 more / most	important – **more** important – **most** important
3음절 이상의 단어		

■ 비교급과 최상급이 불규칙하게 변화하는 단어들도 있다.

many/much – more – most   little – less – least
bad/ill – worse – worst   good/well – better – best
far(거리가 먼) – farther – farthest   far(정도가 심한) – further – furthest

A 다음 밑줄 친 부분을 어법에 맞게 고쳐 쓰시오.

1 He is <u>popularer</u> than Jeremy.

2 Sarah is <u>the most old member</u> of this club.

3 We have <u>little money</u> than they have.

4 Volunteering helps me become <u>more thoughtfuler</u>.

B 다음 우리말과 같은 뜻이 되도록 (   ) 안의 말을 배열하여 문장을 완성하시오.

1 이 오렌지 주스가 네 것보다 더 달다.
(this, yours, orange juice, than, sweeter, is)

_____

2 나는 예상했었던 것보다 더 일찍 회의 장소에 도착했다.
(arrived, than, I, at, I, expected, the meeting place, had, earlier)

_____

3 그는 그의 회사에서 더 멀리 떨어져 있는 지역으로 이사를 갔다.
(his company, moved, he, an area, from, to, farther away)

_____

4 나는 지금이 내 인생 최고의 순간이라고 생각한다.
(of, best, the, moment, this, my life, think, is, I)

_____

비교급+than / 비교급 강조

- 비교급을 이용한 비교 표현은 〈비교급+than〉의 형태로 '~보다 더 …한[하게]'라는 뜻을 나타낸다.
  Sneakers are **more comfortable than** high heels.
- 비교급을 강조할 때는 비교급 앞에 much, even, still, a lot, far 등을 써서 '훨씬'이라는 뜻을 나타낸다.
  My feet are **much bigger than** yours.

★ *PLUS TIP* superior(우수한), inferior(열등한), prior(이전의) 등과 같이 -or로 끝나는 일부 형용사나 동사 prefer의 경우에는 to를 써서 대상을 비교하기도 한다.
She **prefers** winter **to** summer. (prefer A to B: B보다 A를 더 좋아하다)

A   ( ) 안의 말을 이용하여 비교급 문장을 완성하시오.

1 You're talking too fast. Can you speak ＿＿＿＿ ＿＿＿＿? (slowly)

2 Sending an email is much ＿＿＿＿ ＿＿＿＿ sending a letter. (fast)

3 These tomatoes are ＿＿＿＿ ＿＿＿＿ those pears. (fresh)

4 My grandmother is a great cook. Her food is ＿＿＿＿ ＿＿＿＿ ＿＿＿＿ my mom's. (delicious)

5 There are many people in the stadium. It looks ＿＿＿＿ ＿＿＿＿ ＿＿＿＿ ever before. (crowded)

B   다음 우리말과 같은 뜻이 되도록 ( ) 안의 말을 이용하여 문장을 완성하시오.

1 그녀의 방은 내 방보다 훨씬 더 좋다. (a lot, good)
Her room is ＿＿＿＿ ＿＿＿＿ ＿＿＿＿ ＿＿＿＿ ＿＿＿＿.

2 그 표는 내가 예상했던 것보다 훨씬 더 저렴하다. (much, cheap)
The ticket is ＿＿＿＿ ＿＿＿＿ ＿＿＿＿ I expected.

3 중국어는 일본어보다 훨씬 배우기 어렵다. (far, difficult)
Chinese is ＿＿＿＿ ＿＿＿＿ to learn ＿＿＿＿ Japanese.

C   다음 주어진 문장과 같은 뜻이 되도록 문장을 완성하시오.

1 This new stove is not as big as the old one.
→ The old stove was ＿＿＿＿ ＿＿＿＿ this new one.

2 The shop was very clean today. It isn't usually as clean as that.
→ The shop was ＿＿＿＿ ＿＿＿＿ usual today.

3 I like a room with a sea view more than a room with a city view.
→ I prefer a room with ＿＿＿＿ ＿＿＿＿ ＿＿＿＿ ＿＿＿＿ a room
with ＿＿＿＿ ＿＿＿＿ ＿＿＿＿.

최상급 ~ in[of]

■ 최상급을 이용한 비교 표현은 〈the+최상급〉의 형태로, '가장 ~한[하게]'라는 뜻을 나타낸다. 최상급 뒤에 in이나 of를 써서 비교 대상의 범위를 나타내기도 한다.

Sam is **the bravest** boy *in* my class. (in+장소 · 범위를 나타내는 단수명사)

This yellow suitcase is **the lightest** *of* all the suitcases. (of+비교 대상이 되는 명사)

A ( ) 안의 말을 이용하여 최상급 문장을 완성하시오.

1 Which batteries are _____ _____? (cheap)

2 It was _____ _____ day of my life. (bad)

3 Which is _____ _____ island in Korea? (big)

4 She was _____ _____ teacher in the school. (kind)

5 Yesterday was _____ _____ day of the month. (cold)

6 I think history is _____ _____ _____ subject. (boring)

7 How much is _____ _____ model of this vacuum cleaner? (new)

8 She is _____ _____ _____ of her classmates. (intelligent)

B 다음 우리말과 같은 뜻이 되도록 할 때, <u>틀린 부분</u>을 어법에 맞게 고쳐 쓰시오.

1 구할 수 있는 가장 최신 모델의 스마트폰은 무엇인가요?
What is the late smartphone model available?

2 어제는 그녀의 인생에서 가장 행복한 날이었다.
Yesterday was the happier day of her life.

3 그들은 인도에서 가장 가난한 마을을 방문했다.
They visited the most poorest town in India.

C 다음 우리말과 같은 뜻이 되도록 ( ) 안의 말을 이용하여 문장을 완성하시오.

1 이것은 서울에 있는 다리들 중에서 가장 길다. (long)
This is _____ _____ _____ the bridges in Seoul.

2 한국은 세계에서 가장 빠른 인터넷 속도를 가지고 있다. (fast, Internet speed)
Korea has _____ _____ _____ _____ in the world.

3 우리 오빠는 이 식당에서 가장 비싼 요리를 주문했다. (expensive, dish)
My brother ordered _____ _____ _____ _____ in this restaurant.

as+원급+as possible / 배수사+as+원급+as

- 〈as+원급+as possible〉은 '가능한 한 ～한[하게]'라는 뜻으로 〈as+원급+as+주어+can[could]〉로 바꾸어 쓸 수 있다.
  Call me **as soon as possible**. → Call me **as soon as you can**.
- 배수사(three times, four times …)를 〈as+원급+as〉 앞에 써서 '～의 몇 배 …한[하게]'이라는 뜻을 나타낼 수 있고, 이는 〈배수사+비교급+than〉으로 바꾸어 쓸 수 있다. 단, twice는 〈배수사+as+원급+as〉의 형태로만 사용한다.
  He bought **three times as much food as** I did.
  → He bought **three times more food than** I did.

★ 내신만점 TIP 배수사를 이용한 비교 구문의 어순에 유의하자.

A 다음 우리말과 같은 뜻이 되도록 〈보기〉에서 알맞은 말을 골라 빈칸에 적절한 형태로 써넣으시오.

〈보기〉 powerful   many   fast   heavy

1 나는 가능한 한 빨리 여기에 왔다.
  I came here _____ _____ _____ possible.

2 가능한 한 많은 포크와 나이프를 가져와요.
  Bring _____ _____ forks and knives _____ you can.

3 내 개는 내 고양이보다 두 배 더 무겁다.
  My dog is _____ _____ _____ as my cat.

4 저 배터리는 이것보다 세 배 더 강력하다.
  That battery is _____ _____ _____ _____ than this one.

B 다음 우리말과 같은 뜻이 되도록 (   ) 안의 말을 배열하여 문장을 완성하시오.

1 저 건물은 우리 학교보다 두 배 더 높다. (as, as, my school, is, tall, twice)
  That building _____.

2 그는 가능한 한 조용히 집으로 들어왔다. (as, could, he, as, quietly)
  He came in the house _____.

3 Lisa의 머리카락은 내 머리카락보다 세 배 더 길다. (mine, is, longer, three times, than)
  Lisa's hair _____.

4 그녀는 가능한 한 일찍 일어나려고 애썼다. (as, possible, as, early, get up)
  She tried to _____.

176 Chapter 13

비교급＋and＋비교급 / the＋비교급, the＋비교급

- 〈비교급＋and＋비교급〉은 '점점 더 ~한[하게]'라는 뜻이며, 비교급이 'more＋원급'의 형태인 경우에는 〈more and more＋원급〉으로 나타낸다.
Michelle had to speak **louder and louder** at the party.
She becomes **more and more talkative** as time goes by.
- 〈the＋비교급, the＋비교급〉은 '~(하면) 할수록 더 …하다'라는 뜻이다.
The higher I climbed up the mountain, **the colder** I felt.

A 다음 우리말과 같은 뜻이 되도록 ( ) 안의 말을 이용하여 문장을 완성하시오.

1 날씨가 점점 더 따뜻해지고 있다. (warm)
The weather is getting _____ _____ _____.

2 기름은 점점 더 비싸지고 있다. (expensive)
Oil is becoming _____ _____ _____ _____.

3 그 노래는 점점 더 인기를 얻고 있다. (popular)
The song is getting _____ _____ _____ _____.

B 다음 〈보기〉와 같이 주어진 문장을 〈the＋비교급, the＋비교급〉을 이용한 문장으로 바꾸어 쓰시오.

> 〈보기〉 As I sleep more, I get more tired.
> → The more I sleep, the more tired I get.

1 As you read more, you become smarter.
→ _____

2 As it gets hotter, people go swimming more often.
→ _____

3 As I get to know you more, I like you more.
→ _____

C 다음 우리말과 같은 뜻이 되도록 ( ) 안의 말을 배열하여 문장을 완성하시오.

1 그녀는 나이가 들어갈수록, 점점 더 아름다워졌다.
(she, more, the, grew, beautiful, she, the, became, older)

_____

2 그의 영어는 점점 더 나아지고 있다.(better, is, English, better, getting, his, and)

_____

■ 원급과 비교급을 이용해서 최상급의 의미를 나타낼 수 있다.

The sun is **the brightest star**.　　　　　　　　　⟨the+최상급⟩
→ The sun is **brighter than any other star**.　　　⟨비교급+than any other+단수명사⟩
→ **No (other)** star is **brighter than** the sun.　　⟨No (other)+단수명사 ~ 비교급+than⟩
→ **No (other)** star is **as[so] bright as** the sun.　⟨No (other)+단수명사 ~ as[so]+원급+as⟩

A 다음 문장들이 같은 뜻이 되도록 문장을 완성하시오.

1 May is the most beautiful month of the year.

→ May is more beautiful _____ of the year.

→ No other month of the year is _____ than May.

→ No other month of the year is _____ as May.

2 She is the youngest film director in Korea.

→ She is _____ than _____ in Korea.

→ No other film director in Korea is _____ than her.

→ No other film director in Korea is _____ as her.

3 This is the most famous restaurant in Busan.

→ This restaurant is _____ than any other restaurant in Busan.

→ _____ in Busan is _____ than this one.

→ _____ in Busan is _____ as this one.

B 다음 우리말과 같은 뜻이 되도록 ( ) 안의 말을 배열하여 문장을 완성하시오.

1 Mark는 우리 반에서 가장 친절한 소년이다. (Mark, friendliest, is, boy, the)
_____ in my class.

2 그는 사무실에 있는 다른 어떤 사람보다 나이가 더 많다.
(he, older, other, is, any, man, than)
_____ in the office.

3 우리 동아리에 있는 어떤 여자아이도 Jenny만큼 인기가 많지 않다.
(girl, Jenny, is, no, club, popular, other, in, as, as, our)

_____

4 목성은 태양계에 있는 다른 어떤 행성보다 더 크다.
(other, Jupiter, bigger, than, is, any, planet)
_____ in the solar system.

최상급 표현 II — one of the + 최상급 + 복수명사

- 〈one of the + 최상급 + 복수명사〉는 '가장 ~한 것[사람]들 중 하나'라는 의미이다.

  She is **one of the most famous actresses** in Hollywood.
- 그 밖의 최상급 표현은 다음과 같다.

  Amy is **cuter than any other girl** in my class. 〈비교급 + than any other + 단수명사〉

  → Amy is **cuter than all the other girls** in my class. 〈비교급 + than all the other + 복수명사〉

  Pip is **lazier than anybody else** in my family. 〈비교급 + than anybody else〉

  Jay is **the most polite man (that) I've ever seen**. 〈the + 최상급 + (that) + 주어 + have ever v-ed〉

A 다음 ( ) 안에서 알맞은 말을 고르시오.

1 He is one of the nicest (person / people) I know.

2 That is the (good / best) cheesecake I've ever eaten.

3 She is (busier / busiest) than all the other people in my family.

4 Emily is more intelligent than (anybody / nobody) else in her company.

B 다음 두 문장이 같은 뜻이 되도록 문장을 완성하시오.

1 Tony is the bravest person in his school.

→ Tony is _____ anybody else in his school.

2 He is the fastest runner in the world.

→ He runs _____ all the other runners in the world.

3 She is the loveliest girl I've ever met.

→ She is lovelier than _____ girl I've ever met.

C 다음 우리말과 같은 뜻이 되도록 ( ) 안의 말을 이용하여 문장을 완성하시오.

1 그는 세계에서 가장 훌륭한 축구 선수들 중 한 명이다. (good)

He is _____ soccer players in the world.

2 그것은 내가 지금까지 본 것 중 가장 감동적인 영화이다. (touching)

It is _____ _____ _____ _____ I've ever seen.

3 피렌체는 세계에서 가장 흥미로운 도시 중 하나이다. (interesting)

Florence is _____ _____ _____ _____

_____ in the world.

내신대비 TEST

[01-03] 다음 빈칸에 알맞은 말을 고르시오.

01

I ran 100 meters as _____ as I could.

① fast
② faster
③ more fast
④ fastest
⑤ the fastest

02

It's _____ today than it was yesterday.

① mild
② milder
③ mildest
④ more milder
⑤ mildly

03

David is _____ of the players on his team.

① taller
② tallest
③ the tallest
④ more tall
⑤ the most tall

[04-06] 다음 빈칸에 들어갈 수 <u>없는</u> 말을 고르시오.

04

Kay is more _____ than Ben.

① famous
② strong
③ boring
④ patient
⑤ active

05

The population of Seoul is _____ larger than that of New York.

① much
② even
③ a lot
④ very
⑤ far

06

Reading a book is as _____ as watching TV.

① exciting
② better
③ good
④ useful
⑤ interesting

[07-08] 빈칸에 들어갈 말이 순서대로 알맞게 짝지어진 것을 고르시오.

07

• Can you write back to me as soon as
  _____?
• _____ other girl in this town is braver than Sue.

① can – One
② can – No
③ possible – No
④ possible – All
⑤ you can – All

08

• This is the _____ present I've ever received.
• My friend is _____ than anybody else in her class.

① good – beautiful
② better – beautifuler
③ better – more beautiful
④ best – the most beautiful
⑤ best – more beautiful

09

> 그의 가방은 내 것보다 두 배 더 무거웠다.

① His bag was heavier twice as mine.

② His bag was twice heavier as mine.

③ His bag was as twice heavy as mine.

④ His bag was twice as heavy as mine.

⑤ His bag was twice heavier than mine.

10

> 그는 우리 회사에서 가장 중요한 사람들 중 한 명이다.

① He is not so important as people in our company.

② He is more important than nobody else in our company.

③ He is one of the most important person in our company.

④ He is one of the most important people in our company.

⑤ No other person in our company is more important than him.

기출응용

11

다음 표의 내용과 일치하는 것은?

Group A	
Nancy	163 cm
Brian	174 cm
John	182 cm

① Nancy is as tall as Brian.

② John is not so tall as Nancy.

③ Brian is the shortest in Group A.

④ No person in Group A is taller than Brian.

⑤ John is taller than any other person in Group A.

12

> • This dress is _____ longer than that one.
>
> • You can have as _____ as you want.

① very   ② well   ③ good

④ much   ⑤ many

13

> • She got _____ and _____ bored at her job.
>
> • The _____ you practice the piano, the better you can play.

① much   ② many   ③ more

④ little   ⑤ most

14

① Tina isn't as serious as she looks.

② She is the youngest in her family.

③ This hotel is a lot cheaper than that one.

④ This is the best coffee I've ever had.

⑤ He runs faster of anybody else in his class.

15

① She is wiser than her husband.

② The work is getting easier and easier.

③ No other city is more romantic than Prague.

④ The supermarket is a lot more crowded than usual.

⑤ The tulip is one of the most beautiful flower in the world.

16

다음 두 문장의 뜻이 같도록 할 때 빈칸에 알맞은 것은?

> No other boy is as smart as Ken in this school.
> → _____ in this school.

① Ken is the smartest boy
② Other boys are as smart as Ken
③ Ken is one of the smartest boys
④ Any other boy is smarter than Ken
⑤ Ken is not smarter than all the other boys

17

다음 중 의미가 나머지와 <u>다른</u> 것은?

① Picasso is the most creative painter in history.
② No painter in history is as creative as Picasso.
③ Picasso is more creative than all the other painters in history.
④ Picasso is not as creative as other painters in history.
⑤ Picasso is more creative than any other painter in history.

고난도

18

다음 중 어법상 옳은 것을 모두 고르면? (3개)

① Let's go home. It's getting darker and darker.
② Chris ran fast as possible to catch the bus.
③ Do you want to discuss this even further?
④ Junha was more surprised than all the others in the group.
⑤ Jeremy will climb the mountain as higher as he can.

19

다음 우리말을 영어로 옮긴 것 중 잘못된 것은?

① 그녀는 반에서 다른 어떤 학생보다 일찍 온다.
   She comes earlier than any other student in her class.
② 그는 가능한 한 분명하게 내 질문에 답했다.
   He answered my question as clearly as he could.
③ 당신이 행복할수록, 당신은 더 잘 한다.
   The happier you are, the best you do.
④ 어떤 배우도 그만큼 매력적이지 않다.
   No other actor is as attractive as he is.
⑤ 그의 태도는 그녀가 생각했었던 것보다 훨씬 더 불량했다.
   His attitude was far worse than she had thought.

기출응용

20

(A), (B), (C)의 괄호 안에서 알맞은 것끼리 바르게 짝지어진 것은?

> (A) She is as [witty / wittier] as her sister.
> (B) It was the [bigger / biggest] concert I've ever seen.
> (C) No other boy is [fast / faster] than him in his school.

(A)	(B)	(C)
① witty	biggest	faster
② wittier	bigger	fast
③ witty	bigger	faster
④ witty	bigger	fast
⑤ wittier	biggest	faster

서술형 따라잡기

01

주어진 말을 이용하여 우리말과 뜻이 같도록 문장을 완성하시오.

(1) 더 많이 운동하면 할수록, 너는 더 건강해질
   것이다. (healthy)
   → The more you exercise, _____
      _____ you will become.

(2) 그의 기타는 네 것보다 세 배 더 오래되었다. (old)
   → His guitar is _____ _____ _____
      _____ _____ yours.

02

다음 지도를 보고, 형용사 warm과 cold를 이용하여 문장을 완성하시오.

(1) Busan is _____ _____ _____
   _____ Seoul.

(2) Gwangju is _____ _____ city on the
   map.

(3) Dokdo is _____ _____ Daejeon.

03

주어진 말을 이용하여 대화를 완성하시오.

A: What do you like about your boyfriend?
B: _____ _____ boy is _____ than
   him. (smart)

04

**다음 두 문장이 같은 뜻이 되도록 빈칸에 알맞은 말을
쓰시오.**

No other mountain in the world is higher
than Mt. Everest.

→ Mt. Everest is _____ _____ mountain
   in the world.

05

다음 표를 보고, 주어진 말을 이용하여 문장을 완성하시오.

	Starting Time	Running Time	Price
Heroes	7:00 p.m.	4 hrs.	$100
Chicago	4:00 p.m.	2 hrs.	$80
Carmen	2:00 p.m.	3 hrs.	$120

(1) *Heroes* is _____ _____ _____
   _____ *Chicago*. (twice, long)

(2) No other musical starts _____ _____
   _____ *Heroes*. (late)

(3) *Carmen* is _____ _____ _____ any
   other musical. (expensive)

고난도

06

다음 조건에 맞게 우리말을 영어로 옮겨 쓰시오.

〈조건〉 1. 비교급 혹은 최상급을 이용할 것
       2. 어휘 diligent, achieve, useful,
          application을 이용할 것

(1) 너는 부지런할수록, 더 성취할 것이다.

   → _____
      _____ (10단어)

(2) City Map은 가장 유용한 앱들 중 하나이다.

   → _____
      _____ (9단어)

핵심 포인트 정리하기

1 주요 비교 구문

- 원급 비교: 〈① _____ + 형용사/부사의 원급 + _____〉 – '~만큼 …한[하게]'
  〈not as[so] + 형용사/부사의 원급 + as〉 – '~만큼 …하지 않은[않게]'
- 비교급을 이용한 비교: 〈② _____ + _____〉 – '~보다 더 …한[하게]'
  *비교급 강조: much, even, still, a lot, far 등을 사용
- 최상급을 이용한 비교: 〈the + 최상급〉 '가장 ~한[하게]' / 〈the + 최상급 + in[of]〉 '~ 중에서 가장 ~한[하게]'

2 여러 가지 비교 구문

원급	〈as + 원급 + as possible〉 → 〈as + 원급 + as + 주어 + can[could]〉	'가능한 한 ~한[하게]'
	③ 〈_____ + _____ + _____ + _____〉	'~의 몇 배 …한[하게]'
비교급	〈비교급 + and + 비교급〉	'점점 더 ~한[하게]'
	〈the + 비교급, the + 비교급〉	'~(하면) 할수록 더 …하다'
최상급 표현	〈the + 최상급〉 → 〈No (other) + 단수명사 ~ 비교급 + than〉 → 〈No (other) + 단수명사 ~ as[so] + 원급 + as〉 → 〈비교급 + than any other + 단수명사〉 → 〈비교급 + than all the other + ④ _____〉	
	〈비교급 + than anybody else〉	'다른 누구보다 ~한[하게]'
	〈the + 최상급 + (that) + 주어 + have ever v-ed〉	'지금까지 ~한 것 중 가장 …한'
	⑤ 〈_____ + _____ + _____〉	'가장 ~한 것[사람]들 중 하나'

 배수사를 이용한 비교 구문의 어순 기억하기!
원급이나 비교급으로 나타내는 최상급 표현 알아두기!

문제로 개념 다지기

밑줄 친 부분이 어법상 맞으면 O, 틀리면 X 표시하고 바르게 고치시오.

1 Kelly delivered her speech <u>as fluently as</u> I expected.

2 After running, my heart beats <u>more fast</u> than usual.

3 My robot vacuum cleaner is <u>most useful</u> item in my house.

4 This elephant is <u>very bigger</u> than any other elephant in the zoo.

5 My smartphone is <u>as five times expensive</u> as yours.

6 The brighter the room gets, <u>the better we can see.</u>

7 This cookbook is more helpful than <u>any other cookbooks.</u>

8 Scuba diving was <u>one of the most unforgettable experiences</u> of my life.

CHAPTER 14

일치와 화법

개념 쏙쏙

Everything in this shop *is* expensive.	[수의 일치]
I **believed** that he **would take** me to the fancy restaurant.	[시제 일치]
My mother **said to** me, "**Wash** your hands before dinner."	[직접화법]
My mother **told** me **to wash** my hands before dinner.	[간접화법]

일치와 화법

일치에는 주어의 수에 맞게 동사의 형태를 쓰는 수의 일치와, 주절의 시제에 맞게 종속절의 시제를 쓰는 시제 일치가 있습니다. 화법에는 다른 사람이 한 말을 그대로 전달하는 직접화법과 전달자의 입장에 맞게 바꿔 전달하는 간접화법이 있습니다.

수의 일치 I – 단수 취급하는 경우

■ 아래 항목들이 주어인 경우에는 단수 취급하여 단수동사를 쓴다.

- each, every, -thing, -one, -body
  Each of us *has* pictures of the singer.
- (복수 형태의) 학문명, 국가명, 병명
  Mathematics *is* one of my favorite subjects.
- 시간, 거리, 금액, 무게 등을 나타내는 단위
  Ten thousand won a day *is* not enough to live on.
- 동명사구, to부정사구, 명사절
  Traveling with you *is* better than traveling alone.
- 〈the number of+복수명사〉: ~의 수
  The number of students *is* decreasing these days.
- 분수, most, half, some, the rest+of the+단수명사
  Half of the class *is* absent from school.

A ( ) 안의 말을 빈칸에 적절한 형태로 써넣으시오. (단, 현재형으로 쓸 것)

1 Each part of the country _____ different weather. (have)

2 Taking care of a baby _____ a lot of effort. (require)

3 Every student from every town _____ take the test. (have to)

4 Three hours _____ enough time for me to read this book. (be)

B 다음 문장이 어법상 맞으면 O, 틀리면 X 표시하고 바르게 고치시오.

1 Twenty dollars is expensive for a meal.

2 Some students think economics are difficult.

3 Somebody is coming from Australia tomorrow.

4 Every room and bathroom in the hotel have to be cleaned.

C 다음 우리말과 같은 뜻이 되도록 문장을 완성하시오.

1 빙산의 대부분은 물속에 있다.
_____ _____ the iceberg _____ under water.

2 각각의 남자와 여자는 동등한 권리를 가지고 있다.
_____ man and woman _____ equal rights.

3 100미터는 내가 수영하기에 너무 먼 거리이다.
_____ _____ _____ _____ too far for me to swim.

수의 일치 II – 복수 취급하는 경우

- 아래 항목들이 주어인 경우에는 복수 취급하여 복수동사를 쓴다.
  - both A and B: A와 B 둘 다
  Both Jane and I *were* satisfied with the results.
  - ⟨the+형용사⟩: ～한 사람들
  The rich *are* getting even richer.
  - ⟨a number of+복수명사⟩: 많은 ～
  A number of kids *are* exercising on the playground.
  - 분수, most, half, some, the rest+of the+복수명사
  Two-thirds of the apples *have* fallen from the trees due to the storm.

★ 내신만점 *TIP* ⟨부분 표현(분수, most, half, some, the rest)+of the+명사⟩가 주어일 때, 명사의 수에 동사의 수를 일치시킨다는 것을 기억하자.

A ( ) 안의 말을 빈칸에 적절한 형태로 써넣으시오. (단, 현재형으로 쓸 것)

1 The young _____ their own worries. (have)

2 Both Mike and Tom _____ interested in soccer. (be)

3 A number of people _____ swimming on weekends. (go)

4 The number of people in my town _____ decreasing. (be)

B 다음 문장에서 **틀린** 부분을 어법에 맞게 고쳐 쓰시오.

1 The rest of the books is yours.

2 The deaf uses sign language to communicate.

3 The number of overweight children are growing.

4 A number of buildings was destroyed in the earthquake.

C 다음 우리말과 같은 뜻이 되도록 문장을 완성하시오.

1 직원들의 4분의 3은 여성이다.
_____-_____ _____ the workers _____ women.

2 대부분의 집들이 눈으로 덮여 있었다.
_____ _____ the houses _____ covered with snow.

3 많은 학생들이 그의 강의를 듣고 있었다.
_____ _____ _____ _____ _____ listening to his lecture.

시제 일치

- 주절의 시제가 현재일 때, 종속절에 모든 시제가 올 수 있다.
  I **know** she **exercises** in the park. (현재 – 현재)
  I **know** she **exercised** in the park. (현재 – 과거)
  I **know** she **will exercise** in the park. (현재 – 미래)
- 주절의 시제가 과거일 때, 종속절에 과거시제나 과거완료형이 올 수 있다.
  I **knew** she **exercised** regularly. (과거 – 과거)
  I **knew** she **had exercised** regularly. (과거 – 과거완료)

★ **PLUS TIP** 주절의 시제가 과거일 때 종속절에 있는 조동사는 would, could, might, must[had to] 등으로 쓴다.

A ( ) 안의 말을 빈칸에 적절한 형태로 써넣으시오.

1 Mike said that he _____ go fishing the next day. (will)

2 He didn't call her because he _____ to go there alone. (want)

3 She found out that her father _____ a song before she was born. (write)

B 다음 문장을 〈보기〉와 같이 바꿔 쓰시오.

> 〈보기〉 Kevin believes that he will go on a picnic.
> → Kevin believed that he would go on a picnic.

1 Ann thinks that the watch is too expensive to buy.

→ _____

2 The police officer says that we can't park here.

→ _____

C 다음 우리말과 같은 뜻이 되도록 ( ) 안의 말을 이용하여 문장을 완성하시오.

1 그는 그의 부모님이 자신을 신뢰한다는 것을 안다. (trust)
He knows that _____ _____ _____ _____.

2 나는 교실에 내 가방을 두고 왔다는 것을 깨달았다. (leave, bag)
I realized that _____ _____ _____ _____ _____ in the classroom.

3 너는 휴가 기간 동안 인도에 가고 싶었다고 말하지 않았니? (go, India)
Didn't you say that _____ _____ _____ _____ _____ _____ on your vacation?

시제 일치의 예외

- 종속절이 과학적 사실, 변하지 않는 사실, 격언·속담 등을 나타낼 때는 주절의 시제와 관계없이 현재시제를 쓴다.
- 현재에도 지속되는 습관이나 사실은 주절이 과거시제더라도 종속절에 현재시제를 쓸 수 있다.

Galileo **said** that the earth **moves** around the sun.

She **told** me that she **gets up** at six every morning.

- 종속절이 역사적 사실을 나타낼 때는 주절의 시제와 관계없이 과거시제를 쓴다.

We **learned** that the Korean War **ended** in 1953.

A ( ) 안의 말을 빈칸에 적절한 형태로 써넣으시오.

1 The teacher told us that Heo Jun _____ *Donguibogam* in 1610. (write)

2 My brother learned that the sun _____ in the east. (rise)

3 I didn't know that the Gulf War _____ in 1991. (break out)

4 We learned that Antarctica _____ the coldest place on earth. (be)

5 My uncle always said that no news _____ good news. (be)

B 다음 문장에서 **틀린** 부분을 어법에 맞게 고쳐 쓰시오.

1 My grandfather used to say that time flew like an arrow.

2 I wondered why water froze at 0°C.

3 I didn't know that Alexander Bell invents the telephone.

4 This book says that Abraham Lincoln has been the 16th president of the U.S.A.

5 I learned that Brunei was located in the Pacific Ocean.

C 다음 우리말과 같은 뜻이 되도록 ( ) 안의 말을 이용하여 문장을 완성하시오.

1 그 기사에는 빛이 소리보다 더 빨리 이동한다고 쓰여 있었다. (travel, fast)

The article said that _____ _____ _____ than sound.

2 나는 직지심경이 1377년에 인쇄되었다는 것을 배웠다. (print)

I learned that *Jikji* _____ _____ in 1377.

3 할머니는 항상 시간이 돈이라고 말씀하셨다. (be)

My grandmother always said that _____ _____ _____.

4 John은 내게 일요일마다 교회에 다닌다고 말했다. (go to church)

John told me that _____ _____ _____ _____ every Sunday.

평서문의 간접화법 전환

■ 직접화법의 평서문을 간접화법으로 바꾸는 방법

> 간접화법 문장의 형태: say(+that)+주어+동사
>
>   tell+목적어(+that)+주어+동사 (직접화법에서 듣는 사람을 밝히는 경우)
>
> *인용부호 안의 인칭대명사를 전달자의 입장에 맞게 바꾸고, 동사도 시제 일치 원칙에 맞게 바꾼다.

James **said**, "I **will go** shopping." → James **said that he would go** shopping.

My sister **said to** them, "You **have to be** quiet in the library."

→ My sister **told** them that they **had to be** quiet in the library.

■ 지시대명사와 부사(구)의 화법 전환

here → there	this[these] → that[those]	now → then, at that time
ago → before	today → that day	
yesterday → the day before, the previous day		tomorrow → the next[following] day

*단, 지시대명사와 부사(구)는 전달하는 날짜, 시간, 장소 등이 다를 경우에 바꾼다.

A   다음 문장을 간접화법으로 바꾸어 쓰시오.

1   Susan said, "I have to leave in a minute."

     → Susan said _____.

2   My aunt said to me, "I don't feel like making dinner today."

     → My aunt told me _____.

3   David said to Alice, "I will take you to Jim's party tomorrow."

     → David told Alice _____.

4   I said to him, "Someone asked me to give this message to you."

     → I told him _____.

5   Lyla said, "I didn't book a flight to Seattle."

     → Lyla said _____.

B   다음 문장을 직접화법으로 바꾸어 쓰시오.

1   She told me that she was taking a writing class.

     → She said to me, "_____"

2   My mother told me that she would make chicken soup that day.

     → My mother said to me, "_____"

3   He told me that his brother would start middle school the following day.

     → He said to me, "_____"

의문문의 간접화법 전환 I – 의문사가 없는 경우

■ 의문사가 없는 의문문의 직접화법을 간접화법으로 바꾸는 방법

문장의 형태: ask(+목적어)+if[whether]+주어+동사
*인칭, 시제, 지시대명사 및 부사(구) 등은 평서문의 화법 전환에서와 같이 바꾸되 전달동사는 ask를 쓴다.

Mom **said to** me, "Can you finish reading the book by noon?"
→ Mom **asked** me **if I could finish** reading the book by noon.
John **said to** me, "Have you seen this movie?"
→ John **asked** me **if[whether] I had seen** that movie.

A 다음 우리말과 같은 뜻이 되도록 밑줄 친 부분을 어법에 맞게 고쳐 쓰시오.

1 그는 나에게 영국에 가 본 적이 있는지 물었다.
He asked me if I has ever been to England.

2 그녀는 나에게 축구를 좋아하는지 물었다.
She asked me if did I like soccer.

3 Peter는 그녀에게 영화를 보러 갈 수 있는지 물었다.
Peter asked her if she can go to the movies.

4 나는 그들에게 그 마을에 제과점이 있는지 물었다.
I asked them if there is a bakery in the town.

5 그 신사는 그녀에게 그 자리가 비어 있는지 물었다.
The gentleman asked her whether the seat is empty.

6 Nancy는 그에게 커피 한 잔을 마실지 물었다.
Nancy asked him whether he will have a cup of coffee.

B 다음 문장을 ( ) 안의 말을 이용하여 간접화법으로 바꾸어 쓰시오.

1 A man said to me, "Can I use your cell phone?" (if)
→ A man asked me _____.

2 The woman said to me, "Is there a pharmacy nearby?" (if)
→ The woman asked me _____.

3 My father said to us, "Do you have any free time?" (whether)
→ _____

4 Kate said to me, "Have you heard the rumor about Jim?" (whether)
→ _____

의문문의 간접화법 전환 II – 의문사가 있는 경우

■ 의문사가 있는 의문문의 직접화법을 간접화법으로 바꾸는 방법

> 문장의 형태: ask(+목적어)+의문사+주어+동사
> *인칭, 시제, 지시대명사 및 부사(구) 등은 평서문의 화법 전환에서와 같이 바꾸되 전달동사는 **ask**를 쓴다.

The woman **said**, "Where is the nearest subway station?"
→ The woman **asked where the nearest subway station was**.
Annie **said to** me, "When can you help me with this?"
→ Annie **asked** me **when I could help** her with that.

★ *PLUS TIP*   간접의문문은 의문문이 문장 내에서 주어, 보어, 목적어로 쓰인 것으로, 의문사가 있는 간접의문문의 형태는
〈의문사+주어+동사〉이며, 의문사가 없는 간접의문문의 형태는 〈if[whether]+주어+동사〉이다.

A   다음 문장을 간접화법으로 바꾸어 쓰시오.

1   I said to her, "When did your boyfriend give you this?"
→ I asked her _____.

2   Mike said to me, "Who is the woman wearing a hat?"
→ Mike asked me _____.

3   Peter said to me, "What time are you going to meet Jimmy?"
→ Peter asked me _____.

4   My teacher said to me, "Why didn't you finish writing the report?"
→ My teacher asked me _____.

5   My sister said to me, "What have you done with my dress?"
→ My sister asked me _____.

B   다음 우리말과 같은 뜻이 되도록 (   ) 안의 말을 배열하여 문장을 완성하시오.

1   선생님은 우리에게 누가 그 단락을 읽을 것이냐고 물었다.
(would, the passage, who, read)
The teacher asked us _____.

2   너는 그 전시회가 어디서 열리는지 아니? (where, takes place, the exhibition)
Do you know _____?

3   Sharon은 나에게 우리가 언제 배구를 할 것인지 물었다.
(when, play, to, were, we, going, volleyball)
Sharon asked me _____.

명령문의 간접화법 전환

■ 직접화법의 명령문을 간접화법으로 바꾸는 방법

> 문장의 형태: tell[ask, order, advise 등]+목적어+to부정사
> *인칭, 시제, 지시대명사 및 부사(구) 등은 평서문의 화법 전환에서와 같이 바꾸되 인용문의 동사를 to부정사로 바꾼다.
> *부정 명령문일 경우에는 don't나 never를 not+to-v로 바꾼다.

He **said to** me, "Wait here for a moment."
→ He **told** me **to wait** there for a moment.
She **said to** the child, "Don't touch the painting."
→ She **ordered** the child **not to touch** the painting.

★ PLUS TIP   전달동사는 문맥에 맞게 사용한다.
명령할 때: tell, order   충고할 때: advise   요청할 때: ask

A 다음 문장을 간접화법으로 바꾸어 쓰시오.

1 He said to us, "Don't speak during the test."
→ He told us _____.

2 The teacher said to her class, "Repeat after me."
→ The teacher told her class _____.

3 The coach said to me, "Be here at 9 a.m."
→ The coach ordered me _____

4 The captain said to his soldiers, "Keep walking across the river."
→ The captain ordered his soldiers _____.

B 다음 우리말과 같은 뜻이 되도록 (   ) 안의 말을 배열하여 문장을 완성하시오.

1 그들은 나에게 파티에 친구를 데려오라고 말했다.
(told, bring, they, to the party, to, a friend, me)

_____

2 나는 그에게 나중에 다시 전화해 달라고 부탁했다.
(call back, asked, to, later, I, him)

_____

3 그는 나에게 차를 빨리 몰지 말라고 충고했다.
(to, fast, he, not, advised, drive, me)

_____

Chapter 14

내신대비 TEST

[01-03] 다음 빈칸에 알맞은 말을 고르시오.

01

I noticed he _____ a game yesterday.

① play   ② will play
③ has played   ④ has been playing
⑤ was playing

02

He told me a saying: Laughter _____ the best medicine.

① be   ② is   ③ was
④ has been   ⑤ had been

03

The rest of the _____ is going home.

① students   ② group   ③ friends
④ people   ⑤ sick

04

다음 대화의 내용을 한 문장으로 나타낼 때, 빈칸에 들어갈 말이 순서대로 알맞게 짝지어진 것은?

Rachel: How often do you go bowling?
Dan: I go bowling twice a week.
→ Dan _____ that he _____ bowling twice a week.

① told – went   ② said – go
③ told – goes   ④ said – going
⑤ said – goes

[05-07] 빈칸에 들어갈 말이 순서대로 알맞게 짝지어진 것을 고르시오.

05

• Each piece of pizza _____ a different taste.
• Ten minutes _____ enough time to put the puzzle together.

① have – is   ② have – are
③ has – is   ④ has – are
⑤ has – has

06

• Reading this paper in two days _____ almost impossible.
• Both Karen and I _____ excited to go there.

① are – was   ② are – were
③ is – was   ④ is – am
⑤ is – were

07

• I thought that he _____ some problems at school.
• He knew that Korea _____ the 2018 Winter Olympics.

① has – host   ② has – hosts
③ had – hosts   ④ had – hosted
⑤ will have – hosted

[08-09] 다음 문장을 간접화법으로 바꿀 때, 잘못된 것을 고르시오.

08

I said to my sister, "Are you happy with your new classmates?"
→ I ① asked my sister ② that ③ she ④ was happy ⑤ with her new classmates.

09

He said to me, "What time will you be home today?"
→ He ① asked me ② what time ③ I ④ will be home ⑤ that day.

[10-11] 다음 두 문장이 같은 뜻이 되도록 빈칸에 알맞은 말을 고르시오.

10

She said to me, "Fasten your seat belt."
→ She _____.

① said me to fasten my seat belt
② told to me fasten my seat belt
③ told me to fasten my seat belt
④ asked me fastening my seat belt
⑤ asked me if I fasten my seat belt

11

He asked me where I had bought that bag.
→ He said to me, "_____"

① Where did I buy this bag?
② Where did he buy that bag?
③ Where has he bought this bag?
④ Where did you buy this bag?
⑤ Where do you buy that bag?

[12-13] 다음 우리말을 영어로 바르게 옮긴 것을 고르시오.

12

나는 산소가 공기보다 가볍다고 배웠다.

① I learned that oxygen is lighter than air.
② I learned that oxygen be lighter than air.
③ I learned that oxygen was lighter than air.
④ I learned that oxygen has been lighter than air.
⑤ I learned that oxygen had been lighter than air.

13

그는 나에게 밤늦게 음식을 먹지 말라고 말했다.

① He told me not to eat food late at night.
② He told me not eat food late at night.
③ He didn't tell me to eat food late at night.
④ He told me not eating food late at night.
⑤ He told me do not eat food late at night.

14
다음 대화의 빈칸에 알맞은 말은?

A: What did they say about the accident?
B: _____

① They said that a number of people was hurt.
② They said that a number of people were hurt.
③ They said that a number of people is hurt.
④ They said that the number of people are hurt.
⑤ They said that the number of people were hurt.

15

다음 중 문장의 전환이 잘못된 것은?

① He said to me, "Where can I buy this?"

→ He asked me where he could buy that.

② She said to me, "I'll call you tomorrow!"

→ She told me that she would call me the next day.

③ Jason said to me, "Don't tell lies."

→ Jason advised me not to tell lies.

④ He asked me if I minded his answering the phone.

→ He said to me, "Did you mind his answering the phone?"

⑤ John said that he had read the article the previous day.

→ John said, "I read the article yesterday."

[16-18] 다음 중 어법상 틀린 것을 고르시오.

16

① Physics are a difficult subject for me.

② Watching a horror movie is not enjoyable.

③ A number of elephants are living here.

④ Most of his novels have been bestsellers.

⑤ Both my mom and dad were smiling at me.

17

① I told her to wash the dog.

② Everybody needs to wear a black suit.

③ Two kilometers is far for a little boy to walk.

④ Some of the visitors are waiting for the show to start.

⑤ The teacher said Edmund Hillary and Tenzing Norgay have climbed Mt. Everest before anyone else.

18

① She thought I had stolen her textbook.

② The injured have trouble using these chairs.

③ Two-fifths of the students is women.

④ The number of visitors is increasing.

⑤ He told me he didn't have any time to cook.

19

빈칸에 들어갈 말이 나머지와 다른 것은?

① A number of books _____ on the shelves yesterday.

② Everyone _____ waiting for the teacher 10 minutes ago.

③ Five dollars _____ needed to buy bread at that time.

④ The rest of the work _____ done by him last night.

⑤ Writing in English _____ too difficult for me when I was young.

고난도

20

(A), (B), (C)의 괄호 안에서 알맞은 것끼리 바르게 짝지어진 것은?

(A) Half of my friends [know / knows] how to play the piano.

(B) She ordered me [not to / to not] go out at night.

(C) Five kilograms [was / were] the amount that Joe lost by exercising regularly.

	(A)	(B)	(C)
①	knows	not to	was
②	knows	to not	were
③	know	to not	were
④	know	not to	was
⑤	know	not to	were

서술형 따라잡기

01
다음 문장을 간접화법으로 바꾸어 쓰시오.

(1) He said, "I will go camping with Jane."
  → He said that _____.

(2) The man said to me, "Where is this bus going?"
  → The man _____.

02
다음 그림을 보고, 주어진 말을 이용하여 문장을 완성하시오.

(1) A _____ _____ the pieces of fruit _____ oranges. (fifth)

(2) _____ _____ the pieces of fruit _____ apples. (half)

(3) _____ _____ _____ bananas _____ greater than the number of oranges. (number)

03
주어진 말을 알맞게 배열하여 우리말과 뜻이 같도록 문장을 완성하시오.

(1) 그 아이들 중 3분의 2가 열 살 미만이다.
  (of, under ten, are, two-thirds, the kids)
  → _____

(2) 그녀는 내게 내가 그녀를 도울 수 있는지 물었다.
  (her, if, asked, I, me, could, she, help)
  → _____

04
주어진 말을 이용하여 우리말과 뜻이 같도록 문장을 완성하시오.

(1) 그 음식의 대부분은 내 것이다. (food)
  → _____ _____ _____ _____ _____ mine.

(2) 그는 2 더하기 3은 5라고 말했다. (plus, be)
  → He said _____ _____ _____ _____ _____.

05
다음 메모를 보고, 〈보기〉와 같이 문장을 완성하시오.

> **Dr. Kim's Advice**
> · Take this medicine after every meal.
> · (1) Don't drink cold water.
> · (2) Return to the hospital tomorrow.

〈보기〉 Dr. Kim advised me to take that medicine after every meal.

(1) Dr. Kim advised me _____.

(2) Dr. Kim advised me _____ _____.

06
다음 대화를 읽고, 문장을 완성하시오.

Mike: Why were you in Hong Kong a week ago?
Jessie: I go there to see my parents every summer.

→ Mike asked Jessie _____ _____. Jessie told Mike _____.

핵심 포인트 정리하기

1 수의 일치

단수 취급하는 경우	복수 취급하는 경우
each, every, -thing, -one, -body	both A and B: 'A와 B 둘 다'
(복수 형태의) 학문명, 국가명, 병명	
시간, 거리, 금액, 무게 등을 나타내는 단위	〈the+형용사〉: '~한 사람들'
동명사구, to부정사구, 명사절	
〈① _____ number of+복수명사〉	〈② _____ number of+복수명사〉: '많은 ~'

 부분 표현(분수, most, half 등+of the+명사〉가 주어일 때, 명사의 수에 따라 동사의 수를 일치시킨다는 것 기억하기!

2 시제 일치

- 주절의 시제가 현재: 종속절은 모든 시제 가능

  – 주절의 시제가 과거: 종속절은 ③ _____ 또는 과거완료형만 가능

  – 시제 일치의 예외: 과학적 사실, 변하지 않는 사실, 격언·속담, 현재에도 지속되는 습관·사실 → ④ _____ 시제

    역사적인 사실 → ⑤ _____ 시제

 시제 일치의 예외 사항 기억하기!

3 직접화법 → 간접화법 전환

- 평서문: 〈say(+that)+주어+동사〉

    〈tell+⑥ _____ (+that)+주어+동사〉
- 의문문: 의문사가 없는 경우 → 〈ask(+목적어)+⑦ _____ +주어+동사〉

    의문사가 있는 경우 → 〈ask(+목적어)+의문사+주어+동사〉
- 명령문: 〈tell[ask, order, advise 등]+목적어+⑧ _____ 〉

    *부정 명령문일 경우 〈⑨ _____ + _____ 〉

 문장의 종류에 따른 간접화법의 어순 알아두기!

문제로 개념 다지기

밑줄 친 부분이 어법상 맞으면 O, 틀리면 X 표시하고 바르게 고치시오.

1 Ten kilometers <u>are</u> too far for me to run.

2 A number of trash cans <u>was</u> placed throughout the city last week.

3 We learned that giraffes <u>live</u> in the grasslands of Africa.

4 Jina said to John, "Have you ever been to Russia before?"

  → Jina asked John <u>if he had ever been</u> to Russia before.

5 My teacher said to me, "Don't forget to turn in your homework tomorrow."

  → My teacher told me <u>that not forget</u> to turn in my homework the next day.

food truck

CHAPTER 15

특수구문

개념 쏙쏙

It was in June **that** I visited my cousin in Canada.　　　[강조 구문]

Not every animal sleeps in winter.　　　[부정 구문]

Rarely did she talk to her neighbors.　　　[도치 구문]

특수구문

특수구문에는 어떤 내용을 강조할 때 사용하는 강조 구문, 전체나 일부를 부정할 때 사용하는 부정 구문, 부사(구)나 부정어를 강조하기 위해 주어와 동사의 어순을 바꾸는 도치 구문 등이 있습니다.

do를 이용한 강조

■ 조동사 do(do, does, did)를 이용해 동사를 강조하여 문장의 내용임이 사실임을 강조할 수 있다. 주어의 인칭, 수, 그리고 문장의 시제에 따라 〈do[does/did]+동사원형〉의 형태를 쓰고 '정말 ~하다'로 해석한다.
I **do promise** to help you. (내가 정말 너를 돕겠다고 약속할게.)
I **did tell** him the truth! (나는 그에게 정말 사실대로 말했어!)
He **does work** hard. (그는 정말로 열심히 일한다.)

★ 내신만점 TIP ▶ 일반동사 do와 강조의 do를 구분하자.

A 다음 우리말과 같은 뜻이 되도록 빈칸에 조동사 do를 적절한 형태로 써넣으시오.

1 나는 익힌 당근을 정말로 싫어한다.
I _____ hate cooked carrots.

2 그는 수상 스포츠를 정말 좋아한다.
He _____ love water sports.

3 Emma는 그를 정말로 믿었다.
Emma _____ believe him.

4 너는 정말로 열심히 연습해야 해.
You _____ have to practice hard.

5 이 마카롱은 정말 맛이 달콤하다.
This macaron _____ taste sweet.

6 그녀는 강의에 집중하려고 정말로 노력했다.
She _____ try to concentrate on the lecture.

B 다음 ( ) 안의 말과 조동사 do를 이용하여 대화를 완성하시오.

1 A: You failed the exam? Why didn't you study hard?
B: I _____ _____ hard. I don't know why I failed. (study)

2 A: I heard Joe is in the hospital.
B: I _____ _____ he gets better soon. (hope)

3 A: Have you seen any of this actor's movies?
B: Yes. He isn't handsome, but he _____ _____ well. (act)

4 A: Did you send Kalee an invitation by mail?
B: No, but I _____ _____ her an invitation by text message. (send)

5 A: I heard Jenny won first prize in the singing contest again.
B: Wow! She really _____ _____ a talent for music. (have)

⟨It is[was] ~ that …⟩ 강조 구문

- It is[was]와 that 사이에 주어, 목적어, 부사(구) 등 강조하고자 하는 말을 두고, '…한 것은 바로 ~이다[였다]'로 해석한다.

  Ellie found my car keys under the sofa.
  → **It was** *Ellie* **that** found my car keys under the sofa. (주어 강조)
  → **It was** *my car keys* **that** Ellie found under the sofa. (목적어 강조)
  → **It was** *under the sofa* **that** Ellie found my car keys. (부사구 강조)
- 강조하는 대상이 사람일 경우 that 대신 who를 쓸 수 있다.

  It was *David* **who[that]** got a perfect score in science.

★ PLUS TIP   강조하는 대상에 따라 that 대신 which(사물)를 쓸 수 있지만, 거의 사용하지 않는다.

A   다음 밑줄 친 부분을 강조하는 문장을 완성하시오.

1   My uncle encouraged me to become a lawyer.
→ It was _____ to become a lawyer.

2   John called me in the middle of the night.
→ It was _____ John called me.

3   I first met my girlfriend at the cafeteria.
→ It was _____ my girlfriend.

4   My family went on a trip to Taiwan last year.
→ It was _____ to Taiwan.

5   He recommended a toy car as a present for my nephew.
→ It was _____ as a present for my nephew.

B   다음 우리말과 같은 뜻이 되도록 (   ) 안의 말을 배열하여 문장을 완성하시오.

1   내가 엄마를 위해 요리한 것은 바로 브로콜리 수프였다.
(cooked for, that, broccoli soup, it, I, was)

_____ Mom.

2   그 나무 아래에서 울고 있는 사람은 바로 Mike이다. (who, it, crying, is, Mike, is)

_____ under the tree.

3   그녀가 주차장에서 발견한 것은 바로 고양이였다. (that, a cat, found, was, she, it)

_____ in the parking lot.

4   아버지께서 출장에서 돌아오신 것은 바로 어제였다.
(that, yesterday, returned, was, my father, it)

_____ from his business trip.

부분 부정

■ 〈not+all, every, always 등〉은 '모두[항상] ~인 것은 아니다'의 의미로 부분 부정을 나타낸다.
Not all my friends love soccer like I do. (내 친구들 모두가 나처럼 축구를 좋아하는 것은 아니다.)
Not every teen likes the movie. (모든 십 대가 그 영화를 좋아하는 것은 아니다.)

★ PLUS TIP   〈not all+복수명사〉는 복수 취급을, 〈not all+셀 수 없는 명사〉는 단수 취급을 한다.
반면, 〈not every+단수명사〉는 항상 단수 취급을 한다.

A 다음 우리말과 같은 뜻이 되도록 문장을 완성하시오.

1 그들이 항상 바쁜 것은 아니다.
They are _____ _____ busy.

2 모든 아이들이 그 게임을 하고 싶어 하는 것은 아니다.
_____ _____ child wants to play the game.

3 상자 안에 있는 모든 오렌지들이 맛있는 것은 아니었다.
_____ _____ the oranges in the box tasted good.

B 다음 〈보기〉에서 알맞은 말을 골라 대화를 완성하시오.

〈보기〉   all   every   always

1 A: I don't want to eat these mushrooms.
B: They are good for your health. You can't _____ eat what you like.

2 A: I think TV programs are harmful to children.
B: Not _____ of them are bad for kids. There are also educational ones.

3 A: I don't understand why we don't play badminton here.
B: Not _____ student likes it as much as you.

C 다음 우리말과 같은 뜻이 되도록 ( ) 안의 말을 배열하여 문장을 완성하시오.

1 그 모든 책들이 판매용은 아니다. (for sale, all, are, the books, not)

_____

2 그가 항상 직장에 지각하는 것은 아니다. (late, he, always, for, not, work, is)

_____

3 모든 사람이 미래에 대한 목표가 있는 것은 아니다.
(for, not, has, the future, everyone, goals)

_____

전체 부정

■ no, none, neither, never 등은 '아무도[결코] ~하지 않다'의 의미로 전체 부정을 나타낸다.
None of my friends liked my idea. (내 친구들 중 아무도 내 생각을 좋아하지 않았다.) — all의 전체 부정
Neither of them failed the exam. (그들 둘 다 그 시험에 떨어지지 않았다.) — both의 전체 부정

A 다음 우리말과 같은 뜻이 되도록 문장을 완성하시오.

1 그 학생들 중 아무도 손을 들지 않았다.
_____ of the students raised their hands.

2 우리 둘 다 이전에 부산에 가 본 적이 없다.
_____ of us has been to Busan before.

3 우리 아버지는 집 안에서 절대로 담배를 피우지 않으신다.
My father _____ smokes in the house.

B 다음 〈보기〉에서 알맞은 말을 골라 대화를 완성하시오.

〈보기〉	neither	never	none

1 A: Do you really have a talking bird?
B: Yes. But the problem is he _____ talks in front of people.

2 A: Why didn't you buy any shirts at the store?
B: _____ of them looked good on me.

3 A: Do you think Stacy and Diana will join the Spanish club?
B: No, _____ of them is interested in languages.

C 다음 우리말과 같은 뜻이 되도록 ( ) 안의 말을 이용하여 문장을 완성하시오.

1 그는 일요일에는 절대로 공부하지 않는다. (study)
_____ _____ _____ on Sundays.

2 우리 둘 다 어제 캠핑을 가지 않았다. (go)
_____ _____ _____ _____ camping yesterday.

3 그들 중 아무도 그의 질문에 답하지 않았다. (answer)
_____ _____ _____ _____ his question.

- 방향이나 장소를 나타내는 부사구를 강조하기 위해 문장의 맨 앞에 둘 경우, 주어와 동사가 도치되어 〈부사구＋동사＋주어〉의 어순이 된다.
  Under the bed was my old hairpin.
  Over my head passed a bird.
- 부정어(구) never, hardly, little, rarely 등을 강조하기 위해 문장의 맨 앞에 둘 경우, 주어와 동사가 도치된다. be동사나 조동사가 있는 문장은 〈부정어(구)＋be동사/조동사＋주어〉의 어순으로, 일반동사가 있는 문장은 주어 앞에 do[does/did]를 써서 〈부정어(구)＋do[does/did]＋주어＋동사원형〉의 어순으로 쓴다.
  Hardly could I believe my eyes.
  Little did I know that he had changed his name.

★ PLUS TIP 주어가 대명사인 경우 방향이나 장소를 나타내는 부사구가 앞에 나와도 주어와 동사의 도치가 일어나지 않는다.
Here she comes. (O)　　**Here** comes she. (X)

A 다음 문장을 부사구나 부정어를 강조하는 문장으로 바꾸어 쓰시오.

1 The girls danced on the stage.
→ _____

2 I have never seen such a sad movie.
→ _____

3 Dozens of dogs were behind the gate.
→ _____

4 He rarely speaks to others.
→ _____

B 다음 밑줄 친 부분이 강조되도록 (　) 안의 말을 배열하여 문장을 완성하시오.

1 올해는 눈이 <u>거의</u> 오지 않았다. (snow, this year, it, did, scarcely)
_____

2 <u>그 큰 집에</u> 다정한 노부인 한 분이 살았다.
(a, the big house, friendly, in, lived, old woman)
_____

3 <u>금문교 너머로</u> 헬리콥터 한 대가 날아갔다.
(flew, over, a helicopter, the Golden Gate Bridge)
_____

4 나는 집에서 <u>거의</u> 식사를 하지 않는다. (rarely, meals, I, do, at home, eat)
_____

so/neither＋동사＋주어

■ 〈so/neither＋동사＋주어〉는 각각 긍정문과 부정문 다음에 쓰여, '~도 또한 그렇다/그렇지 않다'라는 의미를 나타낸다. 앞에 나온 동사의 종류에 맞추어 be동사, do[does/did], 조동사 중 하나를 쓴다.

A: I **want** to buy a laptop.　　　B: **So do** I. (= I want to buy a laptop, too.)

A: She **will** go to the party.　　　B: **So will** I. (= I will go to the party, too.)

A: He **didn't** have lunch.　　　B: **Neither did** I. (= I didn't have lunch, either.)

A: She **isn't** feeling good.　　　B: **Neither am** I. (= I'm not feeling good, either.)

A　so나 neither를 사용하여 대화를 완성하시오.

1　A: Jenny started learning ballet.　　　B: _____ I.

2　A: Tom is not good at sports.　　　B: _____ I.

3　A: I found this app very useful.　　　B: _____ I.

4　A: He can't move this cabinet alone.　　　B: _____ I.

B　다음 〈보기〉와 같이 B의 말을 풀어 쓰시오.

〈보기〉　A: It's snowing. I don't want to go outside.
　　　　B: Neither do I. → I don't want to go outside, either.

1　A: I'm wearing red sneakers.
　　　B: So am I.　　　→ _____

2　A: Is it raining right now? I don't have an umbrella.
　　　B: Neither do I.　→ _____

3　A: Erin will bring her friends home for dinner.
　　　B: So will I.　　　→ _____

C　다음 우리말과 같은 뜻이 되도록 (　) 안의 말을 이용하여 문장을 완성하시오.

1　우리 엄마는 키가 크신데, 나도 그렇다. (tall)
　　　My mom _____ _____, and _____ _____ _____.

2　Sam은 어젯밤에 돼지들이 나오는 꿈을 꾸었는데, 나도 그랬다. (dream of)
　　　Sam _____ _____ _____ last night, and _____ _____
　　　_____.

3　A: Tom은 정크 푸드를 좋아하지 않아. — B: 나도 그래. (junk food)
　　　A: Tom doesn't _____ _____ _____.
　　　B: _____ _____ _____.

내신대비 TEST

[01-03] 다음 빈칸에 알맞은 말을 고르시오.

01

Hardly _____ how to ski.

① he does know ② does he know
③ do he knows ④ knew he
⑤ he knew

02

I don't like any of the dishes in this restaurant. Neither _____ my father.

① is ② do ③ does
④ don't ⑤ doesn't

03

It was my doll _____ my sister had hidden.

① where ② how ③ when
④ that ⑤ whom

[04-05] 다음 대화의 빈칸에 알맞은 말을 고르시오.

04

A: I saw this documentary last night.
B: _____ Let's change the channel.

① So did I. ② Neither did I.
③ Neither am I. ④ So do I.
⑤ Neither was I.

05

A: I can't go to the museum today.
B: _____ Both of us should go tomorrow.

① So do I. ② So can I.
③ So am I. ④ Neither can I.
⑤ Neither do I.

[06-07] 빈칸에 들어갈 말이 순서대로 알맞게 짝지어진 것을 고르시오.

06

- In the basket _____ the wet towels.
- Not all bakers _____ cakes as well as she.

① is – make ② is – makes
③ are – make ④ are – makes
⑤ are – does make

07

- Not every book _____ worth reading.
- He gave his students homework, but _____ of them turned it in.

① is – all ② is – none
③ is – never ④ are – none
⑤ are – all

08

다음 두 문장의 뜻이 같도록 할 때 빈칸에 알맞은 것은?

Some viewers are disappointed with the ending of the film, but others aren't.
→ _____ viewer is disappointed with the ending of the film.

① Both ② Each ③ None
④ Not every ⑤ Neither

09

> 그는 좀처럼 외식을 하지 않는다.

① Seldom doesn't he eat out.
② He doesn't seldom eat out.
③ Seldom does he not eat out.
④ He seldom not eat out.
⑤ Seldom does he eat out.

10

> 그들 중 아무도 운전 면허증이 없었다.

① Some of them didn't have a driver's license.
② Not all of them had a driver's license.
③ None of them had a driver's license.
④ None of them didn't have a driver's license.
⑤ Neither of them didn't have a driver's license.

기출응용

[11-12] 다음 밑줄 친 부분의 쓰임이 나머지와 다른 것을 고르시오.

11

① You did a really good job.
② He does like his dogs and cats.
③ I did tell him the truth about the case.
④ She does write interesting novels.
⑤ He did oversleep in the morning.

12

① It was rude that she said that to me.
② It was Kevin that recommended me for the job.
③ It was a leather jacket that I bought yesterday.
④ It wasn't Carol that you saw at the bookstore.
⑤ It was in May that we went on a trip.

[13-14] 다음 중 어법상 틀린 것을 고르시오.

13

① Neither of us wanted to be on a diet.
② He did eat the sandwich I made.
③ Across the street is a new flower shop.
④ Not every girl likes to play with dolls.
⑤ It was in this park which I lost my purse.

14

① It was Mike who lent me a cell phone charger.
② Never I have seen such a big cake.
③ On the wall was a painting.
④ I don't like skating. Neither does she.
⑤ She does have difficulty getting up early.

기출응용

15

다음 대화의 밑줄 친 부분을 영어로 바르게 옮긴 것은?

> A: What did you wear to the party last night?
> B: 내가 어젯밤 파티에 입고 간 것은 바로 나의 초록색 드레스였어.

① It is my green dress that I wore it to the party last night.
② It was my green dress that I wore to the party last night.
③ It was my green dress that I wear to the party last night.
④ It was last night that I wore my green dress to the party.
⑤ It was the party that I wore my green dress to last night.

16

다음 밑줄 친 부분을 바르게 강조한 문장은?

> I had <u>never</u> dreamed that he would fail the exam.
>
> → _____ that he would fail the exam.

① Never I had dreamed
② Never had dreamed I
③ Never dreamed I had
④ Never had I dreamed
⑤ Had I never dreamed

17

다음 대화 중 자연스럽지 <u>않은</u> 것은?

① A: You made a mistake again. I don't think you tried your best.
 B: I did try my best.
② A: Where did you see her yesterday?
 B: It was at the dry cleaner's that I saw her.
③ A: Who cooked this Mexican food?
 B: It was my father who cooked it.
④ A: Did any of you wear a uniform?
 B: No. None of us wore a uniform.
⑤ A: I won't go scuba diving this weekend.
 B: So will I. I'm afraid of deep water.

고난도

18

다음 중 어법상 옳은 것끼리 짝지어진 것은?

> (a) Little he realizes that he made her upset.
> (b) Not all of them wanted to go home.
> (c) Here the food comes you ordered.
> (d) It is at six o'clock that she wakes me up.

① (a), (b)　　② (a), (c)　　③ (a), (d)
④ (b), (c)　　⑤ (b), (d)

19

다음 밑줄 친 각 부분을 강조할 때, <u>잘못된</u> 것은?

> ① <u>Charlotte</u> ② <u>read</u> ③ <u>a magazine</u> ④ <u>at the hair salon</u> ⑤ <u>yesterday</u>.

① It was Charlotte that read a magazine at the hair salon yesterday.
② Charlotte does read a magazine at the hair salon yesterday.
③ It was a magazine that Charlotte read at the hair salon yesterday.
④ It was the hair salon that Charlotte read a magazine yesterday.
⑤ It was yesterday that Charlotte read a magazine at the hair salon.

고난도

20

다음 밑줄 친 부분을 바르게 고치지 <u>않은</u> 것은?

① <u>Rarely does Jacob eats</u> rice noodles.
　→ Rarely does Jacob eat
② <u>In her pocket was</u> a few coins.
　→ In her pocket were
③ Bob decided to buy a pet rabbit, and <u>so do I</u>.
　→ so did I
④ <u>Never William has cried</u> while watching a movie.
　→ Never has cried William
⑤ <u>Little dreamed I that</u> I would become a journalist.
　→ Little did I dream that

01

주어진 말을 이용하여 우리말과 뜻이 같도록 문장을 완성하시오.

(1) 모든 사과가 달콤하지는 않다. (apple)

→ _____ _____ _____ is sweet.

(2) 책상 위에 내 책이 있었다. (book)

→ On the desk _____ _____ _____.

02

다음 밑줄 친 부분을 강조하는 문장으로 바꾸어 쓰시오.

(1) Janet <u>exercised</u> every morning to lose weight.

→ _____

(2) He <u>never</u> talks to me during class.

→ _____

03

다음 학급별 동아리 지원 현황표를 보고, 문장을 완성하시오.

Class	Newspaper Club	School Band	Cheerleading Club
A	17	13	0
B	7	18	5
C	27	2	1

(1) _____ of the students in class A applied for the cheerleading club.

(2) _____ _____ of the students in class C applied for the newspaper club.

(3) It is the school band _____ 18 students in class B applied for.

04

다음 두 문장이 같은 뜻이 되도록 문장을 완성하시오.

(1) A: Jeremy doesn't eat meat.

B: I don't eat it, either.

→ A: Jeremy doesn't eat meat.

B: _____ _____ _____.

(2) All of them thought the movie was awful.

→ _____ _____ _____ thought the movie was good.

05

다음 밑줄 친 부분을 강조하는 문장으로 바꾸어 쓰시오.

<u>Mina</u> bought <u>a novel</u> at <u>the bookstore</u>
 (1)   (2)   (3)
<u>this afternoon</u>.
  (4)

(1) _____

(2) _____

(3) _____

(4) _____

고난도

06

다음 편지를 읽고, 틀린 부분을 모두 찾아 바르게 고쳐 쓰시오. (3군데)

It's been a year since I moved to Hong Kong. I am getting used to life here. So my sister is. It is Korean winters where we miss the most. Never it does snow here.

SELF NOTE

핵심 포인트 정리하기

1 강조

- 〈① _____ + 동사원형〉: '정말 ~하다'의 의미로 문장의 내용이 사실임을 강조
- 〈② _____ _____ ~ _____ …〉: '…한 것은 바로 ~이다[였다]'의 의미로 주어, 목적어, 부사(구) 등을 강조
  * 강조하는 대상이 사람일 경우 that 대신 who를 쓸 수 있음

 일반동사 do와 강조의 do 구분하기!

2 부정

- 부분 부정: 〈③ _____ + all, every, always 등〉 '모두[항상] ~인 것은 아니다'
- 전체 부정: 〈no, none, neither, never 등〉 '아무도[결코] ~하지 않다'

3 도치

- 방향·장소 관련 부사구를 강조하는 도치: 〈④ _____ + _____ + _____〉
- 부정어(구)를 강조하는 도치
  〈never, hardly, little, rarely + be동사/조동사 + 주어〉
  〈never, hardly, little, rarely + do[does/did] + 주어 + 동사원형〉

  * 〈⑤ _____ + _____ + _____〉: '~도 또한 그렇다/그렇지 않다'의 의미로 각각 긍정문과 부정문 다음에 사용

 방향·장소 관련 부사구나 부정어(구)가 강조되어 문두에 올 때 어순 알아두기!

문제로 개념 다지기

밑줄 친 부분이 어법상 맞으면 O, 틀리면 X 표시하고 바르게 고치시오.

1 It was Jessica <u>that</u> spilled my juice.

2 It is my neighbor's dog <u>who</u> ruined my soccer ball.

3 Under the table <u>my tennis racket was</u>.

4 Seldom <u>does not he visit</u> his parents.

5 Not <u>every</u> Koreans are kind to foreigners.

6 Never <u>he had heard</u> such a wonderful song.

7 <u>None</u> of us wanted to go swimming.

8 A: I will buy a new cell phone. – B: <u>Neither will I</u>.

9 He <u>do</u> like toy robots. He has hundreds of them in his room.

10 Little <u>didn't I dream</u> that I would break up with him.

MEMO

MEMO

MEMO

MEMO

MEMO

지은이

NE능률 영어교육연구소

NE능률 영어교육연구소는 혁신적이며 효율적인 영어 교재를 개발하고
영어 학습의 질을 한 단계 높이고자 노력하는 NE능률의 연구조직입니다.

문제로 마스터하는 중학영문법 〈LEVEL 3〉

펴 낸 이	주민홍
펴 낸 곳	서울특별시 마포구 월드컵북로 396(상암동) 누리꿈스퀘어 비즈니스타워 10층
	㈜NE능률 (우편번호 03925)
펴 낸 날	2018년 7월 5일 개정판 제1쇄 발행
	2024년 5월 15일 제18쇄
전 화	02 2014 7114
팩 스	02 3142 0356
홈 페 이 지	www.neungyule.com
등 록 번 호	제1-68호
I S B N	979-11-253-2367-9 53740
정 가	11,000원

NE 능률

고객센터

교재 내용 문의 : contact.nebooks.co.kr (별도의 가입 절차 없이 작성 가능)
제품 구매, 교환, 불량, 반품 문의 : 02-2014-7114
☎ 전화문의는 본사 업무시간 중에만 가능합니다.

즐거운 독해가 만드는 실력의 차이!

전국 **온오프 서점** 판매중

초·중등 영어 독해 필수 기본서 주니어 리딩튜터

STARTER 1
(초4-5)

STARTER 2
(초5-6)

LEVEL 1
(초6-예비중)

LEVEL 2
(중1)

LEVEL 3
(중1-2)

LEVEL 4
(중2-3)

최신 학습 경향을 반영한 지문 수록

· 시사, 문화, 과학 등 다양한 소재로 지문 구성
· 중등교육과정의 중요 어휘와 핵심 문법 반영

양질의 문제 풀이로 확실히 익히는 독해 학습

· 지문 관련 배경지식과 상식을 키울 수 있는 다양한 코너 구성
· 독해력, 사고력을 키워주는 서술형 문제 강화

Lexile 지수, 단어 수에 기반한 객관적 난이도 구분

· 미국에서 가장 공신력 있는 독서능력 평가 지수 Lexile 지수 도입
· 체계적인 난이도별 지문 구분, 리딩튜터 시리즈와 연계 강화

NE능률 교재 MAP

문법 구문

초1-2	초3	초3-4	초4-5	초5-6
	그래머버디 1 초등영어 문법이 된다 Starter 1	그래머버디 2 초등영어 문법이 된다 Starter 2 초등 Grammar Inside 1 초등 Grammar Inside 2	그래머버디 3 Grammar Bean 1 Grammar Bean 2 초등영어 문법이 된다 1 초등 Grammar Inside 3 초등 Grammar Inside 4	Grammar Bean 3 Grammar Bean 4 초등영어 문법이 된다 2 초등 Grammar Inside 5 초등 Grammar Inside 6

초6-예비중	중1	중1-2	중2-3	중3
능률중학영어 예비중 Grammar Inside Starter 원리를 더한 영문법 STARTER	능률중학영어 중1 Grammar Zone 입문편 Grammar Zone 워크북 입문편 1316 Grammar 1 문제로 마스터하는 중학영문법 1 Grammar Inside 1 열중 16강 문법 1 쓰기로 마스터하는 중학서술형 1학년 중학 천문장 1	능률중학영어 중2 1316 Grammar 2 문제로 마스터하는 중학영문법 2 Grammar Inside 2 열중 16강 문법 2 원리를 더한 영문법 1 중학영문법 총정리 모의고사 1 중학 천문장 2	Grammar Zone 기초편 Grammar Zone 워크북 기초편 1316 Grammar 3 원리를 더한 영문법 2 중학영문법 총정리 모의고사 2 쓰기로 마스터하는 중학서술형 2학년 중학 천문장 3	능률중학영어 중3 문제로 마스터하는 중학영문법 3 Grammar Inside 3 열중 16강 문법 3 중학영문법 총정리 모의고사 3 쓰기로 마스터하는 중학서술형 3학년

예비고-고1	고1	고1-2	고2-3	고3
문제로 마스터하는 고등영문법 올클 수능 어법 start 천문장 입문	Grammar Zone 기본편 1 Grammar Zone 워크북 기본편 1 Grammar Zone 기본편 2 Grammar Zone 워크북 기본편 2 필히 통하는 고등 영문법 기본편 필히 통하는 고등 서술형 기본편 천문장 기본	필히 통하는 고등 영문법 실력편 필히 통하는 고등 서술형 실전편 TEPS BY STEP G+R Basic	Grammar Zone 종합편 Grammar Zone 워크북 종합편 올클 수능 어법 완성 천문장 완성	

수능 이상/ 토플 80-89· 텝스 600-699점	수능 이상/ 토플 90-99· 텝스 700-799점	수능 이상/ 토플 100· 텝스 800점 이상		
TEPS BY STEP G+R 1	TEPS BY STEP G+R 2	TEPS BY STEP G+R 3		

중학 핵심 문법을
문제로 확실히 끝내는

문제로
마스터하는
중학영문법

LEVEL **3**

정답 및 해설

NE 능률

LEVEL 3

문제로 마스터하는 중학영문법

정답 및 해설

Chapter 01 to부정사 Ⅰ

POINT 01 to부정사의 명사적 용법 Ⅰ - 주어/목적어/보어 p.10

A　1 To make[Making]　2 to teach[teaching]
　　3 to finish　4 To keep[Keeping]　5 to arrive
　　6 to build[building]

B　1 I failed to catch　2 My plan is to study abroad
　　3 She wants to be　4 His wish is to meet
　　5 To read an English novel
　　6 He hopes to learn about

POINT 02 to부정사의 명사적 용법 Ⅱ - 가주어, 가목적어 it p.11

A　1 It is simple to ride the subway in Seoul.
　　2 It is easy to find information on the Internet.
　　3 It is fantastic to achieve one's goals.
　　4 It is difficult to express your opinion in other
　　　languages.

B　1 It is important to exercise regularly.
　　2 It is wonderful to have a true friend.
　　3 I thought it better to study in the morning.
　　4 He found it exciting to speak English.
　　5 Serena found it hard to tell him the truth.

POINT 03 to부정사의 명사적 용법 Ⅲ - 〈의문사+to-v〉 p.12

A　1 when to call her　2 what to do
　　3 where I should hide my pocket money
　　4 how I should decorate the Christmas tree

B　1 when to start　2 who(m) to invite
　　3 how to use　4 what to buy
　　5 where to go　6 what to eat

POINT 04 to부정사의 형용사적 용법 Ⅰ - 명사 수식 p.13

A　1 to sit on[in]　2 news to tell　3 cold to drink
　　4 a pen to write with　5 to talk with[to]
　　6 time to travel　7 way to solve

B　1 anything to do　2 jacket to wear
　　3 town to live in　4 paper to write on
　　5 someone[somebody] to depend on

　　6 friends to play with　7 city to visit

POINT 05 to부정사의 형용사적 용법 Ⅱ - 〈be+to-v〉 용법 p.14

A　1 was to be seen　2 are to be
　　3 are to succeed　4 is to visit　5 was to end

B　1 was to lead　2 are to finish
　　3 was to be found　4 are to fly to Australia
　　5 are to be a writer

POINT 06 to부정사의 부사적 용법 p.15

A　1 to see snow　2 to let us stay　3 To see him
　　4 to go to　5 only to fail

B　1 I'm going to China to learn Chinese.
　　2 She was disappointed to miss the concert.
　　3 You were wise to follow his advice.
　　4 It is too cold to wear a T-shirt and shorts.

내신대비 TEST p.16

01 ③　　02 ④　　03 ⑤　　04 ①　　05 ③　　06 ①
07 ③　　08 ⑤　　09 ⑤　　10 ②　　11 ④　　12 ④
13 ①　　14 ②　　15 ⑤　　16 ⑤　　17 ③
18 ②, ⑤　19 ③　20 ②

서술형 따라잡기 p.19

01 (1) surprised to hear　(2) was, to go back
02 (1) He was rude to make her wait.
　　(2) Did you find someone to work with?
03 (1) to improve my health　(2) to get an A
04 is not good for your health to eat at night
05 (1) it easy to do[wash] the dishes
　　(2) it difficult to clean the bathroom
06 (1) I'll show you how to cook the meat.
　　(2) It is important to know when to apologize.
　　[To know when to apologize is important.]

01 보어 역할을 하는 명사적 용법의 to부정사가 와야 한다.
02 가주어 It이 쓰였으므로 빈칸에는 진주어인 to부정사가 와야
　　한다.

03 some chopsticks를 수식하는 형용사적 용법의 to부정사를 쓴다. '가지고 먹을 젓가락'이라는 의미가 되어야 하므로 to eat 뒤에는 전치사 with가 와야 한다.

04 문맥상 '언제 와야 할지'를 뜻하는 〈when+to-v〉의 형태로 when to come이 와야 한다.

05 첫 번째 빈칸에는 진주어 to make 이하를 대신하는 가주어 It이, 두 번째 빈칸에는 목적어 역할을 하는 명사적 용법의 to부정사가 와야 한다.

06 첫 번째 빈칸에는 '어디로 가야 할지'의 의미가 되어야 하므로 장소를 나타내는 의문사 where가, 두 번째 빈칸에는 진목적어 to become 이하를 대신하는 가목적어 it이 와야 한다.

07 첫 번째 빈칸에는 something을 수식하는 형용사적 용법의 to부정사가, 두 번째 빈칸에는 결과를 나타내는 부사적 용법의 to부정사가 와야 한다.

08 ⑤ 밑줄 친 부분은 진주어 to go 이하를 대신하는 가주어 It으로 쓰인 반면, 나머지는 인칭대명사 It으로 쓰였다.

09 〈보기〉와 ⑤의 to find는 목적을 나타내는 부사적 용법의 to부정사이다. ①, ④는 감정의 원인을 나타내는 부사적 용법, ②는 목적어 역할을 하는 명사적 용법, ③은 진주어로 쓰인 명사적 용법의 to부정사이다.

10 ② 〈의문사+to-v〉는 〈의문사+주어+should+동사원형〉으로 바꾸어 쓸 수 있다.

11 첫 번째 빈칸에는 진주어 to give 이하를 대신하는 가주어 It이, 두 번째 빈칸에는 진목적어 to be honest를 대신하는 가목적어 it이 와야 한다.

12 ④ 〈find+가목적어 it+형용사+진목적어(to make kim-chi)〉 순으로 쓴다.

13 ①은 보어로 쓰인 명사적 용법의 to부정사이고, 나머지는 모두 부사적 용법(②-판단의 근거, ③-목적, ④-감정의 원인, ⑤-결과)의 to부정사이다.

14 ②는 대명사를 수식하는 형용사적 용법의 to부정사이고, 나머지는 모두 명사적 용법(①, ③-목적어, ④-보어, ⑤-진주어)의 to부정사이다.

15 〈보기〉와 ⑤의 it은 가목적어로 쓰인 반면, ①과 ③은 비인칭 주어, ②는 가주어, ④는 인칭대명사로 쓰였다.

16 ⑤ to write 뒤에 전치사 on이 와야 한다.

17 ③ thought 뒤에 가목적어 it이 필요하다.

18 ① 주어로 쓰인 that은 to save 이하를 대신하는 가주어 It이 되어야 한다.
③ 명사인 two sisters를 수식하는 형용사적 용법의 to부정

사로 to take care 뒤에 전치사 of가 와야 한다.
④ 동사 know의 목적어로 '무엇을 해야 할지'의 의미인 what to do가 와야 한다.

19 ③ to sit 뒤에 전치사 on이 와야 한다.

20 (b) be는 결과를 나타내는 부사적 용법의 to부정사 to be가 되어야 한다.
(c) jump rope는 진목적어로 쓰였으므로 to jump rope가 되어야 한다.

서술형 따라잡기

01 (1) 형용사 surprised 뒤에 감정(놀람)의 원인을 나타내는 부사적 용법의 to부정사가 와야 한다.
(2) 운명을 나타내는 〈be+to-v〉 용법을 쓴다.

02 (1) 판단의 근거를 나타내는 부사적 용법의 to부정사로 to make her wait를 rude 뒤에 쓴다.
(2) someone 뒤에 형용사적 용법의 to부정사 to work with를 쓴다.

03 (1) 목적을 나타내는 부사적 용법의 to부정사를 쓴다.
(2) 주어 자리에 가주어 it이 있으므로, 진주어인 to부정사는 문장 뒤에 쓴다.

04 가주어 It을 주어 자리에 쓸 경우 주어로 쓰인 to부정사(구)는 문장 뒤에 쓴다.

05 〈it(가목적어)+형용사+to부정사(진목적어)〉의 순으로 쓴다.

06 (1) 동사 show의 직접목적어로 '~하는 법'의 의미인 〈how+to-v〉를 쓴다.
(2) 동사 know의 목적어로 '언제 ~할지'의 의미인 〈when+to-v〉를 쓴다. 문장의 주어로 쓰인 to부정사구는 문장 뒤로 보내고 주어 자리에 가주어 It을 써서 표현할 수 있다.

SELF NOTE   p.20

A 핵심 포인트 정리하기
① 명사적 ② it ③ 의문사, 주어, should, 동사원형
④ 형용사, to-v ⑤ be, to-v ⑥ 부사적 ⑦ 목적

B 문제로 개념 다지기
1 X, it difficult to stay in shape 2 O
3 X, someone strong to carry
4 X, to sit on[in] 5 O 6 O 7 X, It is wise to pay

Chapter 02 to부정사 II

A 1 tall enough to reach the top of the bookcase

2 too tired to move

3 so smart that she can solve that difficult problem

4 so busy that they can't go on vacation

B 1 This soup is too hot to eat.

2 It is bright enough to read a book

3 The wallet is too big to put in my pocket.

4 Julie is so shy that she can't sing

5 Tim is brave enough to travel

A 1 X, to stay 2 O 3 X, to become

4 X, to wait 5 O 6 X, to take 7 X, to brush

B 1 expected you to be 2 ordered his dog to sit

3 tell him to stop 4 advised me to swim

5 want me to travel 6 helped her prepare

7 allow us to enter

A 1 go 2 know 3 to get 4 return

B 1 tell 2 to bring 3 look 4 use

5 buy 6 to come

C 1 had me do 2 made her cancel

3 got him to wear 4 didn't let me join

5 asked him to take

A 1 sing[singing] 2 (to) cross 3 to bring

4 touch[touching] 5 kick[kicking] 6 go

7 cry[crying]

B 1 steal[stealing] 2 laugh[laughing]

3 move[moving] 4 to come

5 play[playing] 6 train

C 1 feel the wind blow[blowing]

2 saw them smile[smiling]

3 heard his son shout[shouting]

A 1 for 2 for 3 of 4 of 5 for

B 1 to be 2 him 3 me 4 of you

C 1 It was silly of Helen to lose her bag.

2 It will be difficult for him to speak English.

3 It will be easy for you to find a drugstore around here.

A 1 him 2 not to touch 3 for us

4 not to skip 5 a few minutes

B 1 promised not[never] to miss the class again

2 told me not[never] to read the story

3 decided not[never] to buy an outdoor jacket

C 1 took five hours for us to climb

2 lucky for her to pass

3 tell your son not to go

A 1 that he has a secret

2 to have made a mistake

3 seems to be a good teacher

4 seem to have enjoyed the movie

5 seem to be allowed here

B 1 They seem to be old friends.

2 Matthew wanted them not to worry.

3 Alice seems to have lost weight.

4 Your room needs to be cleaned.

A 1 so to speak 2 To begin with

3 To make matters worse 4 To be frank

5 Strange to say

B 1 그는 잘생긴 것은 말할 것도 없고 똑똑하다.

2 사실대로 말하면, 그가 나에게 네 이름을 물었다.

3 간단히 말하면, 나는 혼자 있는 시간이 필요하다.

4 말할 필요도 없이, 그는 곧 나를 보러 올 것이다.

5 확실히, 이것은 내가 가장 좋아하는 영화는 아니다.

내신대비 TEST
p.30

01 ④	02 ⑤	03 ②	04 ③	05 ④	06 ⑤
07 ②	08 ①	09 ③	10 ②	11 ⑤	12 ③
13 ③	14 ①	15 ③	16 ④	17 ④	18 ⑤
19 ①	20 ①				

서술형 따라잡기
p.33

01 (1) told me to water (2) got him to drive

02 (1) It took me an hour to get to the library.

   (2) It is impossible for me to leave now.

03 (1) to have lost it (2) them not to say

04 (1) (to) learn how to play the violin

   (2) of you to tell him a lie

05 (1) too fast for the boy to follow

   (2) light enough for her to carry

06 (1) for Maria to run 10 km

   (2) three hours to read the book

01 〈형용사/부사+enough+to-v〉는 '…할 만큼 충분히 ~하다'라는 의미이다.

02 to부정사의 의미상의 주어는 주로 〈for+목적격〉을 쓴다.

03 사역동사 make는 목적격 보어로 원형부정사를 취한다.

04 to부정사의 의미상의 주어는 주로 〈for+목적격〉을 쓴다.

05 to부정사의 의미상의 주어로 〈of+목적격〉이 쓰일 때는 앞에 사람의 성격이나 성품을 나타내는 형용사가 와야 한다.

06 사역동사와 지각동사는 목적격 보어로 원형부정사를 취하는 반면, order는 목적격 보어로 to부정사를 취한다.

07 첫 번째 문장은 '너무 ~해서 …할 수 없다'라는 의미의 〈too+형용사/부사+to-v〉 구문이 쓰였고, 두 번째 문장에서 사역동사 have는 목적격 보어로 원형부정사를 취한다.

08 첫 번째 문장은 to부정사의 의미상의 주어로 〈for+목적격〉이 와야 하고, 두 번째 문장은 의미상의 주어인 more exciting stories가 행위의 영향을 받으므로 to부정사의 수동태인 〈to

be v-ed〉를 써야 한다.

09 to begin with: 우선, 먼저
strange to say: 이상한 이야기지만

10 ② 지각동사 feel은 목적격 보어로 원형부정사 혹은 현재분사를 취한다.

11 '~였던 것 같다'라는 의미는 〈seem to have v-ed〉 구문으로 나타낸다. 주어진 말을 배열하면 'Brian seems to have fallen in love.'가 되므로 네 번째에 오는 단어는 have이다.

12 ③은 '너무 ~해서 …할 수 있다'의 의미인 반면, 나머지는 모두 '너무 ~해서 …할 수 없다'의 뜻이다.

13 동사 advise는 목적격 보어로 to부정사를 취하며, to부정사의 부정형은 to부정사 앞에 not이나 never를 쓴다.

14 ① nice는 사람의 성격이나 성품을 나타내는 형용사이므로 to부정사의 의미상의 주어로 〈of+목적격〉을 쓴다. 나머지는 모두 to부정사의 의미상의 주어로 〈for+목적격〉을 쓴다.

15 ③ '(~가) …하는 데 (시간이) 걸리다'라는 의미는 〈It takes (+목적격)+시간+to-v〉의 형태로 나타내므로 getting을 to get으로 고쳐야 한다.

16 ④ 지각동사 hear는 목적격 보어로 원형부정사 혹은 현재분사를 취하므로 to come을 come이나 coming으로 고쳐야 한다.

17 ④ 사역동사 have는 목적격 보어로 원형부정사를 취하므로 to fix를 fix로 고쳐야 한다.

18 (A) 지각동사는 목적격 보어로 원형부정사 혹은 현재분사를 취한다.

   (B) 사역동사 make는 목적격 보어로 원형부정사를 취한다.

   (C) '~인 것 같다'라는 의미는 〈seem to-v〉 구문으로 나타낸다.

19 ① to부정사의 시제가 문장의 시제보다 앞설 경우에는 완료부정사(to have v-ed)를 쓰므로 to be를 to have been으로 고쳐야 한다.

20 (b) '너무 ~해서 …할 수 없다'라는 의미는 〈too+형용사/부사+to-v〉의 형태로 나타내므로 to wearing을 to wear로 고쳐야 한다.

서술형 따라잡기

01 (1) 동사 tell은 목적격 보어로 to부정사를 취한다.
   (2) 동사 get은 '~하게 하다'라는 사역의 의미를 갖지만 목적격 보어로 to부정사를 취한다.

02 (1) 〈It takes+목적격+시간+to-v〉는 '~가 …하는 데 (시간) 이 걸리다'라는 의미이다.

(2) 가주어 It을 주어 자리에 쓰고 진주어인 to부정사구는 문장 뒤에 쓴다. to부정사의 의미상의 주어는 〈for+목적격〉의 형태로 to부정사 앞에 쓴다.

03 (1) to부정사의 시제가 문장의 시제보다 앞설 경우, 완료부정사(to have v-ed)를 쓴다.

(2) 동사 ask는 목적격 보어로 to부정사를 취하며, to부정사의 부정형은 to부정사 앞에 not을 쓴다.

04 (1) 동사 help는 목적격 보어로 원형부정사 혹은 to부정사를 취한다.

(2) 가주어 It이 쓰였으므로, 진주어에 해당하는 to부정사를 문장 뒤에 쓴다. 사람의 성격이나 성품을 나타내는 형용사 (stupid)가 보어로 쓰였으므로, to부정사의 의미상의 주어는 〈of+목적격〉의 형태로 쓴다.

05 (1) 〈too+형용사/부사+to-v〉: 너무 ~해서 …할 수 없다

(2) 〈형용사/부사+enough+to-v〉: …할 만큼 충분히 ~하다

06 '~가 …하는 데 (시간)이 걸리다'는 〈It takes+시간+for+목적격+to-v〉 혹은 〈It takes+목적격+시간+to-v〉로 나타낸다.

SELF NOTE　　　　　　　　　　p.34

A 핵심 포인트 정리하기

① too, to-v ② enough, to-v ③ 원형부정사
④ to부정사 ⑤ of ⑥ for ⑦ to have v-ed
⑧ seem to-v ⑨ so to speak ⑩ to be frank

B 문제로 개념 다지기

1 X, too salty to eat 2 X, for me
3 X, seem to expect 4 X, know
5 O 6 X, for him to read

Chapter 03 동명사

POINT 01 동명사의 역할 – 주어/보어/목적어　　p.36

A 1 Walking around the lake
2 doing puzzles
3 Sending text messages during class
4 taking yoga classes
5 having any dessert

B 1 Exercising regularly 2 interested in going
3 is climbing 4 playing the piano
5 doesn't like talking

POINT 02 동명사의 의미상의 주어/부정　　p.37

A 1 her 2 his[him] 3 my[me]

B 1 his[him] returning to the hospital
2 my[me] turning off the light

C 1 Not driving too fast
2 about his coming to Seoul
3 by his not answering my calls
4 for not coming on time
5 about her not remembering his birthday

POINT 03 동명사의 시제와 수동태　　p.38

A 1 having a barbecue party tonight
2 being stuck in traffic
3 not having taken care of herself
4 having spilled water on your notebook

B 1 having made a mistake 2 being bothered
3 having fallen down 4 being invited

POINT 04 동명사와 현재분사　　p.39

A 1 현재분사 2 현재분사 3 현재분사 4 동명사
5 현재분사 6 동명사 7 동명사 8 동명사
9 동명사 10 현재분사 11 동명사 12 현재분사

B 1 만화를 그리고 있는 소녀는 내 친구이다.
2 수면제를 복용하는 것은 위험할 수 있다.
3 바다에서 수영하고 있는 사람들이 많다.
4 그의 취미 중 하나는 이탈리아 음식을 요리하는 것이다.

5 그는 대기자 명단에서 자신의 이름을 찾았다.

6 이 식당에는 흡연 구역이 없다.

POINT 05 동명사 목적어 vs. to부정사 목적어　　p.40

A 1 to persuade　2 leaving　3 reading　4 to let
5 to take　6 telling　7 to listen　8 to become
9 staying　10 to make it

B 1 gave up buying
2 plans to have
3 avoid going shopping
4 keep calling me
5 enjoys talking to
6 quit[stopped] drinking coffee

POINT 06 동명사와 to부정사를 목적어로 취하는 동사　　p.41

A 1 to rain　2 learning　3 giving　4 to eat

B 1 regretted laughing at
2 tried to lose
3 stopped to ask
4 remembered to do
5 forgot to return

POINT 07 동명사 주요 구문 I　　p.42

A 1 go climbing
2 was busy answering
3 is worth watching
4 wasn't used to eating
5 look forward to meeting

B 1 She felt like going to bed.
2 I'm used to reading Chinese.
3 The issue is worth discussing.
4 We were busy cleaning the kitchen.
5 It's no use complaining about the service

POINT 08 동명사 주요 구문 II　　p.43

A 1 There is no avoiding
2 How[What] about eating
3 couldn't help skipping class

4 have trouble[difficulty] (in) speaking
5 kept[prevented] the airplane from taking off

B 1 had trouble[difficulty] getting
2 There is no helping
3 spent much money fixing
4 On[Upon] returning home
5 couldn't help calling your name

내신대비 TEST　　p.44

01 ③　02 ③　03 ⑤　04 ①　05 ③　06 ④
07 ⑤　08 ③　09 ④　10 ⑤　11 ④　12 ②
13 ④　14 ②　15 ③　16 ③　17 ④　18 ②
19 ②　20 ①

서술형 따라잡기　- - - - - - - - - - - - - - -　p.47

01 (1) being given (2) no use apologizing
02 (1) his[him] working at a restaurant
(2) couldn't help speaking loudly
03 kept my son from running
04 (1) to send an email (2) from playing tennis
(3) an hour running
05 (1) Not eating vegetables
(2) having gotten[got] an A in science
06 to live → to living / keeping → to keep /
to hear → to hearing

01 enjoy는 동명사만을 목적어로 취하는 동사이다.

02 〈spend+시간[돈]+(on) v-ing〉는 '~하는 데 시간[돈]을 쓰
다'라는 의미이다.

03 동명사의 의미상의 주어는 소유격 혹은 목적격의 형태로 쓴다.

04 hope는 to부정사만을 목적어로 취하는 동사이다.

05 give up은 동명사만을 목적어로 취하는 동사이다.

06 ④는 진행형으로 쓰인 현재분사이고, 나머지는 모두 동명사이다.

07 ⑤는 수식하는 명사의 진행·능동을 나타내는 현재분사이고,
나머지는 모두 뒤에 오는 명사의 용도나 목적을 나타내는 동명
사이다.

08 만리장성이 어땠는지를 묻는 질문에 놀랍다고 했으므로, 그 뒤
에 이어질 말은 '만리장성을 본 것을 잊지 못할 것이다'가 와야

자연스럽다. 따라서 forget의 목적어로 동명사가 쓰인 ③이 가장 적절하다.

09 On v-ing: ~하자마자
What about v-ing?: ~하는 게 어때?

10 be used to v-ing: ~하는 것에 익숙하다
be worth v-ing: ~할 가치가 있다

11 decide는 to부정사를 목적어로 취한다. '~한 것을 후회하다'의 의미일 때 regret은 동명사를 목적어로 취한다.

12 ② 동명사의 의미상의 주어는 소유격이나 목적격으로 쓴다.

13 ④ consider는 동명사를 목적어로 취하는 동사이다.

14 ② deny는 동명사를 목적어로 취하는 동사이다.

15 ③ 〈have difficulty (in) v-ing〉는 '~하는 데 어려움을 겪다'라는 의미이다.

16 (a) avoid는 동명사를 목적어로 취하는 동사이다.
(d) '식후에 약을 먹을 것'을 잊지 말라고 하는 것이므로 forget의 목적어로 to부정사가 와야 한다.

17 (a) 〈be used to v-ing〉는 '~하는 것에 익숙하다'라는 의미이다.
(b) 전치사의 목적어로는 동명사를 쓰므로 being을 써서 동명사의 수동태 표현으로 바꿔야 한다.
(d) mind는 동명사만을 목적어로 취한다.

18 ① try to-v: ~하려고 노력하다
try v-ing: 시험 삼아 ~해보다
③ look forward to v-ing: ~하기를 고대하다
④ feel like v-ing: ~하고 싶다
⑤ have trouble (in) v-ing: ~하는 데 어려움을 겪다

19 (A) refuse는 to부정사를 목적어로 취하는 동사이다.
(B) '~하는 것을 멈추다'의 의미가 되어야 하므로 〈stop+v-ing〉로 써야 한다.
(C) 동명사의 의미상의 주어는 소유격이나 목적격의 형태로 나타낸다.

20 ① 〈be busy v-ing〉는 '~하느라 바쁘다'라는 의미이다.

서술형 따라잡기 -

01 (1) 전치사의 목적어는 동명사를 쓰며 '생일 선물을 받다'라는 의미로 동명사의 수동태를 쓴다.
(2) 〈It's no use v-ing〉는 '~해 봐야 소용없다'라는 의미이다.

02 (1) 전치사의 목적어로는 동명사를 쓰고, 동명사의 의미상의 주어는 동명사 앞에 소유격이나 목적격의 형태로 쓴다.

(2) 〈can't (help) but+동사원형〉은 '~하지 않을 수 없다'라는 의미로 〈can't help v-ing〉로 바꾸어 쓸 수 있다.

03 〈keep+목적어+from v-ing〉는 '~가 …하는 것을 막다'라는 의미이다.

04 (1) 이메일을 '보낼' 것을 잊은 것이므로 forget의 목적어로 to부정사가 와야 한다.
(2) 〈prevent+목적어+from v-ing〉는 '~가 …하는 것을 막다'라는 의미이다.
(3) 〈spend+시간+v-ing〉는 '~하는 데 시간을 쓰다'라는 의미이다.

05 (1) 문장의 주어로 동명사를 쓴다. 동명사의 부정은 동명사 앞에 Not을 붙여 나타낸다.
(2) 전치사의 목적어로는 동명사를 쓴다. 동명사의 시제가 문장의 시제보다 앞선 시점이므로 〈having v-ed〉의 형태로 쓴다.

06 • '~하는 것에 익숙하다'라는 의미인 be used to의 to는 전치사로 뒤에 동명사가 와야 한다.
• promise는 to부정사를 목적어로 취하는 동사이다.
• look forward to의 to는 전치사로 뒤에 동명사가 와야 한다.

SELF NOTE p.48

A 핵심 포인트 정리하기
① 소유격, 목적격 ② having v-ed ③ 형용사
④ 동명사 ⑤ to부정사 ⑥ be used to, 동명사
⑦ be worth, 동명사

B 문제로 개념 다지기
1 X, not having visited 2 X, running 3 O
4 X, Not recycling[Not to recycle]
5 X, to taking 6 X, kept me from wasting

Chapter 04 분사 I

POINT 01 현재분사/과거분사   p.50

A   **1** locked   **2** named   **3** standing   **4** barking

     5 used   **6** repaired   **7** sitting   **8** broken

     9 walking   **10** made   **11** written   **12** leaving

B   **1** is ringing   **2** was built   **3** was burned[burnt]

     4 lost children[kids]   **5** shaking voice

     6 were invited

POINT 02 능동의 v-ing vs. 수동의 v-ed   p.51

A   **1** boring, bored   **2** confused, confusing

     3 disappointed, disappointing

     4 satisfying, satisfied   **5** exciting, excited

B   **1** amazing   **2** embarrassed   **3** depressing

     4 shocked   **5** tired

POINT 03 분사의 역할 I – 명사 수식   p.52

A   **1** hurt in the accident   **2** waiting for the bus

     3 sitting next to Julie   **4** parked outside

     5 taken by her husband

B   **1** Who is that smiling girl?

     2 He got an email written in English.

     3 She was surprised to see a broken window.

     4 Laura has a brother working in a bank.

     5 The people invited to the party didn't come.

     6 They have a painting painted by Picasso.

POINT 04 분사의 역할 II – 보어   p.53

A   **1** called   **2** tired   **3** cut   **4** boring

     5 interesting   **6** surprised   **7** closed

     8 depressed   **9** waving   **10** repaired

B   **1** looked disappointed

     2 had her tooth pulled out

     3 smelled, burning   **4** found, playing

     5 heard him calling[call]   **6** had, painted white

POINT 05 분사구문 만드는 법   p.54

A   **1** (Being) Tired   **2** Coming home

     3 Finding the keys   **4** Turning right

     5 Knowing them both   **6** Cooking his dinner

     7 (Being) Angry with me

B   **1** Saving   **2** Feeling hot   **3** Doing his homework

     4 remembering

POINT 06 분사구문의 의미 I – 때/이유   p.55

A   **1** watching TV   **2** (Being) Interested in pets

     3 finishing her work

B   **1** When he left home

     2 Because he was very sick

     3 While I was waiting[While I waited] for my

     homeroom teacher

C   **1** 그녀에게 이야기할 때, 나는 긴장했다.

     2 할 일이 너무 많았기 때문에, 그는 외출할 수 없었다.

     3 비용을 지불한 후에, 너는 영수증을 받아야 한다.

POINT 07 분사구문의 의미 II – 동시동작/연속상황   p.56

A   **1** Taking off his shoes   **2** Listening to music

     3 Putting on her swimming goggles

     4 Waving to the driver

B   **1** Opening the door, he walked in.

     2 Sitting on the sofa, I read a book.

     3 He sang a song, impressing everyone.

C   **1** 차에서 내리며, 그녀는 나에게 미소를 보냈다.

     2 야구를 하다가 그는 갑자기 어지러움을 느꼈다.

     3 그 기차는 5시에 출발해서 서울에 9시에 도착한다.

POINT 08 분사구문의 의미 III – 조건/양보   p.57

A   **1** Though driving a car

     2 Though breathing heavily

     3 Making a blog

     4 Though having a bicycle

     5 Though enjoying taking pictures

     6 Getting some fresh air

     7 Looking to your left

B 1 이 버스를 타면, 당신은 놀이공원에 가게 될 거예요.

2 나이가 나보다 어린데도, 그녀는 나의 언니인 것처럼 행동한다.

3 오른쪽으로 돌면, 당신의 왼편에 그 가게가 보일 거예요.

내신대비 TEST
p.58

01 ③ 02 ⑤ 03 ⑤ 04 ④ 05 ③ 06 ②
07 ② 08 ① 09 ① 10 ② 11 ④ 12 ②
13 ③ 14 ③ 15 ①, ④ 16 ④ 17 ④
18 ②, ④ 19 ⑤ 20 ⑤

서술형 따라잡기
p.61

01 Running along the river

02 (1) reading a[the] newspaper
　 (2) holding a[her / the] dog

03 (1) painting → painted
　 (2) Look → Looking / counts → counting

04 (1) Listening to classical music, she fell asleep.[She fell asleep listening to classical music.]
　 (2) There is a client waiting for you in the office.[There is a client in the office waiting for you.]

05 (1) moving (2) downloaded (3) Being bored

06 (1) I saw her crossing the road.
　 (2) Being thirsty, she drank a glass of water.

01 문맥상 Emily에게 '이야기하고 있는'의 의미로 the man을 수식하는 현재분사 talking이 와야 한다.

02 문맥상 '삶은' 계란을 먹었다는 의미가 되어야 하므로 과거분사 boiled가 와야 한다.

03 문맥상 이유를 나타내는 분사구문이 되어야 하므로 Walking이 와야 한다.

04 동사 had의 목적어인 her wallet은 '도난당한' 것이므로 목적격 보어 자리에 수동의 의미를 나타내는 과거분사 stolen을 쓴다.

05 첫 번째 빈칸에는 '표를 산 후에'라는 의미로 때를 나타내는 분사구문이 되어야 하므로 Buying이 알맞다. 두 번째 빈칸

에는 누군가가 Robert라고 '이름지어진' 것이므로 Some-body를 수식하는 분사로 수동의 의미를 나타내는 과거분사 named가 알맞다.

06 첫 번째 빈칸에는 The jazz concert가 감정을 유발하는 주체이므로 amazing이 와야 하고, 두 번째 빈칸에는 The teacher가 감정을 느끼는 주체이므로 satisfied가 와야 한다.

07 ②는 문장에서 주어로 쓰인 동명사인 반면, 나머지는 모두 분사구문을 이끄는 현재분사이다.

08 ①은 전치사의 목적어로 쓰인 동명사인 반면, 나머지는 모두 앞의 명사를 수식하는 현재분사이다.

09 이유를 나타내는 분사구문이므로, '~ 때문에'의 의미를 가진 접속사 As가 와야 한다.

10 조건을 나타내는 분사구문이므로, '~하면'의 의미를 가진 접속사 If가 와야 한다.

11 '가방을 내려놓은 후에'라는 의미로 때를 나타내는 분사구문이 되어야 하므로 접속사 After로 시작하는 문장이 와야 한다.

12 ②는 때를 나타내는 분사구문이다.

13 〈보기〉와 ③은 이유를 나타내는 분사구문이고, ①, ②, ④는 때나 동시동작을, ⑤는 조건을 나타내는 분사구문이다.

14 〈보기〉와 ③은 조건을 나타내는 분사구문이고, ①, ②는 이유를, ④, ⑤는 동시동작을 나타내는 분사구문이다.

15 ② day가 피로한 감정을 유발하는 주체이므로 현재분사 tiring이 와야 한다.
③ 목적어(us)가 감정을 느끼는 주체이므로, 목적격 보어 자리에 과거분사 annoyed가 와야 한다.
⑤ Jeremy가 감정을 느끼는 주체이므로 과거분사 interested가 와야 한다.

16 ④ 동시동작을 나타내는 분사구문이 되도록 Shaking이 와야 한다.

17 ④ 목적어(the information)가 혼란을 유발하는 주체이므로 목적격 보어 자리에 현재분사 confusing이 와야 한다.

18 우리말이 조건을 나타내고 있으므로, 분사구문이나 접속사 If로 시작하는 부사절이 올 수 있다.

19 ⑤ 분사구문을 부사절로 바꿀 때는 주절의 시제와 일치시켜야 하므로 eats는 ate가 되어야 한다.

20 (A) 문맥상 때를 나타내는 분사구문을 이끄는 Going이 와야 한다.
(B) The service는 감정을 유발하는 주체이므로, 현재분사

satisfying이 와야 한다.

(C) 목적어(me)가 감정을 느끼는 주체이므로, 목적격 보어 자리에 과거분사 depressed가 와야 한다.

서술형 따라잡기 -

01 접속사 및 주절의 주어와 같은 주어를 지우고, 동사를 v-ing 형태로 바꾼다.

02 동시동작을 나타내는 분사구문을 이용해 문장을 완성한다.

03 (1) 목적어 it(= a new house)은 '페인트칠 되는' 것이므로 목적격 보어 자리에 수동의 의미를 나타내는 과거분사 painted가 와야 한다.

(2) 문맥상 Look은 조건을 나타내는 분사구문을 이끌어야 하므로 분사 Looking으로 고친다. counts는 동시동작을 나타내는 분사구문을 이끌어야 하므로 counting으로 고친다.

04 (1) 동시동작을 나타내는 분사구문으로 쓴다.

(2) 분사(waiting)가 다른 수식어구와 함께 쓰이고 있으므로 a client를 뒤에서 수식하도록 배열한다.

05 (1) 목적어(the movie)가 감정을 유발하는 주체이므로 현재분사 moving을 쓴다.

(2) 동영상 파일은 '내려받아지는' 것이므로 목적격 보어로 과거분사 downloaded를 쓴다.

(3) 문맥상 이유를 나타내는 분사구문으로 쓴다.

06 (1) 목적어(her)가 길을 건너고 있는 것이므로 현재분사 crossing을 이용한다.

(2) 이유를 나타내는 분사구문으로 쓴다.

SELF NOTE p.62

A 핵심 포인트 정리하기
① 능동·진행 ② 수동태 ③ 수동 ④ 뒤
⑤ 이유 ⑥ ~하고 나서

B 문제로 개념 다지기
1 X, broken 2 X, carrying 3 X, embarrassed
4 O 5 X, Standing up
6 X, Though getting wet 7 O

Chapter 05 분사 II

POINT 01 분사구문의 부정 p.64

A 1 Not wanting to go there alone
2 Not getting enough sleep
3 Not having a car
4 Though not liking the food
5 Not having enough time
6 Not knowing the passcode
7 Not wanting to disturb others

B 1 Not feeling well   2 Not feeling hungry
3 Not having tickets   4 Not knowing where to go

POINT 02 완료 분사구문 p.65

A 1 Having forgotten his lines in the play
2 Having had great fun in Japan
3 As[Because/Since] I wrote an email to him
4 Having left home when she was young
5 Having left my cell phone at home
6 As[Because/Since] he studied history in university

B 1 Having lost   2 Having earned
3 Having grown up in   4 Not having graduated
5 Having listened to

POINT 03 being / having been의 생략 p.66

A 1 (Being) Surprised at the news
2 (Being) Confused
3 Though (having been) accepted by the university
4 (Having been) Given an invitation
5 (Being) Interested in photos

B 1 Asked   2 Satisfied with   3 Elected
4 Careful not   5 Not having warmed up

POINT 04 독립분사구문 p.67

A 1 The weather getting hotter
2 The rain being heavy

3 My brother having taken my car

4 It being my turn to sing

5 Nobody wanting to talk

6 There being no one in the office

B 1 The dog barking loudly

2 The traffic being bad

3 There being many people

4 The road being dark

5 The children taking a nap

POINT 05 비인칭 독립분사구문   p.68

A 1 Strictly speaking   2 Speaking of

3 Generally speaking   4 Roughly speaking

5 Taking everything into consideration

6 Considering

B 1 Strictly speaking   2 Generally speaking

3 Roughly speaking   4 Speaking of

5 Judging from   6 Frankly speaking

POINT 06 with+(대)명사+분사   p.69

A 1 with, turned   2 with her cat sitting

3 with her mother calling

4 with their fans waving

5 with his friends singing

B 1 with her clothes folded   2 with the taxi waiting

3 with the door closed

4 with the washing machine running

5 with my friends sitting

내신대비 TEST   p.70

01 ③   02 ②   03 ④   04 ④   05 ③   06 ②
07 ④   08 ②   09 ②   10 ①   11 ⑤   12 ⑤
13 ④   14 ③   15 ④   16 ③   17 ③   18 ⑤
19 ④   20 ②, ③, ⑤

서술형 따라잡기 ----------------------------- p.73

01 (1) (Being) Alone

(2) There being no subway station

02 Not having slept well

03 (1) with his eyes closed

(2) with her arms folded

04 Having fallen from the tree

05 (1) Having finished writing my essay

(2) Henry having come back from the trip

06 Walked → Walking

Buying → Having bought

having not → not having

01 부사절의 시제가 주절의 시제보다 앞선 경우에는 완료 분사구문 〈having+v-ed〉를 쓴다. 주절의 주어인 she가 많은 나라에서 '살았던' 것이므로 Having lived가 알맞다.

02 '몰라서'라는 의미의 이유를 나타내는 분사구문의 부정은 분사 앞에 not을 써서 Not knowing으로 나타낸다.

03 부사절의 주어가 주절의 주어와 다른 경우 주어를 생략하지 않고 분사 앞에 남겨둔다.

04 '~가 …된 채로'라는 의미의 〈with+명사+과거분사〉 구문이다.

05 speaking of: ~ 이야기가 나왔으니 말인데
generally speaking: 일반적으로 말해서

06 첫 번째 빈칸에는 '~가 …한 채로'라는 의미의 〈with+명사+현재분사〉 구문이므로 clapping이, 두 번째 빈칸에는 이유를 나타내는 분사구문으로 Being surprised가 와야 한다. 이때 Being은 생략이 가능하므로 Surprised가 적절하다.

07 첫 번째 빈칸에는 주절보다 이전에 일어난 일을 나타내는 완료 분사구문으로, 모든 돈이 '쓰인' 것이므로 having been spent가 와야 한다. 두 번째 빈칸에는 문맥상 '~을 고려하면'의 의미인 Considering이 적절하다.

08 첫 번째 빈칸에는 주절의 주어인 내가 물을 '마시는' 것이므로 Drinking이, 두 번째 빈칸에는 주절의 주어인 the book이 프랑스어로 '쓰인' 것이므로 Written이 적절하다. Written 앞에는 Being이 생략되었다.

09 분사구문의 부정은 분사 앞에 not이나 never를 써서 나타낸다.

10 주절보다 이전에 일어난 일을 나타내는 완료 분사구문으로 Having been born이 되어야 하지만, Having been은 생략이 가능하므로 Born이 적절하다.

11 ⑤ 주절보다 이전에 일어난 일을 나타내는 완료 분사구문으로

Having been이 되어야 한다.

12 ⑤ 주절의 시제보다 이전에 일어난 일을 나타내는 완료 분사구문으로 Having worked가 적절하다.

13 ④ 부사절의 주어가 주절의 주어와 다르므로 부사절의 주어 (The bus)를 생략하지 않고 분사 앞에 남겨두며, 부사절과 주절의 시제가 같으므로 부사절의 동사를 v-ing 형태로 바꾼다.

14 ③ '필요하지 않아서'라는 의미의 이유를 나타내는 분사구문은 접속사 Because로 시작하는 부사절로 바꿔 쓸 수 있다.

15 주절보다 이전에 일어난 일을 나타내는 완료 분사구문으로, 문맥상 '그 영화를 두 번 봤기 때문에'라는 의미가 되어야 하므로 ④가 적절하다.

16 (a) Considering: ~을 고려하면
(b) I가 감정을 느끼는 주체이므로 Being shocked가 와야 한다.

17 ③ 분사구문의 부정은 분사 앞에 not이나 never를 써서 나타내므로 Not having money가 되어야 한다.

18 ⑤ judging from: ~로 판단하건대

19 ④ 열심히 연습한 것은 완벽하게 연기하고 있는 것보다 이전의 일이므로 완료 분사구문인 Having practiced hard가 되어야 한다.

20 ① 〈with+(대)명사+분사〉 구문에서 명사(the candles)와 분사의 관계가 능동이므로 burning이 와야 한다.
④ Taking everything into consideration: 모든 것을 고려해 볼 때

서술형 따라잡기 --------------------------------

01 (1) 접속사 및 주절의 주어와 같은 부사절의 주어를 지우고, 부사절과 주절의 시제가 같으므로 was alone을 Being alone으로 고친다. 이때 Being은 생략이 가능하다.
(2) 접속사를 지우고, 부사절의 주어와 주절의 주어가 다르므로 주어 There는 분사 being 앞에 남겨둔다.

02 주절보다 이전에 일어난 일을 나타낼 때는 완료 분사구문 〈having+v-ed〉를 쓴다. 분사구문의 부정은 분사 앞에 Not을 써서 나타낸다.

03 '~가 …된 채로'라는 의미의 〈with+명사+과거분사〉 구문을 쓴다.

04 나무에서 떨어진 것은 병원에 입원한 것보다 이전의 일이므로 완료 분사구문인 Having fallen을 이용한다.

05 주절보다 이전의 일을 나타낼 때는 완료 분사구문

〈having+v-ed〉를 쓴다. 부사절의 주어가 주절의 주어와 다를 때는 분사 앞에 부사절의 주어를 남겨둔다.

06 주어인 I가 걷고 있었던 것이므로 Walked는 Walking으로 고친다. 스마트폰을 산 것은 주절의 시점보다 이전의 일이므로 Buying은 Having bought로 고친다. 분사구문의 부정은 분사 앞에 not을 붙여 나타내므로, having not을 not having으로 고친다.

SELF NOTE ◀   p.74

A 핵심 포인트 정리하기
① not/never ② having, 과거분사(v-ed)
③ being/having been ④ Judging from
⑤ Generally speaking ⑥ 현재분사 ⑦ 과거분사

B 문제로 개념 다지기
1 X, Not knowing
2 X, The flight having been delayed
3 X, Having failed 4 O 5 X, Disappointed
6 O 7 X, Judging from his tone of voice
8 X, with the crowd cheering

Chapter 06 시제

POINT 01 현재완료의 계속 / 경험 용법　　p.76

A 1 have never driven　2 has taken
　3 have visited　4 has seen

B 1 has rained　2 have met him
　3 have loved you　4 Have you, won

C 1 Cindy는 2주째 계속 아프다.
　2 너는 전에 롤러코스터를 타 본 적이 있니?
　3 나는 7살 이래로 발레를 춰 오고 있다.

POINT 02 현재완료의 완료 / 결과 용법　　p.77

A 1 has been to　2 has lost
　3 have not[haven't] decided

B 1 hasn't sent　2 has just ended　3 have had
　4 has already arrived　5 has bought
　6 has improved

POINT 03 현재완료 진행형　　p.78

A 1 have been cleaning the house
　2 has been ringing　3 has been staying
　4 has been doing his homework
　5 has been driving

B 1 have, been working　2 have been writing
　3 has been talking　4 have been walking
　5 has been teaching English
　6 has been waiting for

POINT 04 과거완료의 계속 / 경험 용법　　p.79

A 1 has tried　2 had been　3 had never read
　4 had known　5 has taught　6 Had Sarah won

B 1 had practiced　2 had never read
　3 had never been　4 had seen
　5 had been　6 had had few friends

POINT 05 과거완료의 완료 / 결과 용법　　p.80

A 1 had left　2 has been　3 had broken

　4 quit　5 had already cleaned

B 1 He had hurt his leg a month before
　2 I had left my bag at home
　3 When the man had finished playing
　4 Ann had already left
　5 she had already ordered her food

POINT 06 과거완료 진행형　　p.81

A 1 had been raining　2 had been watching
　3 had been playing　4 had been reading
　5 had been chatting

B 1 had been snowing　2 has never[not] been
　3 had gone　4 had been shouting
　5 had been walking　6 had been waiting
　7 had been sleeping

내신대비 TEST　　p.82

01 ①　02 ③　03 ②　04 ③　05 ④　06 ②
07 ⑤　08 ④　09 ③　10 ①　11 ②　12 ④
13 ⑤　14 ①　15 ⑤　16 ⑤　17 ④　18 ⑤
19 ③　20 ④

서술형 따라잡기　　p.85

01 (1) has gone　(2) has been coughing
02 (1) Have you finished reading the book?
　(2) She had never swum until she was
　　twelve.
03 (1) has been playing　(2) had been raining
04 How long have, known
05 (1) have had a baseball game　(2) have won
06 had never been → have never been / have
　heard → heard / watched → have been
　watching[have watched]

01 문맥상 경험을 나타내는 현재완료를 써야 한다.
02 문맥상 계속을 나타내는 과거완료 진행형을 써야 한다.
03 문맥상 계속을 나타내는 현재완료를 써야 한다.
04 계속을 나타내는 현재완료나 현재완료 진행형 문장에서 동작이

나 상태가 시작된 시점 앞에 since를 쓴다.

05 첫 번째 빈칸에는 과거 이전부터 과거의 어느 시점까지 계속 아팠던 것이므로 과거완료를, 두 번째 빈칸에는 과거 이전부터 과거의 어느 시점까지의 경험을 나타내므로 과거완료를 쓴다.

06 첫 번째 빈칸에는 과거 이전부터 과거의 어느 시점까지의 경험을 나타내므로 과거완료를, 두 번째 빈칸에는 과거보다 이전에 일어난 일을 나타내는 대과거를 써야 하므로 had visited가 와야 한다.

07 과거부터 현재까지 얼마나 오랫동안 이곳에서 일해오고 있는지 묻고 답하는 대화로 현재완료 또는 현재완료 진행형을 이용한다.

08 내가 문을 열기 이전부터 그는 계속 컴퓨터 게임을 하고 있었으므로 종속절에는 과거, 주절에는 과거완료 진행형을 쓴다.

09 ③ 과거부터 현재까지 얼마나 오랫동안 TV를 보고 있었는지 묻고 있으므로 현재완료 진행형이나 현재완료가 되어야 한다. 따라서 빈칸에는 been watching이나 watched가 와야 한다.

10 ①은 현재완료의 경험을 나타내고, 나머지는 모두 현재완료의 계속을 나타낸다.

11 ②는 현재완료의 결과를 나타내고, 나머지는 모두 현재완료의 완료를 나타낸다.

12 ④는 과거완료의 완료를 나타내고, 나머지는 모두 과거완료의 경험을 나타낸다.

13 ⑤ 과거부터 현재까지 계속 진행 중인 일을 나타내므로 현재완료 진행형인 have been sleeping으로 쓴다.

14 ① 과거 이전에 시작된 일이 과거의 어느 시점에 막 완료되었음을 나타내므로, 완료를 나타내는 과거완료를 쓴다.

15 과거부터 현재까지 계속 진행 중인 일을 나타내므로 현재완료 진행형을 쓴다.

16 ⑤에는 과거부터 현재까지 계속되어 온 일을 나타내는 현재완료 have been이 오는 반면, 나머지에는 과거의 어느 시점 이전의 일을 나타내는 과거완료나 과거완료 진행형을 만드는 had been이 온다. ②, ③은 before 등의 접속사와 함께 쓰여 시간의 전후 관계가 비교적 분명하므로 과거진행형을 만드는 was도 올 수 있다.

17 ④ 과거 어느 특정 시점보다 이전의 일을 이야기하고 있으므로 과거완료 hadn't had가 와야 한다.

18 ⑤ 과거 이전의 일을 이야기하는 과거완료 had finished가 와야 한다. 접속사 after와 함께 쓰여 시간의 전후 관계가 분명하므로 과거시제인 finished도 올 수 있다.

19 ③ 과거부터 현재까지 계속 진행 중인 일이 무엇인지 묻고 있으므로 현재완료 진행형으로 답해야 한다.

20 (a) yesterday와 같이 특정 과거 시점을 나타내는 말은 과거 시제에 쓴다.

서술형 따라잡기

01 (1) 문맥상 결과를 나타내는 현재완료를 써야 한다.
  (2) 문맥상 계속을 나타내는 현재완료 진행형을 써야 한다.

02 (1) 과거에 시작된 일이 현재에 완료되었음을 나타내므로 현재완료를 쓴다. 현재완료의 의문문은 〈Have+주어+v-ed ~?〉의 어순으로 쓴다.
  (2) 과거 이전부터 과거까지의 경험을 나타내므로 주절에는 과거완료를, 종속절에는 과거시제를 쓴다.

03 (1) 과거에 시작된 일이 현재에도 계속 진행 중임을 나타내므로 현재완료 진행형을 쓴다.
  (2) 과거 이전에 시작된 일이 과거에도 진행 중임을 나타내는 과거완료 진행형을 쓴다.

04 B가 현재완료로 Jessie를 알아온 기간을 이야기하고 있으므로, 의문사 how long과 현재완료를 이용해 〈How long +have+주어+v-ed ~?〉의 어순으로 질문을 완성한다.

05 (1) Bears는 수요일부터 오늘까지 매일 경기를 했으므로 현재완료를 쓴다.
  (2) Bears는 지난 두 경기 연속 승리를 했으므로 현재완료를 쓴다.

06 문맥상 '(과거부터 현재까지) 다녀온 적이 없다'가 되어야 하므로 had never been을 have never been으로 고친다. yesterday라는 과거를 나타내는 부사가 있으므로 have heard는 heard가 되어야 한다. watched는 과거부터 현재까지 계속되고 있는 일을 나타내는 현재완료 have watched나 현재완료 진행형 have been watching으로 써야 한다.

SELF NOTE   p.86

A 핵심 포인트 정리하기
① have[has], v-ed ② had, v-ed ③ ~한 적이 있다
④ 벌써/이미/막 ~했다 ⑤ have[has], been, v-ing
⑥ had, been, v-ing

B 문제로 개념 다지기
1 X, have been 2 X, have not seen 3 O 4 O
5 X, had just finished

Chapter 07 수동태

POINT 01 수동태의 의미   p.88

A 1 wasn't[was not] called by his friends
   2 will be opened to the public (by them)
   3 were baked in the oven
   4 is offered to all employees
   5 is usually used as a camera (by people)

B 1 will be served   2 Is, owned
   3 will be cleaned   4 will be delivered
   5 was produced

POINT 02 수동태의 형태   p.89

A 1 is being examined   2 have been used
   3 should be repeated

B 1 Our proposal may be accepted by the school.
   2 His birthday must not be forgotten again by us.
   3 Sand castles were being built on the beach by the kids.

C 1 can be eaten   2 has been treated
   3 is being asked   4 should be taken

POINT 03 4형식 문장의 수동태   p.90

A 1 → were given an impressive lesson in Korean history class by Mrs. Park
     → was given to us in Korean history class by Mrs. Park
   2 → were told an interesting story by the man
     → was told to the children by the man
   3 → was handed my travel schedule by my secretary
     → was handed to me by my secretary

B 1 were sent to her   2 was made for him
   3 were shown to Mark   4 was given to me
   5 was bought for Julie

POINT 04 5형식 문장의 수동태 I   p.91

A 1 The boy is considered clever (by everyone).

2 The baby tigers were kept warm by the zookeeper.
3 He was found to be satisfied with the results by Serena.
4 The man was asked to empty all the boxes by them.
5 We were told not to make noise during the test by the teacher.

B 1 considered him an expert
   → He was considered an expert (by people).
   2 allowed me to travel
   → I was allowed to travel by my parents.
   3 advised me to take a taxi
   → I was advised to take a taxi by her.
   4 asked me to tell a scary story
   → I was asked to tell a scary story by the children.

POINT 05 5형식 문장의 수동태 II   p.92

A 1 made to wear
   2 heard to whisper[whispering]
   3 seen to jog[jogging]
   4 was seen to enter[entering]

B 1 The couple was seen holding hands by her.
   2 I am[I'm] always made to clean my room by my mom.
   3 The people were seen to cheer for the baseball team by a reporter.

C 1 He was made to stay
   2 They were heard talking
   3 She was seen to carry
   4 was heard crying

POINT 06 주의해야 하는 수동태 I
– by 이외의 전치사를 쓰는 수동태   p.93

A 1 am worried about   2 was surprised at
   3 were known to   4 was crowded with
   5 is filled with

B 1 am satisfied with   2 is made of

3 was covered with[in]   4 interested in

A 1 (turned off), was turned off by my father
  2 (found out), was found out by Mr. Kim
  3 (look up to), are looked up to by many people

B 1 I closely resemble my grandmother.
  2 The report was handed in this morning.
  3 Beyonce's concert was sold out in a day.

C 1 The baby was taken care of by Kelly.
  2 The school trip to Taiwan was called off by
    the principal.
  3 His strange hat is laughed at all the time by
    the kids.

A 1 are thought to be very sensitive
  2 is believed to determine personality
  3 is reported to be effective for losing weight

B 1 is thought that Mr. Kang is humorous
  2 is reported that flowers will begin to bloom
    earlier than last year
  3 is said that he won the medal to please his
    sick mother

C 1 is said to help   2 It is believed that
  3 was reported to increase

내신대비 TEST   p.96

01 ①	02 ④	03 ②	04 ②, ③	05 ④	06 ③
07 ④	08 ③	09 ④	10 ⑤	11 ②	12 ③
13 ②	14 ③	15 ④	16 ⑤	17 ①, ②, ⑤	
18 ①	19 ②	20 ⑤			

서술형 따라잡기 ------------------------- p.99

01 (1) was bought for me by my mom
   (2) will be fixed by tomorrow by him
02 (1) Luggage should be sent to the ship.
   (2) Your coat is being washed now.

03 (1) The house is being painted by John.
   (2) The bookshelf will be filled with books
       by Holly.
04 She was helped out
05 (1) to be looking for a new member
   (2) is reported to be preparing a special
       lunch today
   (3) that a pop singer is coming to our
       school festival
06 have just been arrived → have just arrived /
   deliver → to deliver / by → about

01 현재완료형 수동태는 〈have[has]+been+v-ed〉의 형태
   이다.
02 미래시제의 수동태는 〈will+be+v-ed〉의 형태이다.
03 be covered with: ~로 덮여 있다
04 문장의 동사가 say일 때 〈It is+v-ed that …〉 형태의 수동
   태 문장을 만들 수 있다. 또한 that절의 주어를 수동태 문장의
   주어로 할 때는 that절의 동사가 to부정사로 바뀐다.
05 Mark에 의해 이 슬라이드 쇼가 '보여질' 것이므로 첫 번째 빈
   칸에는 be presented가 와야 한다. 소포가 어제 나에게 '배
   송된' 것이고, 4형식 동사 deliver가 직접목적어를 주어로 하
   는 수동태 문장에서는 간접목적어 앞에 전치사 to를 써야 하므
   로 두 번째 빈칸에는 was delivered to가 적절하다.
06 첫 번째 빈칸에는 내가 '꾸지람을 듣는' 것이므로 전치사 of 뒤
   에 동명사의 수동태인 being scolded를 쓴다. 동사 suit는
   수동태로 쓸 수 없는 동사이므로 두 번째 빈칸에는 suits가 알
   맞다.
07 내가 '존경을 받는' 것을 좋아한다는 의미가 되어야 하므로 첫
   번째 빈칸에는 동명사의 수동태인 being respected를 쓴
   다. 그가 득점하는 것이 '예상된다'라는 의미가 되어야 하므로
   두 번째 빈칸에는 수동태인 is expected가 와야 한다.
08 5형식 문장의 수동태에서는 동사를 〈be+v-ed〉의 형태로 바
   꾸고 목적격 보어는 동사 뒤에 그대로 쓴다.
09 지각동사(see)의 목적격 보어가 현재분사인 경우, 수동태에서
   도 현재분사를 그대로 둔다.
10 ⑤ 콩이 암을 예방한다고 '보도되는' 것이므로 are reported
   to prevent가 되어야 한다.

11 ② '준비되고 있다'라는 의미가 되어야 하므로 진행형의 수동태인 is being prepared가 되어야 한다.

12 ③ 별은 '보일' 수 있는 것이므로 can be seen이 되어야 한다.

13 ② 사역동사(make)의 목적격 보어가 원형부정사인 경우, 수동태 문장에서 to부정사로 바뀐다. 따라서 made eat은 made to eat이 되어야 한다.

14 ③ 미래시제의 수동태는 〈will+be+v-ed〉의 형태로 쓴다.

15 ④ 동사 believe의 목적어로 쓰인 that절의 주어가 수동태 문장의 주어로 쓰일 때, that절의 동사는 to부정사로 바뀐다. 따라서 study는 to study가 되어야 한다.

16 (A) 5형식 문장에서 목적격 보어로 쓰인 to부정사는 수동태가 되어도 그 형태가 변하지 않는다.
(B) 수프는 '데워지고 있는' 것이므로 진행형의 수동태인 is being heated가 알맞다.
(C) be pleased with: ~로 즐거워하다

17 ③ 동사 resemble은 수동태로 쓸 수 없는 동사이므로, I resemble my mother.로 써야 한다.
④ 5형식 문장에서 목적격 보어로 쓰인 to부정사는 수동태가 되어도 그 형태가 변하지 않는다. 따라서 helping은 to help가 되어야 한다.

18 (a) be filled with: ~로 가득 차다
(b) be made from: ~로 만들어지다(화학적 변화)
(c) be worried about: ~에 대해 걱정하다
(d) be interested in: ~에 관심이 있다

19 ② 사역동사(make)의 목적격 보어로 쓰인 원형부정사는 수동태 문장에서 to부정사로 바뀐다. 따라서 made to focus on이 되어야 한다.

20 ⑤ be crowded with: ~로 붐비다

서술형 따라잡기 -

01 (1) 4형식 동사 buy의 직접목적어를 주어로 해서 수동태 문장을 만들 때, 간접목적어 앞에는 전치사 for를 쓴다.
(2) 미래시제의 수동태는 〈will+be+v-ed〉의 형태이다.

02 (1) 조동사의 수동태는 〈조동사+be+v-ed〉의 형태이다.
(2) 진행형의 수동태는 〈be동사+being+v-ed〉의 형태이다.

03 (1) 집이 칠해지고 있으므로 진행형의 수동태를 쓴다.
(2) 책장이 책으로 가득 찰 것이므로 미래시제의 수동태를 쓴다.

04 동사구(help out)의 수동태에서는 동사만 〈be+v-ed〉의 형태로 바꾸고, 동사구에 포함된 부사나 전치사는 그대로 쓴다.

05 문장의 동사가 report일 때 〈It is reported that …〉 형태의 수동태가 가능하다. 또한 that절의 주어를 수동태 문장의 주어로 쓸 수 있는데, 이때 that절의 동사는 to부정사로 바뀐다.

06 arrive는 목적어가 필요 없는 동사이고 내가 '도착한' 것이므로 have just been arrived는 능동태인 have just arrived가 되어야 한다. 5형식 문장에서 목적격 보어로 쓰인 to부정사는 수동태가 되어도 그 형태가 변하지 않으므로 was told 뒤의 deliver는 to deliver로 고쳐야 한다. 동사 worry는 수동태가 되면 행위자를 나타낼 때 전치사 by 대신 about을 쓴다.

SELF NOTE   p.100

A 핵심 포인트 정리하기
① be동사, v-ed ② was/were, v-ed
③ will, be, v-ed ④ been ⑤ being ⑥ be
⑦ to ⑧ to부정사 ⑨ to부정사
⑩ be satisfied with ⑪ to부정사

B 문제로 개념 다지기
1 X, to bark[barking] 2 X, is being made
3 X, taken care of by experts 4 O
5 X, be given 6 X, to mean

Chapter 08 조동사

3 must have missed

4 should not have studied

5 may[might] have checked in

01 ④	02 ②	03 ④	04 ①	05 ⑤	06 ④
07 ①	08 ③	09 ⑤	10 ①	11 ③	12 ⑤
13 ②	14 ③	15 ②	16 ①	17 ⑤	18 ③
19 ④	20 ②, ⑤				

서술형 따라잡기 ----------------------- p.113

01 (1) used to be (2) had to look after

02 (1) He will be able to come back to Seoul.

(2) I would rather not join the debate club.

03 (1) should have studied

(2) can't have cleaned

04 (1) used to have curly hair

(2) used to drive a car

05 (1) not eat too much junk food

(2) help her mom prepare dinner

06 had not better → had better not /

must have checked → should have checked

01 '~일지도 모른다'라는 의미의 may를 쓴다.

02 '~할 필요가 없다'는 don't have to를 써서 표현한다.

03 '~하는 게 좋겠다'는 had better를 써서 표현한다.
had better의 부정형은 had better not이다.

04 '~임이 틀림없다'로 강한 추측을 나타낼 때는 must를 쓴다.

05 과거의 일에 대한 후회를 나타내므로 '~했어야 했다'라는 의미의 〈should+have+v-ed〉를 쓴다.

06 '~하곤 했다'로 과거의 습관을 나타낼 때는 조동사 would나 used to를 쓴다.

07 '~했을지도 모른다'라는 의미의 〈may+have+v-ed〉를 쓰는 것이 알맞다.

08 'B하느니 차라리 A하겠다'는 would rather A than B로 나타내므로 첫 번째 빈칸에는 would rather가 알맞다. 두 번째 빈칸에는 '~일 리가 없다'라는 의미의 cannot이 와야 한다.

09 첫 번째 빈칸에는 '~할 필요가 없다'라는 의미의 don't have

to가 와야 한다. 두 번째 빈칸에는 '~이었음이 틀림없다'라는 의미의 〈must+have+v-ed〉가 와야 한다.

10 첫 번째 빈칸에는 '~했어야 했다'라는 의미의 〈should+have +v-ed〉 중 should가, 두 번째 빈칸에는 '(마땅히) ~해야 한다'라는 의미의 should가 와야 한다.

11 주절의 시제가 과거이므로 첫 번째 빈칸에는 will의 과거형인 would가, 두 번째 빈칸에는 'B하느니 차라리 A하겠다'의 would rather A than B 중 would가 와야 한다.

12 '~했어야 했다'는 〈should+have+v-ed〉를 써서 표현한다.

13 ②의 may는 약한 추측을 나타내고, 나머지는 모두 허가의 의미를 나타낸다.

14 ③의 must는 의무를 나타내고, 나머지는 모두 강한 추측을 나타낸다.

15 ② '~일 리가 없다'라는 의미의 부정적 추측은 cannot을 써서 표현한다.

16 ① 그녀가 책상에서 잠들었다는 문장 뒤에 그녀가 업무로 인해 피곤했을 리가 없다는 내용은 어울리지 않는다. '~했을지도 모른다'라는 의미의 〈may+have+v-ed〉나 '~이었음이 틀림 없다'라는 의미의 〈must+have+v-ed〉 등을 쓰는 것이 알 맞다.

17 ⑤ 과거를 나타내는 부사 yesterday가 있으므로 과거의 필요·의무를 나타내는 had to를 써야 한다.

18 ③ had better 뒤에는 동사원형이 오므로 to use를 use로 고쳐야 한다.

19 ④ 앞으로의 가능성을 묻는 질문에 '~이었을 리가 없다'라며 과거의 일에 대한 강한 의심을 나타내는 답변은 어울리지 않는다.

20 ① would rather 뒤에는 동사원형이 오므로 to teach를 teach로 고쳐야 한다.

③ ought to의 부정형은 ought not to이다.

④ 과거의 상태를 나타낼 때는 used to를 쓴다. would는 과거의 습관을 나타낸다.

서술형 따라잡기 --------------------------------

01 (1) '~이었다'로 과거의 상태를 나타낼 때는 used to를 쓴다.
(2) 과거의 필요·의무를 나타낼 때는 had to를 쓴다.

02 (1) 조동사 will과 can을 연이어 쓸 수 없으므로 can 대신 be able to를 쓴다.
(2) would rather의 부정형은 would rather not이다.

03 (1) '~했어야 했다'의 〈should+have+v-ed〉가 와야 한다.

(2) '~이었을 리가 없다'의 〈can't+have+v-ed〉가 와야 한다.

04 과거의 상태나 습관을 나타낼 때는 used to를 쓴다.

05 '~하는 게 좋겠다'는 had better를 써서 표현하고, had better 뒤에는 동사원형을 쓴다. had better의 부정형은 had better not이다.

06 had better의 부정형은 had better not이다.
문맥상 일기예보를 '확인했어야 했는데'가 되어야 하므로 must have checked를 should have checked로 고쳐야 한다.

Chapter 09 가정법

POINT 04 I wish+가정법 과거완료   p.119

A   1 had gotten   2 had been   3 were

B   1 he had listened to the doctor's advice

    2 my mother had bought me a new jacket

    3 my school had not[hadn't] canceled its plan to build a gym

C   1 she had gone shopping

    2 I had made a reservation

    3 I had not told him

POINT 05 as if+가정법 과거   p.120

A   1 it were Christmas   2 she were angry

    3 he knew my brother   4 he were a doctor

    5 I were a child

B   1 as if it were my fault

    2 as if she were a model

    3 as if he owned this house

    4 as if he knew everything

    5 as if they were athletes

POINT 06 as if+가정법 과거완료   p.121

A   1 he had seen me

    2 he had been in a fight

    3 he had been in New York

    4 she had not[hadn't] liked my present

    5 he had paid for your lunch

B   1 as if he had been crying

    2 as if she had lived in China

    3 as if she had visited Paris

    4 as if he had won the game[match]

POINT 07 Without[But for] ～+가정법 과거   p.122

A   1 Without air   2 Without the bus

    3 But for your jokes

B   1 If it were not for the map application, I could not find my way around the city.

    2 If it were not for my alarm clock, I could not wake up early in the morning.

    3 If it were not for the Internet, we could not get information quickly.

C   1 If it were not for water, no one could survive.

    2 Without Betty, we could not win our soccer games.

POINT 08 Without[But for] ～+가정법 과거완료   p.123

A   1 not have finished this project

    2 not have tried it   3 have gotten[got] lost

B   1 If it had not been for your reminder, I could not have remembered his birthday.

    2 If it had not been for Jamie, I would not have enjoyed going to school.

C   1 Without a personal trainer, I couldn't have lost weight.

    2 But for your help, I might have failed the exam.

내신대비 TEST   p.124

01 ③   02 ②   03 ②   04 ④   05 ③   06 ⑤

07 ⑤   08 ④   09 ③   10 ①   11 ④   12 ④

13 ③   14 ④   15 ③   16 ②   17 ⑤   18 ④

19 ⑤   20 ①, ②, ③

서술형 따라잡기 - p.127

01 (1) would have played basketball

    (2) could not have graduated

02 (1) had a kite, fly

    (2) didn't have an umbrella, get wet

03 Without[But for] this boat

04 Lucy acted as if nothing had happened.

05 (1) had finished, would have gone

    (2) it had not been for, would have spent

06 (1) I wish they had fixed my smartphone.

    (2) If we had closed the window, we would not be cold now.

01 가정법 과거 문장에서 if절의 be동사는 주어의 인칭과 수에 상관없이 were를 쓴다.

02 가정법 과거완료 문장에서 if절의 동사는 〈had v-ed〉를 쓴다.

03 주절의 시제와 같은 시점의 상황을 반대로 가정할 때 〈as if+가정법 과거〉를 쓴다.

04 주절의 시제보다 앞선 시점의 상황을 반대로 가정할 때 〈as if+가정법 과거완료〉를 쓴다.

05 현재는 이루기 어려운 소망을 나타낼 때 〈I wish+가정법 과거〉를 쓴다.

06 과거 사실과 반대되는 상황을 가정하는 가정법 과거완료 〈If+주어+had v-ed ~, 주어+조동사의 과거형+have v-ed …〉를 쓴다.

07 과거에 실현되지 못한 일이 현재까지 영향을 미치는 상황을 가정하는 혼합 가정법 〈If+주어+had v-ed ~, 주어+조동사의 과거형+동사원형 …〉을 쓴다.

08 현재는 이루기 어려운 소망을 나타낼 때 〈I wish+가정법 과거〉를 쓴다.

09 첫 번째 빈칸에는 주절의 시제와 같은 시점의 상황을 반대로 가정하는 〈as if+가정법 과거〉가 와야 한다. 두 번째 빈칸에는 과거에 실현되지 못한 일이 현재까지 영향을 미치는 상황을 가정하는 혼합 가정법 〈If+주어+had v-ed ~, 주어+조동사의 과거형+동사원형 …〉이 와야 한다.

10 첫 번째 빈칸에는 현재는 이루기 어려운 소망을 나타내는 〈I wish+가정법 과거〉가 와야 한다. 두 번째 빈칸에는 과거 사실과 반대되는 상황을 가정하는 가정법 과거완료가 와야 한다.

11 첫 번째 빈칸에는 주절의 시제보다 앞선 시점의 상황을 반대로 가정하는 〈as if+가정법 과거완료〉가, 두 번째 빈칸에는 과거 사실과 반대되는 상황을 가정하는 가정법 과거완료가 와야 한다.

12 과거에 있었던 것이 없었다고 가정하는 〈Without ~+가정법 과거완료〉에서 Without은 If it had not been for ~로 바꾸어 쓸 수 있다.

13 문맥상 주절의 시제보다 앞선 시점의 상황을 반대로 가정하는 〈as if+가정법 과거완료〉가 와야 한다.

14 과거에 이루지 못한 일에 대한 소망이나 아쉬움을 나타낼 때 사용하는 〈I wish+가정법 과거완료〉가 와야 한다.

15 ③ 과거에 실현되지 못한 일이 현재까지 영향을 미치는 상황을 가정하는 혼합 가정법 〈If+주어+had v-ed ~, 주어+조동사의 과거형+동사원형 …〉이 와야 한다.

16 ② 주절의 시제와 같은 시점의 상황을 반대로 가정하는 〈as if+가정법 과거〉가 와야 한다.

17 ① 주절의 시제와 같은 시점의 상황을 반대로 가정하는 〈as if+가정법 과거〉나 주절의 시제보다 앞선 시점의 상황을 반대로 가정하는 〈as if+가정법 과거완료〉가 되어야 하므로 has been을 were 또는 had been으로 고쳐야 한다.
② 현재 사실과 반대되거나 실현 가능성이 희박한 일을 가정하는 가정법 과거 문장이 되어야 하므로 can see를 could see로 고쳐야 한다.
③ 과거에 이루지 못한 일에 대한 소망이나 아쉬움을 나타내는 〈I wish+가정법 과거완료〉 문장이 되어야 하므로 bought를 had bought로 고쳐야 한다.
④ 현재 사실과 반대되거나 실현 가능성이 희박한 일을 가정하는 가정법 과거 문장이 되어야 하므로 will take를 would take로 고쳐야 한다.

18 ④ 가정법 과거완료 문장이므로 would go는 would have gone으로 써야 한다.

19 ⑤ had를 had had로 바꾸어 가정법 과거완료로 표현하거나, could have bought를 could buy로 바꾸어 가정법 과거로 표현한다.

20 ④ knew를 had known으로 바꾸어 가정법 과거완료 문장으로 만들거나, would have called를 would call로 바꾸어 가정법 과거 문장으로 만들어야 한다.
⑤ 〈But for ~+가정법〉 문장으로 didn't know는 would not know 혹은 would not have known이 되어야 한다.

서술형 따라잡기 -

01 (1) 과거 사실과 반대되는 상황을 가정하는 가정법 과거완료를 쓴다.
(2) 과거에 있었던 것이 없었다고 가정할 때는 〈Without+가정법 과거완료〉를 쓴다.

02 현재 사실과 반대되거나 실현 가능성이 희박한 일을 가정하는 가정법 과거를 쓴다.

03 If it had not been for는 Without 혹은 But for로 바꾸어 쓸 수 있다.

04 주절의 시제보다 앞선 시점의 상황을 반대로 가정하는 〈as if+가정법 과거완료〉를 쓴다.

05 과거 사실과 반대되는 상황을 가정하는 가정법 과거완료를 쓴다.

06 (1) 과거에 이루지 못한 일에 대한 소망이나 아쉬움을 나타내는 〈I wish+가정법 과거완료〉를 쓴다.
(2) 과거에 실현되지 못한 일이 현재까지 영향을 미치는 상황을 가정하는 혼합 가정법 〈If+주어+had v-ed ~, 주어+조동사

의 과거형+동사원형 …)을 쓴다.

SELF NOTE   p.128

A 핵심 포인트 정리하기

① 동사의 과거형 ② 조동사의 과거형, 동사원형

③ had v-ed ④ 조동사의 과거형, have v-ed

⑤ had v-ed ⑥ 조동사의 과거형, 동사원형

⑦ ~했더라면 좋을 텐데 ⑧ as if ⑨ Without

B 문제로 개념 다지기

1 O 2 X, If it had not been for 3 X, drove

4 X, had already lost

5 X, could not have opened

Chapter 10 접속사

POINT 01 시간, 이유를 나타내는 종속 접속사 I
– when / while / as / since   p.130

A 1 since 2 while 3 As 4 When

B 1 while you were taking a shower

  2 As he went up higher

  3 since she moved to

POINT 02 시간, 이유를 나타내는 종속 접속사 II
– until[till] / every time / as soon as   p.131

A 1 since 2 Every[Each] time 3 until[till]

  4 As soon as

B 1 On[Upon] lying down 2 until[till], went off

  3 Every[Each] time he goes

  4 until[till] the delivery man comes

  5 Whenever I take an umbrella

  6 As soon as, got off

POINT 03 조건을 나타내는 종속 접속사 – if / unless   p.132

A 1 Unless I write it down, I'll forget about it.

  2 If you don't wear a coat, you'll catch a cold.

  3 Unless you have a receipt, we can't give you a refund.

B 1 O 2 X, will arrive → arrives

  3 X, supports → will support

C 1 Unless it rains 2 If she tells

  3 Unless he needs money 4 If you visit

POINT 04 양보를 나타내는 종속 접속사
– though / even though / even if   p.133

A 1 Even though 2 even if 3 If 4 Even though

B 1 Even if you are busy

  2 Even though the cake looked awful

  3 Although I don't like him

  4 Even if it was your fault

POINT 05 결과, 목적을 나타내는 종속 접속사 – so ~ that … / so that ~ p.134

A 1 so cold that we stayed
2 so that I can travel abroad
3 so quickly that, understand
4 so that I can talk

B 1 so angry that I want to run out of here
2 so hungry that she decided to make some snacks
3 the TV so that he could focus on his studying
4 in order that we can have a better life

POINT 06 상관 접속사 I – both A and B / not only A but also B p.135

A 1 both, and   2 as well as
3 both, and   4 not only, but also

B 1 was → were   2 like → likes   3 were → was

C 1 not only, but also   2 both, and
3 not only, but also   4 as well as

POINT 07 상관 접속사 II – either A or B / neither A nor B p.136

A 1 wears   2 but   3 is   4 and   5 either

B 1 Either, or   2 neither, nor   3 either, or

C 1 neither smokes nor drinks
2 neither exciting nor successful
3 either take a bus or walk
4 neither looked at me nor talked to me

POINT 08 명령문+and / 명령문+or p.137

A 1 and   2 or   3 and   4 or

B 1 Come to the party, and you will see him.
2 Give it a try, or you will regret it later.
3 Read this article, and you'll understand my point of view.
4 Go to bed early, or you'll wake up late tomorrow.
5 Fasten your seat belt, and you'll have a safe flight.

C 1 이 약을 먹어라, 그러면 너는 나아질 것이다.
2 그의 생일을 축하해 주어라, 그러면 그가 기뻐할 것이다.
3 너무 많이 먹지 마라, 그러지 않으면 너는 배가 아플 것이다.

내신대비 TEST p.138

01 ⑤   02 ①   03 ⑤   04 ④   05 ②   06 ④
07 ③   08 ④   09 ②   10 ①   11 ⑤   12 ③
13 ②   14 ②   15 ①   16 ③   17 ⑤   18 ③
19 ④   20 ②

서술형 따라잡기 ----------------------------------- p.141

01 (1) On[Upon] getting   (2) Every[Each] time
02 He writes poems as well as novels.
03 (1) so that he could pass the test
(2) or, forget to buy something
04 (1) both fruit and vegetables
(2) neither run nor ride a bike
05 (1) The TV show was so boring that Dad turned off the TV.
(2) Mike is boiling water so that he can cook some noodles.
06 and → or / will return → return / or → nor

01 문맥상 '~ 때문에'의 의미인 종속 접속사 as가 와야 한다.
02 문맥상 '비록 ~이지만'의 의미인 종속 접속사 Though가 와야 한다.
03 'A도 B도 아닌'의 의미인 상관 접속사 〈neither A nor B〉를 쓴다.
04 첫 번째 빈칸에는 '~ 이래로', 두 번째 빈칸에는 '~ 때문에'의 의미인 종속 접속사 since가 와야 한다.
05 첫 번째 빈칸에는 'A와 B 중 하나'의 의미인 상관 접속사 〈either A or B〉 구문에서 or가, 두 번째 빈칸에는 '~해라, 그러지 않으면 …할 것이다'의 〈명령문+or …〉 구문에서 or가 와야 한다.
06 문맥상 '비록 ~이지만'의 의미인 양보를 나타내는 종속 접속사 Even though가 와야 한다.
07 'A와 B 둘 다'의 의미인 상관 접속사 〈Both A and B〉가 적절하다. *cf.* 〈not A but B〉: A가 아니라 B

08 '~할 때마다'의 의미인 whenever는 every time, each time 등으로 바꾸어 쓸 수 있다.

09 ② '~해라, 그러지 않으면 …할 것이다'의 〈명령문+or …〉 구문이 적절하다.

10 첫 번째 빈칸에는 상관 접속사 〈neither A nor B〉 구문의 nor가 알맞다. 두 번째 빈칸에는 '~하기 위해서'의 의미로 목적을 나타내는 종속 접속사 〈so that ~〉이 적절하다.

11 첫 번째 빈칸에는 '~할 때마다'의 의미인 Whenever가 알맞다. 두 번째 빈칸에는 '~하자마자'의 의미인 as soon as가 적절하다.

12 '~하지 않으면'의 의미인 종속 접속사 Unless를 쓴다.

13 ②의 if는 '~인지'의 의미로 명사절을 이끄는 접속사인 반면, 나머지는 모두 '만약 ~라면'의 의미로 부사절을 이끄는 조건을 나타내는 종속 접속사 if이다.

14 ②의 as는 '~함에 따라'의 의미인 반면, 나머지는 모두 '~ 때문에'의 의미이다.

15 ①의 while은 '~인 데 반하여'의 의미인 반면, 나머지는 모두 '~하는 동안'의 의미이다.

16 ③에는 '~ 이래로'의 의미인 종속 접속사 since가 적절하고, 나머지는 모두 '비록 ~이지만'의 의미인 종속 접속사 although [though, even though]가 적절하다.

17 ⑤ 〈명령문+or …〉 구문으로, '개에게 먹이를 너무 많이 주지 마라, 그러지 않으면 개가 살이 찔 것이다.'라는 의미의 문장과 같은 뜻이 되려면 '만약 개에게 먹이를 너무 많이 주면, 개가 살이 찔 것이다.'가 되어야 하므로 Unless가 아닌 If가 와야 한다.

18 ③ 상관 접속사 〈both A and B〉는 복수 취급한다.

19 ④ 조건의 부사절에서는 미래의 일도 현재시제로 나타낸다.

20 (d) 상관 접속사 〈not only A but also B〉는 B에 동사의 수를 일치시킨다.

서술형 따라잡기

01 (1) 〈As soon as+주어+동사〉는 〈On[Upon] v-ing〉로 바꾸어 쓸 수 있다.
   (2) 〈Whenever+주어+동사〉는 〈Every[Each] time+주어+동사〉로 바꾸어 쓸 수 있다.

02 'A뿐만 아니라 B도'는 상관 접속사 〈B as well as A〉 구문을 쓴다.

03 (1) '~할 수 있도록'의 의미로 목적을 나타내는 종속 접속사

〈so that ~〉을 쓴다.
   (2) '~해라, 그러지 않으면 …할 것이다'의 의미로 〈명령문+or …〉를 쓴다. '살' 것을 잊어버린다는 의미를 나타내기 위해서는 forget 뒤에 to부정사를 써야 한다.

04 (1) 'A와 B 둘 다'의 의미인 상관 접속사 〈both A and B〉를 이용한다.
   (2) 'A도 B도 아닌'의 의미인 상관 접속사 〈neither A nor B〉를 이용한다.

05 (1) '너무 ~해서 …하다'의 결과를 나타내는 종속 접속사 〈so ~ that …〉을 이용한다.
   (2) '~할 수 있도록'의 목적을 나타내는 종속 접속사 〈so that ~〉을 이용한다.

06 문맥상 '~해라, 그러지 않으면 …할 것이다'의 의미가 되어야 하므로 and를 or로 고친다. 조건의 부사절에서는 미래의 일도 현재시제로 나타내므로 will return을 return으로 고친다. 'A도 B도 아닌'의 의미는 상관 접속사 〈neither A nor B〉 구문으로 나타내므로, or를 nor로 고친다.

SELF NOTE
p.142

A 핵심 포인트 정리하기
① as ② since ③ as soon as ④ if
⑤ even if ⑥ so that ⑦ not only A but also B
⑧ either ⑨ nor ⑩ and
B 문제로 개념 다지기
1 O 2 X, or 3 X, don't see 4 O
5 X, and 6 X, is 7 X, so long that 8 X, or

POINT 01 주격 관계대명사   p.144

A 1 Which → What 2 what → which[that]
   3 which → who[that] 4 who → that
   5 what → which[that]

B 1 Bring me the pencil case which[that] is on my desk.
   2 I saw a girl who[that] was crying in the street.
   3 She gave me a tiny doll which[that] was made of paper.
   4 Lily introduced me to a boy who[that] was wearing glasses.
   5 Logan has two cats and a dog which[that] are friendly.
   6 I have a comic book which[that] is very popular with teenagers.

POINT 02 소유격 관계대명사   p.145

A 1 Have you seen a book whose cover is red?
   2 I chose a puppy whose ears were white.
   3 He met a woman whose husband is a pianist.
   4 She knows a man whose family lives in Sweden.

B 1 Do you have a hat whose ribbon is pink?
   2 She has a friend whose job is teaching science.
   3 Mr. Shin is a comedian whose wife is a producer.
   4 He talked about a girl whose name is the same as mine.

POINT 03 목적격 관계대명사   p.146

A 1 You will like the movie which[that] I saw yesterday.
   2 This is the girl who(m)[that] I like the most of all my friends.
   3 I ate lunch with the boy who(m)[that] you introduced me to the other day.[I ate lunch with the boy to whom you introduced me the other day.]
   4 When can you give me the money which[that] you borrowed last week?

B 1 Here is the key which you were looking for.
   2 I know a friendly woman who works at the library.
   3 The sandwiches which you made were delicious.
   4 What is the name of the computer game that you like the most?

POINT 04 관계대명사 what   p.147

A 1 What 2 who[that] 3 what 4 which[that]
   5 what

B 1 X, were → was
   2 X, the teacher → what the teacher
   3 X, that → what 4 O
   5 X, what → which[that]

C 1 What you said 2 what he did
   3 what she enjoys watching
   4 what I want to wear

POINT 05 주로 관계대명사 that을 쓰는 경우   p.148

A 1 whose 2 that 3 that

B 1 I want to buy something that I can wear to the party.
   2 This is the only article that I read last month.
   3 Did you see the old man and the cat that were sitting on the bench?

C 1 the most serious problem that
   2 the first woman that won
   3 something that is low

POINT 06 관계부사 when / where   p.149

A 1 when 2 where 3 when 4 when 5 where

B 1 The day when my midterms ended was the happiest day of my life.
   2 He showed me the place where he had hidden for an hour.

3 They found a wounded dolphin in the area where people were swimming.

C 1 The classroom where his sister studies is full of books.

2 I miss the time when my family traveled to Jeju Island.

POINT 07 관계부사 why / how　　　　p.150

A 1 the reason　2 why　3 how　4 the way
5 why　6 how　7 the reason

B 1 how he shoots a basketball
2 why he was moving to another town
3 how she cooks such delicious ramen
4 how the waiters at this restaurant act
5 why her boyfriend didn't call her
6 why I need to live with my grandparents

POINT 08 관계부사와 선행사의 생략　　　　p.151

A 1 O　2 O　3 X　4 O　5 O

B 1 This is where my friend works.
2 There are several reasons why I entered this college.
3 I will never forget when Jim won the world championship.
4 I saw Megan at the restaurant where we used to eat lunch.
5 We talked about how she studied for her exams.

내신대비 TEST　　　　p.152

01 ①　02 ③　03 ⑤　04 ④　05 ②　06 ⑤
07 ④　08 ①　09 ③　10 ④　11 ②　12 ②
13 ③　14 ③　15 ⑤　16 ①　17 ④　18 ③
19 ②, ③, ④　20 ③

서술형 따라잡기 - p.155

01 (1) when I won the speech contest
(2) whose father was a famous lawyer

02 (1) I have a relative whose house is on the coast.
(2) I visited the bank where he works.

03 (1) who[that] is wearing gloves
(2) where a dog is sleeping

04 (1) What he gave me
(2) I know the reason why

05 (1) where Ryu Hyun Jin was born
(2) whose height is
(3) when Ryu Hyun Jin won 14 games

06 the reason how → the reason why / which → that

01 문맥상 선행사를 포함한 관계대명사 what이 와야 한다.

02 The street를 선행사로 하는 목적격 관계대명사 which가 와야 한다. 전치사 on이 있으므로 관계부사는 올 수 없다.

03 선행사가 장소를 나타내므로 관계부사 where를 쓴다.

04 ④ 관계부사 when은 시간을 나타내는 선행사와 함께 쓸 수 있다.

05 the first나 every를 포함하는 선행사와 함께 쓸 수 있는 주격 관계대명사는 that이다.

06 문맥상 선행사를 포함한 관계대명사 what이 와야 한다.

07 사람과 사물 모두를 선행사로 취할 수 있는 관계대명사 that이 와야 한다.

08 ① 사람 선행사(The woman)와 현재분사(reading) 사이에 〈주격 관계대명사+be동사〉가 생략되었으며, 선행사가 단수이므로 that is가 적절하다.

09 첫 번째 빈칸에는 문맥상 방법을 나타내는 관계부사 how가, 두 번째 빈칸에는 선행사가 the reason이므로 이유를 나타내는 관계부사 why가 와야 한다.

10 첫 번째 빈칸에는 선행사가 the evening이므로 시간을 나타내는 관계부사 when이, 두 번째 빈칸에는 문맥상 선행사를 포함한 관계대명사 what이 와야 한다.

11 ②에는 선행사를 포함한 관계대명사 what이 와야 하는 반면, ①, ③, ④에는 주격 관계대명사 that, ⑤에는 목적격 관계대명사 that이 와야 한다.

12 ② 주격 관계대명사는 생략할 수 없다. ①과 ③은 목적격 관계대명사, ④는 시간을 나타내는 일반적인 명사가 선행사인 관계

부사, ⑤는 〈주격 관계대명사+be동사〉로 생략이 가능하다.

13 관계대명사 what은 선행사를 포함하므로 각각 earphones 와 the only thing을 선행사로 하는 (b)와 (c)의 빈칸에 올 수 없다.

14 ③ 선행사 the way와 관계부사 how는 함께 쓰지 않으므로 둘 중 하나만 와야 한다.

15 ⑤ 선행사가 사람일 경우에는 소유격 관계대명사로 whose가 와야 한다.

16 ①은 명사적 용법의 to부정사 앞에 쓰인 의문사 where인 반면, 나머지는 장소를 나타내는 선행사와 함께 쓰인 관계부사 where이다.

17 ④는 명사절을 이끄는 종속 접속사 that인 반면, 나머지는 모두 관계대명사 that이다.

18 (A) the wallet을 선행사로 하는 목적격 관계대명사 that이 와야 한다.
(B) '~하는 것'의 의미로 선행사를 포함한 관계대명사 what 이 와야 한다.
(C) 장소 a park를 선행사로 하는 관계부사 where가 와야 한다.

19 ① The printer를 선행사로 하는 주격 관계대명사 which 또 는 that이 있어야 한다.
⑤ 선행사 the lady와 black hair가 소유의 관계에 있으므 로 that은 소유격 관계대명사 whose가 되어야 한다.

20 ③ 선행사가 -thing으로 끝나는 경우 관계대명사 that을 쓴다.

서술형 따라잡기 -

01 (1) 선행사가 the day이므로 시간을 나타내는 관계부사 when을 이용한다.
(2) 선행사 a girl과 Her father는 소유의 관계에 있으므로 소유격 관계대명사 whose를 이용한다.

02 (1) 선행사 a relative와 house는 소유의 관계에 있으므로 소유격 관계대명사 whose를 이용한다.
(2) 선행사가 the bank로 장소를 나타내므로 관계부사 where를 써서 문장을 배열한다.

03 (1) a girl을 선행사로 하는 주격 관계대명사 who를 이용한다.
(2) a doghouse를 선행사로 하는 관계부사 where를 이용한다.

04 (1) 선행사를 포함한 관계대명사 What을 써서 표현한다.
(2) 선행사 the reason과 관계부사 why를 이용해 표현한다.

05 (1) 선행사가 the city로 장소를 나타내므로 관계부사 where 를 이용해서 문장을 완성한다.
(2) 소유격 관계대명사 whose가 height를 수식하는 구조 로 문장을 완성한다.
(3) 선행사가 the year로 때를 나타내므로 관계부사 when 을 이용해서 문장을 완성한다.

06 선행사가 the reason이므로 how는 관계부사 why로 고친 다. 선행사가 the very thing이므로 관계대명사 which는 that으로 고친다.

SELF NOTE   p.156

A 핵심 포인트 정리하기
① whose ② which[that] ③ that ④ what
⑤ when ⑥ where ⑦ why

B 문제로 개념 다지기
1 X, who(m)[that] 혹은 which 삭제   2 X, that
3 O   4 X, where   5 O
6 X, the way와 how 중 하나 삭제

Chapter 12 관계사 II

01 ③ 02 ④ 03 ① 04 ③ 05 ③ 06 ⑤

07 ① 08 ④ 09 ④ 10 ② 11 ⑤ 12 ②

13 ②, ④ 14 ③, ⑤ 15 ④ 16 ⑤ 17 ②

18 ③ 19 ①, ③, ④ 20 ④

서술형 따라잡기 -------------------------- p.169

01 (1) Whoever arrives last (2) in which

02 (1) Wherever you work

　　(2) Whoever visits this museum

03 (1) However cold it is, they will go fishing.

　　(2) However early you arrive, you cannot

　　　　enter the room until 10.

04 in which I got my hair cut[which I got my

　　hair cut in]

05 (1) which is a national holiday

　　(2) whoever[anyone who] has a ticket

06 (1) Whatever he says, I don't agree with

　　　him.

　　(2) I went to the department store, where

　　　toys were on sale.

01 문맥상 '언제 ~하더라도'라는 의미의 복합관계부사
　　Whenever가 알맞다.

02 '서점에서' 소설책을 산 것이므로 〈전치사+관계대명사〉인 in
　　which가 와야 한다.

03 Stephen Hawking을 선행사로 하며 선행사에 대한 부가적
　　인 정보를 제공하는 계속적 용법의 주격 관계대명사 who가 와
　　야 한다.

04 계속적 용법의 관계대명사는 〈접속사+대명사〉로 바꿔 쓸 수
　　있다. 문맥상 앞뒤 관계가 순조롭게 연결되며 주격 관계대명사
　　who가 선행사 an Austrian couple을 가리키므로 and
　　they로 바꿔 쓸 수 있다.

05 첫 번째 빈칸에는 '~하는 곳은 어디든지'라는 의미의 복합관계
　　부사 Wherever가 와야 한다. 두 번째 빈칸에는 '~하는 것
　　은 어느 것이든지'라는 의미의 복합관계대명사 Whichever
　　가 와야 한다.

06 첫 번째 빈칸에는 Café Prince를 선행사로 하며 선행사에 대

한 부가적인 정보를 제공하는 계속적 용법의 주격 관계대명사
which가 와야 한다. 내가 '도시에서' 자란 것이므로 두 번째 빈
칸에는 〈전치사+관계대명사〉인 in which가 와야 한다.

07 첫 번째 빈칸에는 '~하는 사람은 누구든지'의 whoever가 와
　　야 한다. 두 번째 빈칸에는 앞의 절 전체를 선행사로 하는 계속
　　적 용법의 주격 관계대명사 which가 와야 한다.

08 ④ 네가 가는 곳이 어디든지 너와 함께 하겠다는 말에, 나는 전
　　에 그곳에 가본 적이 있다는 답변은 어울리지 않는다.

09 첫 번째 빈칸에는 didn't even say hello to me를 선행사
　　로 하는 계속적 용법의 주격 관계대명사 which가, 두 번째 빈
　　칸에는 today's special을 선행사로 하는 계속적 용법의 목
　　적격 관계대명사 which가 와야 한다.

10 '아무리 ~하더라도'라는 의미의 복합관계부사 However가 와
　　야 한다.

11 ⑤ 관계대명사 앞에 전치사가 쓰인 경우 관계대명사는 생략할
　　수 없다.

12 ② the country 뒤에는 장소를 나타내는 관계부사 where
　　가 오거나, 관계대명사 which 앞 혹은 관계사절 끝에 전치사
　　in이 와야 한다.

13 '무엇을 ~하더라도'라는 의미의 복합관계대명사 Whatever
　　또는 No matter what이 와야 한다.

14 The airplane을 선행사로 하는 주격 관계대명사 which와
　　진행형 〈be동사+현재분사〉의 is가 와야 한다. 〈주격 관계대명
　　사+be동사〉는 뒤에 분사구가 올 경우 생략할 수 있다.

15 ④ that은 계속적 용법의 주격 관계대명사로 쓸 수 없으므로
　　사람을 나타내는 주격 관계대명사 who가 와야 한다.

16 ⑤ 주격 관계대명사만 생략할 수 없으므로 the girl who[that]
　　is standing이 되어야 한다. 혹은 〈주격 관계대명사+be동
　　사〉는 생략할 수 있으므로 the girl standing이 되어야 한다.

17 (a)와 (c)에는 '아무리 ~하더라도'라는 의미의 However, (b)
　　에는 '~할 때는 언제나'라는 의미의 Whenever, (d)에는 '~하
　　는 사람은 누구든지'라는 의미의 Whoever가 와야 한다.

18 ③에는 선행사를 포함하는 관계대명사 what이나 복합 관계대
　　명사 whatever 또는 whichever가 와야 한다. ①과 ②에
　　는 전치사의 목적어 역할을 하는 관계대명사 which가, ④와
　　⑤에는 계속적 용법의 관계대명사 which가 적절하다.

19 ② 관계대명사 앞에 전치사가 쓰인 경우 관계대명사는 생략할
　　수 없다.
　　⑤ 전치사 뒤에는 관계대명사 who가 올 수 없다.

20 (a) her blue dress를 선행사로 하며 선행사에 대한 부가적

인 정보를 제공하는 계속적 용법의 주격 관계대명사 which가 알맞다.

(b) 문맥상 '~할 때는 언제나'라는 의미의 복합관계부사 whenever가 적절하다.

(c) 우리가 '리조트에서 머문' 것이므로 〈전치사+관계대명사〉인 at which로 쓰거나 관계사절 끝에 전치사 at이 와야 한다.

서술형 따라잡기

01 (1) No matter who는 '누가 ~하더라도'라는 의미로 Whoever로 바꾸어 쓸 수 있다.
(2) 관계대명사가 전치사의 목적어인 경우, 전치사는 관계대명사 앞에 올 수 있다. 이때 전치사 뒤에 관계대명사 that이 올 수 없으므로 which를 써야 한다.

02 (1) '어디서 ~하더라도'라는 의미의 복합관계부사 Wherever를 쓴다.
(2) '~하는 사람은 누구든지'라는 의미의 복합관계대명사 Whoever를 쓴다.

03 '아무리 ~하더라도'는 〈However+형용사/부사+주어+동사〉의 어순으로 쓴다.

04 관계대명사가 전치사의 목적어인 경우, 전치사는 관계대명사 앞이나 관계사절 끝에 올 수 있다.

05 (1) October 3를 선행사로 하며 선행사에 대한 부가적인 정보를 제공하는 계속적 용법의 주격 관계대명사 which를 쓴다.
(2) '~하는 사람은 누구든지'라는 의미의 복합관계대명사 whoever 또는 anyone who를 쓴다.

06 (1) '무엇을 ~하더라도'라는 의미의 〈Whatever+주어+동사〉를 쓴다.
(2) the department store를 선행사로 하며 선행사에 대한 부가적인 정보를 제공하는 계속적 용법의 관계부사 where를 쓴다.

SELF NOTE
p.170

A 핵심 포인트 정리하기
① whoever ② whichever ③ whatever
④ whenever ⑤ wherever ⑥ however
⑦ who, which ⑧ when, where
⑨ 주격 관계대명사, be동사

B 문제로 개념 다지기
1 O 2 X, which 3 O 4 X, which 5 O

Chapter 13 비교 구문

POINT 01 as+원급+as
p.172

A 1 as rich as 2 as funny as 3 not as[so] tall as
4 is not as[so] difficult as
5 as many comic books as

B 1 as good as 2 not as[so] old as
3 as large as 4 as fast as
5 not as[so] comfortable as
6 not as[so] smart as

POINT 02 비교급과 최상급 만드는 방법
p.173

A 1 more popular 2 the oldest member
3 less money 4 more thoughtful

B 1 This orange juice is sweeter than yours.
2 I arrived at the meeting place earlier than I had expected.
3 He moved to an area farther away from his company.
4 I think this is the best moment of my life.

POINT 03 비교급+than / 비교급 강조
p.174

A 1 more slowly 2 faster than 3 fresher than
4 more delicious than 5 more crowded than

B 1 a lot better than my room
2 much cheaper than
3 far more difficult, than

C 1 bigger than 2 cleaner than
3 a sea view to, a city view

POINT 04 최상급 ~ in[of]
p.175

A 1 the cheapest 2 the worst 3 the biggest
4 the kindest 5 the coldest 6 the most boring
7 the newest 8 the most intelligent

B 1 late → latest 2 happier → happiest
3 the most poorest → the poorest

C 1 the longest of

2 the fastest Internet speed

3 the most expensive dish

POINT 05 as+원급+as possible / 배수사+as+원급+as
p.176

A 1 as fast as   2 as many, as

3 twice as heavy

4 three times more powerful

B 1 is twice as tall as my school

2 as quietly as he could

3 is three times longer than mine

4 get up as early as possible

POINT 06 비교급+and+비교급 / the+비교급, the+비교급
p.177

A 1 warmer and warmer

2 more and more expensive

3 more and more popular

B 1 The more you read, the smarter you become.

2 The hotter it gets, the more often people go swimming.

3 The more I get to know you, the more I like you.

C 1 The older she grew, the more beautiful she became.

2 His English is getting better and better.

POINT 07 최상급 표현 I – 원급과 비교급 이용
p.178

A 1 than any other month, more beautiful, as[so] beautiful

2 younger, any other film director, younger, as[so] young

3 more famous, No (other) restaurant, more famous, No (other) restaurant, as[so] famous

B 1 Mark is the friendliest boy

2 He is older than any other man

3 No other girl in our club is as popular as Jenny.

4 Jupiter is bigger than any other planet

POINT 08 최상급 표현 II – one of the+최상급+복수명사
p.179

A 1 people   2 best   3 busier   4 anybody

B 1 braver than   2 faster than   3 any other

C 1 one of the best

2 the most touching movie[film]

3 one of the most interesting cities

내신대비 TEST
p.180

01 ①   02 ②   03 ③   04 ②   05 ④   06 ②
07 ③   08 ⑤   09 ④   10 ④   11 ⑤   12 ④
13 ③   14 ⑤   15 ⑤   16 ①   17 ④
18 ①, ③, ④   19 ③   20 ①

서술형 따라잡기
p.183

01 (1) the healthier (2) three times as old as

02 (1) not as[so] warm as (2) the warmest
(3) colder than

03 No other, smarter

04 the highest

05 (1) twice as long as (2) as[so] late as
(3) more expensive than

06 (1) The more diligent you are, the more you will achieve.
(2) City Map is one of the most useful applications.

01 '가능한 한~한[하게]'는 〈as+원급+as+주어+can[could]〉로 표현한다.

02 '~보다 더 …한[하게]'는 〈비교급+than〉을 쓴다. 형용사/부사의 비교급은 주로 단어 뒤에 '-(e)r'를 붙인다.

03 '~ 중에서 가장 …한[하게]'는 〈the+최상급+of[in]〉으로 표현한다.

04 strong의 비교급은 stronger이므로 앞에 more가 필요 없다.

05 비교급을 강조할 때는 비교급 앞에 much, even, still, a lot, far 등을 쓰며 very는 쓸 수 없다.

06 〈as+형용사/부사의 원급+as〉의 형태로 빈칸에는 원급이 들어가야 한다.

07 첫 번째 빈칸에는 〈as+원급+as possible〉 구문의 possible이 들어가야 한다. 두 번째 빈칸에는 최상급 표현 중 하나인 〈No (other)+단수명사 ~ 비교급+than〉 구문의 No가 들어가야 한다.

08 첫 번째 문장은 〈the+최상급+(that)+주어+have ever v-ed〉 구문으로 빈칸에는 best가 들어가야 한다. 두 번째 문장은 최상급 표현 중 하나인 〈비교급+than anybody else〉 구문으로, 빈칸에는 more beautiful이 들어가야 한다.

09 '~의 몇 배 …한[하게]'는 〈배수사+as+원급+as〉 또는 〈배수사+비교급+than〉으로 나타낸다. 단, twice는 〈배수사+as+원급+as〉의 형태로만 사용한다.

10 '가장 ~한 것[사람]들 중 하나'는 〈one of the+최상급+복수명사〉를 쓴다.

11 A그룹에서 John이 다른 어떤 사람보다 키가 크므로 〈비교급+than any other+단수명사〉를 써서 최상급으로 나타낼 수 있다.

12 첫 번째 빈칸에는 비교급을 강조하는 much, 두 번째 빈칸에는 〈as+형용사/부사의 원급+as〉 구문의 원급 자리에 들어가는 much가 와야 한다.

13 첫 번째 문장은 '점점 더 ~한[하게]'의 〈비교급+and+비교급〉 구문으로, 비교급이 'more+원급'일 경우에는 〈more and more+원급〉의 형태로 쓴다. 두 번째 문장은 '~(하면) 할수록 더 …하다'의 〈the+비교급, the+비교급〉 구문이다.

14 ⑤ 〈비교급+than anybody else〉의 형태로 of를 than으로 고쳐야 한다.

15 ⑤ 〈one of the+최상급+복수명사〉의 형태로 flower를 flowers로 고쳐야 한다.

16 〈No (other)+단수명사 ~ as[so]+원급+as〉는 최상급 표현 중 하나이다.

17 ④는 '피카소는 다른 화가들만큼 독창적이지 않다.'라는 의미인 반면, 나머지는 모두 '피카소가 가장 독창적이다.'라는 최상급의 의미이다.

18 ② 〈as+원급+as possible〉 구문이므로 fast 앞에 as가 와야 한다.
⑤ '~만큼 …한[하게]'는 〈as+원급+as〉를 쓰므로, as high as가 되어야 한다.

19 ③ '~(하면) 할수록 더 …하다'는 〈the+비교급, the+비교급〉이므로 the best는 the better가 되어야 한다.

20 (A) '~만큼 …한[하게]'는 〈as+원급+as〉를 쓰므로 witty가 와야 한다.

(B) 〈the+최상급+(that)+주어+have ever v-ed〉는 최상급 표현 중 하나로 biggest가 와야 한다.
(C) 〈No (other)+단수명사 ~ 비교급+than〉은 최상급 표현 중 하나로 faster가 와야 한다.

서술형 따라잡기

01 (1) '~(하면) 할수록 더 …하다'는 〈the+비교급, the+비교급〉을 쓴다.
(2) '~의 몇 배 …한[하게]'는 〈배수사+as+원급+as〉를 쓴다.

02 (1) 부산은 서울만큼 따뜻하지 않으므로 warm을 이용하여 〈not as[so]+형용사/부사의 원급+as〉 구문으로 나타낸다.
(2) 지도상에서 광주가 가장 따뜻하므로 warm을 이용하여 최상급 문장으로 나타낸다.
(3) 독도는 대전보다 추우므로 cold를 이용하여 비교급 문장으로 나타낸다.

03 문맥상 최상급의 의미를 갖는 〈No (other)+단수명사 ~ 비교급+than〉을 쓴다.

04 〈No (other)+단수명사 ~ 비교급+than〉은 최상급의 의미이다.

05 (1) *Heroes*가 *Chicago*보다 공연 시간이 두 배 더 길다. 따라서 〈배수사+as+원급+as〉를 쓴다.
(2) *Heroes*가 가장 늦게 시작하므로, 최상급의 의미를 갖는 〈No (other)+단수명사 ~ as[so]+원급+as〉를 쓴다.
(3) *Carmen*은 다른 어떤 뮤지컬보다 가격이 비싸므로, 〈비교급+than any other+단수명사〉를 쓴다.

06 (1) '~(하면) 할수록 더 …하다'의 〈the+비교급, the+비교급〉 구문을 쓴다.
(2) '가장 ~한 것[사람]들 중 하나'는 〈one of the+최상급+복수명사〉를 쓴다.

SELF NOTE
p.184

A 핵심 포인트 정리하기
① as, as ② 비교급, than ③ 배수사, as, 원급, as
④ 복수명사 ⑤ one of the, 최상급, 복수명사

B 문제로 개념 다지기
1 O 2 X, faster 3 X, the most useful
4 X, much[even, still, a lot, far] bigger
5 X, five times as expensive
6 O 7 X, any other cookbook 8 O

POINT 01 수의 일치 I – 단수 취급하는 경우 p.186

A 1 has 2 requires 3 has to 4 is

B 1 ○ 2 X, are → is 3 ○ 4 X, have → has

C 1 Most of, is 2 Each, has
   3 One hundred meters is

POINT 02 수의 일치 II – 복수 취급하는 경우 p.187

A 1 have 2 are 3 go 4 is

B 1 is → are 2 uses → use 3 are → is
   4 was → were

C 1 Three-fourths of, are 2 Most of, were
   3 A number[lot] of students were

POINT 03 시제 일치 p.188

A 1 would 2 wanted 3 had written

B 1 Ann thought that the watch was too expensive
     to buy.
   2 The police officer said that we couldn't park
     here.

C 1 his parents trust him 2 I had left my bag
   3 you wanted to go to India

POINT 04 시제 일치의 예외 p.189

A 1 wrote 2 rises 3 broke out 4 is 5 is

B 1 flew → flies 2 froze → freezes
   3 invents → invented 4 has been → was
   5 was → is

C 1 light travels faster 2 was printed
   3 time is money 4 he goes to church

POINT 05 평서문의 간접화법 전환 p.190

A 1 (that) she had to leave in a minute
   2 (that) she didn't feel like making dinner that
     day
   3 (that) he would take her to Jim's party the

next[following] day
   4 (that) someone had asked me to give that
     message to him
   5 (that) she hadn't booked a flight to Seattle

B 1 I am[I'm] taking a writing class.
   2 I will make chicken soup today.
   3 My brother will start middle school tomorrow.

POINT 06 의문문의 간접화법 전환 I – 의문사가 없는 경우 p.191

A 1 if I had ever been to England
   2 if I liked soccer
   3 if she could go to the movies
   4 if there was a bakery 5 was empty
   6 would have a cup of coffee

B 1 if he could use my cell phone
   2 if there was a pharmacy nearby
   3 My father asked us whether we had any free
     time.
   4 Kate asked me whether I had heard the rumor
     about Jim.

POINT 07 의문문의 간접화법 전환 II – 의문사가 있는 경우 p.192

A 1 when her boyfriend had given her that
   2 who the woman wearing a hat was
   3 what time I was going to meet Jimmy
   4 why I hadn't finished writing the report
   5 what I had done with her dress

B 1 who would read the passage
   2 where the exhibition takes place
   3 when we were going to play volleyball

POINT 08 명령문의 간접화법 전환 p.193

A 1 not to speak during the test
   2 to repeat after her 3 to be there at 9 a.m.
   4 to keep walking across the river

B 1 They told me to bring a friend to the party.
   2 I asked him to call back later.
   3 He advised me not to drive fast.

01 ⑤	02 ②	03 ②	04 ⑤	05 ③	06 ⑤
07 ④	08 ②	09 ④	10 ③	11 ④	12 ①
13 ①	14 ②	15 ④	16 ①	17 ⑤	18 ③
19 ①	20 ④				

서술형 따라잡기 ----------------------------- p.197

01 (1) he would go camping with Jane
　　(2) asked me where that bus was going

02 (1) fifth of, are　(2) Half of, are
　　(3) The number of, is

03 (1) Two-thirds of the kids are under ten.
　　(2) She asked me if I could help her.

04 (1) Most of the food is
　　(2) two plus three is five

05 (1) not to drink cold water
　　(2) to return to the hospital the next[following] day

06 why she had been in Hong Kong a week before, (that) she goes there to see her parents every summer

01 주절의 시제가 과거일 때 종속절에는 과거시제나 과거완료형이 올 수 있다. 따라서 과거진행형인 was playing이 적절하다.

02 종속절이 격언·속담 등을 나타낼 때는 주절의 시제와 관계없이 현재시제를 쓴다.

03 〈the rest+of the+단수명사〉는 단수 취급하므로 is가 와야 한다.

04 목적어가 없으므로 첫 번째 빈칸에는 said가 온다. 현재에도 지속되는 습관은 주절의 시제가 과거더라도 종속절에 현재시제를 쓸 수 있다.

05 Each와 시간을 나타내는 단위가 각각 주어로 올 때 동사는 단수 취급한다.

06 동명사구가 주어로 올 때 동사는 단수 취급한다. 〈Both A and B〉는 복수 취급한다.

07 주절의 시제가 과거일 때 종속절에는 과거시제나 과거완료형이 올 수 있다. 역사적 사실은 항상 과거시제로 쓴다.

08 의문사가 없는 의문문을 간접화법으로 바꾸면 〈ask(+목적어)+if[whether]+주어+동사〉의 형태가 되므로 that을 if나 whether로 고쳐야 한다.

09 의문사가 있는 의문문의 직접화법을 간접화법으로 전환하면 〈ask(+목적어)+의문사+주어+동사〉의 어순이 된다. 주절의 시제가 과거이므로 종속절의 will be home은 would be home이 되어야 한다.

10 직접화법의 명령문을 간접화법으로 바꾸면 〈tell+목적어+to-v〉의 형태가 된다.

11 의문사가 있는 의문문의 간접화법을 직접화법으로 전환하면 주어와 동사의 순서가 바뀌고, 인칭대명사와 동사의 시제는 주절의 주어의 관점에 맞게 바뀐다. 또 지시대명사 that은 this로 바뀐다.

12 종속절이 과학적 사실을 나타낼 때는 주절의 시제와 관계없이 항상 현재시제를 쓴다.

13 ① 부정 명령문을 간접화법으로 바꾸면 〈told+목적어+not+to-v〉 형태가 된다.

14 문맥상 '많은 사람들이 다쳤다'라고 하는 것이 적절하므로 〈a number of+복수명사+복수동사〉가 와야 한다. 주절의 시제가 과거이므로 종속절의 동사도 과거형인 were를 쓴다.

15 ④ 의문사가 없는 의문문의 간접화법에서 종속절의 과거시제는 직접화법에서 현재시제로 바꿔야 한다. 간접화법에서 인칭대명사 I와 his는 주절의 주어의 관점에 맞게 바꿔야 하므로 직접화법에서 you와 my가 되어야 한다.

16 ① 학문명은 '-s'로 끝나더라도 단수 취급한다. 따라서 are는 is로 고친다.

17 ⑤ 종속절이 역사적인 사실을 나타낼 때는 주절의 시제와 관계없이 과거시제를 쓴다. 따라서 have climbed는 climbed로 고친다.

18 ③ 〈분수+of the+복수명사〉는 복수 취급한다. 따라서 is는 are로 고친다.

19 ① 〈a number of+복수명사〉는 복수 취급하므로 빈칸에는 were를 쓴다. every, 금액을 나타내는 단위, 〈the rest+of the+단수명사〉, 동명사구는 모두 단수 취급하므로 나머지 빈칸에는 was를 쓴다.

20 (A) 〈half+of the+복수명사〉는 복수 취급하므로 know가 와야 한다.
　　(B) 부정 명령문을 간접화법으로 바꾸면 〈order+목적어+not+to-v〉 형태가 되므로 not to가 와야 한다.
　　(C) 무게를 나타내는 단위는 단수 취급하므로 was가 와야 한다.

01 (1) 주절의 시제가 과거이므로, 종속절의 will은 would로 바꾸고, 인칭대명사도 주절의 주어의 관점에 맞게 바꾼다.
(2) 의문사가 있는 의문문을 간접화법으로 전환하면 〈ask+목적어+의문사+주어+동사〉의 형태가 된다. 주절의 시제가 과거이므로 동사 is는 was로 바꾸고, this는 that으로 바꾼다.

02 (1) 과일의 1/5이 오렌지이므로 a fifth를 이용한다. 〈분수+of the+복수명사〉는 복수 취급한다.
(2) 과일의 절반이 사과이므로 half를 이용한다. 〈half+of the+복수명사〉는 복수 취급한다.
(3) 바나나의 수가 오렌지의 수보다 많으므로 the number of(~의 수) 구문을 이용한다. 〈The number of+복수명사〉는 단수 취급한다.

03 (1) 〈분수+of the+복수명사〉는 복수 취급한다.
(2) 의문사가 없는 의문문을 간접화법으로 바꾸면 〈ask+목적어+if+주어+동사〉의 어순이 된다.

04 (1) 〈most+of+단수명사〉는 단수 취급한다.
(2) 종속절이 변하지 않는 사실을 나타낼 때는 주절의 시제와 관계없이 현재시제를 쓴다.

05 명령문을 간접화법으로 바꾸면 〈advise+목적어+to-v〉 형태가 되며, 부정 명령문을 간접화법으로 바꾸면 〈advise+목적어+not+to-v〉 형태가 된다. tomorrow는 간접화법으로 바꾸면 the next[following] day가 된다.

06 의문사가 있는 의문문을 간접화법으로 전환하면 〈ask+목적어+의문사+주어+동사〉의 형태가 된다. 주절의 시제보다 이전에 일어난 일을 묻고 있으므로 과거완료형을 쓰고, ago는 before로 바꾼다. 간접화법에서 주절이 과거시제일 경우 종속절에는 원칙적으로 과거시제 또는 과거완료형이 오지만, 전달 시점에도 지속되는 습관이라 볼 경우 현재시제로 쓸 수 있다. 인칭대명사는 주절의 주어의 관점에 맞추어 바꾼다.

SELF NOTE p.198

A 핵심 포인트 정리하기
① the ② a ③ 과거시제 ④ 현재 ⑤ 과거
⑥ 목적어 ⑦ if[whether] ⑧ to부정사
⑨ not, to-v

B 문제로 개념 다지기
1 X, is 2 X, were 3 O 4 O 5 X, not to forget

Chapter 15 특수구문

POINT 01 do를 이용한 강조 p.200

A 1 do 2 does 3 did 4 do 5 does 6 did

B 1 did study 2 do hope 3 does act
4 did send 5 does have

POINT 02 〈It is[was] ~ that …〉 강조 구문 p.201

A 1 my uncle that[who] encouraged me
2 in the middle of the night that
3 at the cafeteria that I first met
4 last year that my family went on a trip
5 a toy car that he recommended

B 1 It was broccoli soup that I cooked for
2 It is Mike who is crying
3 It was a cat that she found
4 It was yesterday that my father returned

POINT 03 부분 부정 p.202

A 1 not always 2 Not every 3 Not all

B 1 always 2 all 3 every

C 1 Not all the books are for sale.
2 He is not always late for work.
3 Not everyone has goals for the future.

POINT 04 전체 부정 p.203

A 1 None 2 Neither 3 never

B 1 never 2 None 3 neither

C 1 He never studies 2 Neither of us went
3 None of them answered

POINT 05 장소 부사구 도치 / 부정어 도치 p.204

A 1 On the stage danced the girls.
2 Never have I seen such a sad movie.
3 Behind the gate were dozens of dogs.
4 Rarely does he speak to others.

B 1 Scarcely did it snow this year.

2 In the big house lived a friendly old woman.

3 Over the Golden Gate Bridge flew a helicopter.

4 Rarely do I eat meals at home.

POINT 06 so/neither+동사+주어   p.205

A 1 So did   2 Neither am   3 So did

   4 Neither can

B 1 I'm wearing red sneakers, too.

   2 I don't have an umbrella, either.

   3 I will bring my friends home for dinner, too.

C 1 is tall, so am I   2 dreamed of pigs, so did I

   3 like junk food, Neither do I

내신대비 TEST   p.206

01 ②	02 ③	03 ④	04 ①	05 ④	06 ③
07 ②	08 ④	09 ⑤	10 ③	11 ①	12 ①
13 ⑤	14 ②	15 ②	16 ④	17 ⑤	18 ⑤
19 ②, ④	20 ④				

서술형 따라잡기 - p.209

01 (1) Not every apple (2) was my book

02 (1) Janet did exercise every morning to
       lose weight.

   (2) Never does he talk to me during class.

03 (1) None (2) Not all (3) that

04 (1) Neither do I (2) None of them

05 (1) It was Mina that[who] bought a novel at
       the bookstore this afternoon.

   (2) It was a novel that Mina bought at the
       bookstore this afternoon.

   (3) It was at the bookstore that Mina
       bought a novel this afternoon.

   (4) It was this afternoon that Mina bought a
       novel at the bookstore.

06 So my sister is. → So is my sister. /
   where → that / Never it does → Never does it

01 부정어(Hardly)가 강조되어 문두에 오면 주어와 동사의 도

치가 일어나는데, 일반동사가 쓰였으므로 〈Hardly+does
+주어+동사원형〉의 어순이 되어야 한다.

02 부정문에 동의하는 말은 〈Neither+동사+주어〉의 형태이다.
앞에 일반동사의 현재형이 쓰였으므로 does가 와야 한다.

03 〈It was ~ that …〉 강조 구문에서 강조되는 말이 사물일 때
that을 쓴다.

04 긍정문에 동의하는 말은 〈So+동사+주어〉의 형태이다. 앞에
일반동사의 과거형이 쓰였으므로 So did I가 와야 한다.

05 부정문에 동의하는 말은 〈Neither+동사+주어〉로 앞에 조동
사 can이 쓰였으므로 Neither can I가 와야 한다.

06 첫 번째 문장은 〈장소의 부사구+동사+주어〉의 도치 구문으로,
주어가 복수명사이므로 빈칸에는 are가 적절하다. 두 번째 문
장에서 부분 부정을 나타내는 〈Not all+복수명사〉는 복수 취
급하므로 빈칸에는 make를 쓴다.

07 첫 번째 문장에서 〈Not every+단수명사〉는 단수 취급하므
로 빈칸에 is를 쓴다. 두 번째 문장의 빈칸에는 them을 전체
부정하는 none이 와야 한다.

08 관객들이 모두 영화의 결말에 실망한 것은 아니므로 부분 부정
을 나타내는 Not every를 쓴다.

09 부정어(Seldom)가 강조되어 문두에 오면 주어와 동사의 도
치가 일어나는데, 현재시제의 일반동사가 쓰였고 주어가 3인칭
단수이므로 〈Seldom does+주어+동사원형〉의 어순이 되
어야 한다.

10 them을 전체 부정하는 None을 쓴다.

11 ①의 do는 '하다'의 의미를 지닌 일반동사이고, 나머지는 모두
본동사를 강조하기 위해 쓰인 조동사 do이다.

12 ①은 가주어 It, 나머지는 모두 〈It was ~ that …〉 강조구문
의 It이다.

13 ⑤ 〈It was ~ that …〉 강조 구문으로 부사구가 강조되었으므
로 which를 that으로 고쳐야 한다.

14 ② 부정어(never)가 강조되어 문두에 오면 주어와 동사의 도
치가 일어나므로 〈Never+조동사+주어〉의 어순인 Never
have I seen이 되어야 한다.

15 〈It is[was] ~ that …〉 강조 구문을 이용하여 강조하고자 하
는 목적어(my green dress)를 It was와 that 사이에 둔
다.

16 부정어(never)가 강조되어 문두에 오면 주어와 동사의 도치가
일어나므로 〈Never+조동사+주어〉의 어순인 Never had I
dreamed가 되어야 한다.

17 ⑤ 부정문에 동의하는 말은 〈Neither+동사+주어〉이므로, So will I는 Neither will I가 되어야 한다.

18 (a) 부정어(Little)가 강조되어 문두에 오면 주어와 동사의 도치가 일어나는데, 현재시제의 일반동사가 쓰였고 주어가 3인칭 단수이므로 〈Little does+주어+동사원형〉의 어순인 Little does he realize ~가 되어야 한다.
(c) 장소의 부사구(Here)가 강조되어 문두에 오면 〈장소의 부사구+동사+주어〉의 어순인 Here comes the food ~가 되어야 한다.

19 ② 과거시제이므로 조동사 did를 이용해 〈did+동사원형〉 형태가 되어야 한다.
④ Charlotte이 잡지를 읽은 것은 '미용실에서'였다는 문장이 되어야 하므로 the hair salon 앞에 전치사 at이 와야 한다.

20 ④ 부정어(never)가 강조되어 문두에 오면 주어와 동사의 도치가 일어나므로 〈Never+조동사+주어〉의 어순인 Never has William cried가 되어야 한다.

서술형 따라잡기 -

01 (1) '모두 ~인 것은 아니다'의 부분 부정으로 단수동사가 왔으므로 〈Not every+단수명사〉의 형태가 되어야 한다.
(2) 장소의 부사구가 강조되어 문두에 왔으므로 〈부사구+동사+주어〉의 어순이 되어야 한다.

02 (1) 과거시제이므로 조동사 did를 이용해 동사를 강조한다.
(2) 부정어(Never)가 강조되어 문두에 오면 주어와 동사의 도치가 일어나는데, 현재시제의 일반동사가 쓰였고 주어가 3인칭 단수이므로 〈Never does+주어+동사원형〉의 어순이 되어야 한다.

03 (1) class A에서 cheerleading club에 지원한 사람이 아무도 없으므로, 전체 부정을 나타내는 None을 쓴다.
(2) class C의 학생들이 모두 newspaper club에 지원한 것은 아니므로, 부분 부정을 나타내는 Not all을 쓴다.
(3) the school band를 강조하는 〈It is ~ that …〉 강조 구문이므로 that을 쓴다.

04 (1) 부정문에 동의하는 말은 〈Neither+동사+주어〉로 앞에 일반동사의 현재형이 쓰였으므로 Neither do I로 쓴다.
(2) '그들은 모두 그 영화가 좋다고 생각하지 않았다.'라는 의미가 되어야 하므로, 전체 부정인 None of them이 와야 한다.

05 〈It was ~ that …〉 강조 구문으로, 강조되는 말이 사람일 경우 that 대신 who를 쓸 수 있다.

06 '~도 또한 그렇다'의 의미로 긍정문 다음에 쓰인 So my sis-

ter is.는 So is my sister.가 되어야 한다. 문장의 목적어인 Korean winters를 강조하는 〈It is ~ that …〉 강조 구문이므로 where를 that으로 고쳐야 한다. 부정어(Never)가 문두에 오면 주어와 조동사의 도치가 일어나므로 Never it does는 Never does it으로 고쳐야 한다.

SELF NOTE　　　　　　　　　　　p.210

A 핵심 포인트 정리하기
① do[does/did] ② It is[was], that ③ not
④ 부사구, 동사, 주어 ⑤ so/neither, 동사, 주어

B 문제로 개념 다지기
1 O　2 X, that　3 X, was my tennis racket
4 X, does he visit　5 X, all　6 X, had he heard
7 O　8 X, So will I　9 X, does
10 X, did I dream

01 ③ **02** ② **03** ③ **04** will be sent to my father tomorrow by me **05** ⑤ **06** ②

07 more fans than any other young actor

08 ⑤ **09** ③ **10** are to make

11 as carefully as I could **12** It is this safety pin that I have been looking for. **13** ④

14 ② **15** would → used to **16** was → were

17 ④ **18** Not all children[kids] want to have

19 ④ **20** ③ **21** ②, ③, ⑤

22 (1) hadn't been, would have gone
(2) had played, wouldn't have lost

01 '경기가 비로 인해 연기된 사실'이 좋은 소식이라는 의미이므로, 앞에 나온 절 전체를 선행사로 취하는 계속적 용법의 관계대명사 which가 와야 한다.

02 뒤에 비교급이 왔으므로, 비교급을 강조하는 말 much, even, still, a lot, far 등이 와야 한다.

03 첫 번째 빈칸에는 '~에 만족하다'를 나타내는 be satisfied with의 with가 와야 하고, 두 번째 빈칸에는 '~로 가득 차다'를 나타내는 be filled with의 with가 와야 한다.

04 4형식 능동태 문장을 직접목적어를 주어로 하는 수동태 문장으로 바꾸어 써야 하므로, 동사는 will be sent로 바꾸고, 간접목적어 my father 앞에는 전치사 to를 쓴다.

05 부정문에 대한 응답으로 '~도 그렇지 않다'라는 의미를 나타내는 〈neither+동사+주어〉 구문을 쓴다. A에서 일반동사의 과거형이 쓰였으므로 B의 답변으로 Neither did I가 와야 한다.

06 문맥상 '그녀가 그곳에 있었을 리가 없어.'라는 의미가 되어야 하므로 과거 사실에 대한 강한 의심을 나타내는 〈can't have v-ed〉인 can't have been이 와야 한다.

07 '다른 어떤 ~보다 더 많은'은 〈비교급+than any other+단수명사〉로 나타내므로 more fans than any other young actor로 쓴다.

08 〈보기〉와 ⑤의 to부정사는 각각 앞의 명사(구) time과 a good house를 꾸미는 형용사적 용법의 to부정사이다. ①은 형용사를 꾸미는 부사적 용법, ②와 ③은 진주어로 쓰인 명사적 용법, ④는 목적어로 쓰인 명사적 용법의 to부정사이다.

09 '~하는 것은 불가능하다'는 〈There is no v-ing〉로 나타낸다.

10 be동사 뒤에 to부정사가 쓰여 '~하려고 하다'라는 의도의 의미를 나타낼 수 있으므로 〈be+to부정사〉인 are to make를 쓴다.

11 '가능한 한 ~한[하게]'라는 의미의 〈as+원급+as possible〉은 〈as+원급+as+주어+can[could]〉으로 바꾸어 쓸 수 있다. 문장의 시제가 과거이므로 as carefully as I could 로 쓴다.

12 '…한 것은 바로 ~이다'를 나타내는 강조 구문 〈It is ~ that〉 사이에 밑줄 친 부분을 넣어 나타낸다. 따라서 It is this safety pin that I have been looking for.로 쓴다.

13 '아무리 ~하더라도'는 복합관계부사 however 또는 no matter how를 써서 However sleepy you are 또는 No matter how sleepy you are로 나타낸다.

14 목적어가 that절인 문장을 수동태로 써야 하므로, It is said that taking deep breaths is effective ~ 또는 Taking deep breaths is said to be effective ~가 되어야 한다.

15 '(전에는) ~이었다'라는 과거의 상태를 나타낼 때는 would를 쓸 수 없고 used to를 써야 한다.

16 〈a number of+복수명사〉가 주어로 오면 동사는 복수 취급하므로 was는 were가 되어야 한다.

17 부사절의 접속사를 없애고, 부사절의 주어가 주절의 주어와 다르므로 부사절의 주어를 분사 앞에 남겨 둔 후, 주절과 시제가 같으므로 were는 being으로 고친다. 따라서 빈칸에 There being so many cars가 와야 한다.

18 '모두 ~인 것은 아니다'라는 의미의 부분 부정은 not all을 써서 나타낸다.

19 ④ 내가 교실에 들어갔을 때 수업은 이미 시작했었으므로 주절에 과거완료를 쓴다.

20 부정 명령문을 간접화법으로 전환할 때는 〈not to-v〉의 형태로 나타낸다.

21 ① 상관 접속사 〈neither A nor B〉는 B에 동사의 주어를 일치시키므로 have가 되어야 한다.
④ 과거 이전에 시작된 일이 과거에도 진행 중임을 나타내는 과거완료 진행형을 써야 한다.

22 과거 사실과 반대되는 상황을 가정하는 가정법 과거완료 문장이므로 〈If+주어+had v-ed ~, 주어+조동사의 과거형+have v-ed …〉로 나타낸다.

01 ③ 02 ⑤ 03 ② 04 two hours decorating
05 ④ 06 ③ 07 So was I 08 ⑤
09 has been taking a bath 10 ③ 11 ②
12 ⑤ 13 were → was 14 ⑤ 15 ③
16 The penguins are being trained by a tall man. 17 Having taken a nap an hour ago
18 ③ 19 ④ 20 Seldom does he make phone calls to 21 ③ 22 (1) four times higher than (2) twice as high

01 '모든 불이 꺼진 채로'라는 의미로 the lights와 분사가 수동의 관계이므로 〈with+(대)명사+과거분사〉를 써서 나타낸다. 따라서 turned가 와야 한다.

02 과거 사실과 반대되는 상황을 가정하는 가정법 과거완료 문장이므로 〈If+주어+had v-ed ~, 주어+조동사의 과거형+have v-ed …〉를 써야 하고, 빈칸에는 had known이 와야 한다.

03 문맥상 '헬멧을 썼어야 했다'라는 과거의 일에 대한 유감을 나타내므로 should have worn이 와야 한다.

04 '장식하는 데 두 시간을 쓰다'라는 의미이므로 〈spend+시간+v-ing〉를 써서 two hours decorating으로 쓴다.

05 '~하지 않으면'은 unless를 쓰고, 조건을 나타내는 부사절에서는 미래의 일도 현재시제로 나타내므로 Unless there is가 와야 한다.

06 '점점 더 ~한[하게]'는 〈비교급+and+비교급〉으로 나타내므로 high의 비교급을 쓴 higher and higher가 와야 한다.

07 긍정문에 대한 답변으로 '~도 (또한) 그렇다'라는 의미를 나타내는 〈so+동사+주어〉 구문을 쓴다. A에서 be동사의 과거형이 쓰였으므로 So was I가 와야 한다.

08 5형식 문장에서 목적격 보어로 쓰인 to부정사는 수동태 문장에서도 동사 뒤에 그대로 쓴다. 따라서 was asked to sing이 알맞다.

09 30분 전에 목욕을 시작해서 여전히 목욕을 하고 있는 중이므로 현재완료 진행형 has been taking a bath를 쓴다.

10 첫 번째 빈칸에는 '사람들이 생각하는 것'이라는 의미로 전치사 from의 목적어가 되는 선행사를 포함한 관계대명사 what이 와야 하고, 두 번째 빈칸에는 '무엇을 입어야 할지'라는 의미로 〈의문사+to부정사(to wear)〉의 의문사 what이 와야 한다.

11 ②는 '이 호텔의 다른 모든 방은 이 방만큼 크다.'라는 의미인 반면, 나머지는 모두 '이 방은 이 호텔에서 가장 크다.'라는 최상급의 의미를 나타낸다.

12 첫 번째 빈칸에는 사람의 성격이나 성품을 나타내는 형용사 kind가 보어로 쓰였으므로 to부정사의 의미상의 주어로 of him이 와야 하고, 두 번째 빈칸에는 동명사의 의미상의 주어로 소유격 또는 목적격이 와야 하므로 their나 them이 와야 한다.

13 〈half of+the+단수명사〉는 단수형 동사를 쓰므로 were spent는 was spent가 되어야 한다.

14 '~하지 않을 수 없다'는 〈can't help v-ing〉 또는 〈can't (help) but+동사원형〉으로 나타내므로 ⑤가 알맞다.

15 의문사가 있는 의문문을 간접화법으로 전환할 때는 전달동사는 ask로 바꾸고 인용문은 〈의문사+주어+동사〉의 어순으로 써야 하므로 ③이 알맞다.

16 능동태 문장의 목적어 the penguins가 수동태 문장의 주어로 오고, 진행형으로 쓰인 동사 is training은 수동태에서 are being trained가 된다. 능동태 문장의 주어 A tall man은 수동태에서는 〈by+행위자〉로 문장 뒤에 쓴다.

17 부사절을 분사구문으로 만들 때는 부사절의 접속사와 주어를 생략(주절과 부사절의 주어가 같은 경우)하고 동사를 v-ing형으로 바꾼다. 이때 부사절의 시제가 주절의 시제보다 앞설 경우에는 완료형 분사구문 〈having v-ed〉의 형태로 쓴다.

18 〈so ~ that+주어+can't〉는 '너무 ~해서 …할 수 없다'라는 의미로 〈too+형용사/부사+to-v〉로 바꾸어 쓸 수 있다. 따라서 too short to use가 적절하다.

19 ④ 전치사 뒤에는 관계대명사 that이 올 수 없으므로 in that은 in which가 되거나 전치사 in을 관계사절 끝으로 보내야 한다.

20 부정어 seldom을 강조하기 위해 문장의 앞에 두면 주어와 동사가 도치된다. 일반동사가 쓰였으므로, 〈부정어+do[does/did]+주어+동사원형〉 형태인 Seldom does he make phone calls to가 되어야 한다.

21 (a) be used to v-ing: ~하는 것에 익숙하다
   (e) deny는 동명사를 목적어로 취하는 동사이다.

22 (1) Jason의 수학 점수 100점은 Mina의 수학 점수 25점보다 네 배 높다. '~의 몇 배 …한[하게]'은 〈배수사+as+원급+as〉 또는 〈배수사+비교급+than〉으로 나타내므로 four times as high as 또는 four times higher than으로 쓴다. 빈칸이 4개이므로 four times higher than으로 쓴다.

(2) Chris의 영어 점수 90점은 Jason의 영어 점수 45점보다 두 배 높다. 원급의 as가 있으므로 twice as high로 쓴다.

01 ④ 02 ③ 03 ② 04 had ended 05 ③
06 It is no use giving advice 07 became
more and more exciting 08 ④ 09 ③
10 kept us from swimming 11 ④ 12 ⑤
13 for these batteries, it were not for these
batteries 14 reported that drinking too
much soda, is reported to be 15 ⑤ 16 ③
17 ④ 18 that → which 19 meet → meeting
20 She asked me if[whether] I could deliver
that to her house. 21 ⑤ 22 (1) Being a little
dizzy (2) Not[Never] having done her
homework last night (3) nodding her head

01 '마치 ~인 것처럼'의 의미로 주절의 시제와 같은 시점의 상황을 반대로 가정할 때 〈as if+주어+동사의 과거형〉을 쓴다.

02 '(과거에) 만약 ~했다면, (지금) …할 텐데'의 의미로 과거에 실현되지 못한 일이 현재까지 영향을 미치는 상황을 가정할 때 사용하는 혼합 가정법(〈If+주어+had v-ed ~, 주어+조동사의 과거형+동사원형 …〉) 문장이므로, If절의 동사로 had bought가 와야 한다.

03 '그가 저 카레를 맛보기 전까지는 평생 그렇게 양념 맛이 강한 음식을 먹어본 적이 없었다.'라는 의미로 과거완료 had tasted가 와야 한다. 부정어 never를 강조하기 위해 문장의 맨 앞에 두면 주어와 동사가 도치되므로 〈부정어+조동사+주어〉의 형태를 써서 had he tasted가 되어야 한다.

04 '내가 도착했을 때 식은 이미 끝난 상태였다'라는 의미가 되어야 하므로 완료의 의미를 나타내는 과거완료 had ended를 써야 한다.

05 첫 번째 빈칸에는 분사구문의 주어로 날씨를 나타내는 비인칭 주어 It이 와야 하고, 두 번째 빈칸에는 뒤의 진주어 that절을 대신하는 가주어 It이 와야 한다.

06 '~해 봐야 소용없다'는 〈It is no use v-ing〉로 나타낸다.

07 '점점 더 ~한[하게]'는 〈비교급+and+비교급〉으로 나타내는데, 비교급이 〈more+원급〉의 형태인 경우에는 〈more and more+원급〉이 된다. 따라서 became more and more exciting으로 쓴다.

08 첫 번째 빈칸에는 사역동사 let의 목적격 보어인 원형부정사 take가 와야 하고, 두 번째 빈칸에는 want의 목적격 보어인 to부정사 to ask가 와야 한다.

09 과거 사실과 반대되는 상황을 가정하는 가정법 과거완료 문장이므로 〈If+주어+had v-ed ~, 주어+조동사의 과거형+have v-ed …〉로 나타낸다. 따라서 If절의 동사 형태는 had run이, 주절의 동사 형태는 would have voted가 되어야 한다.

10 '높은 파도로 우리는 바다에서 수영을 할 수 없었다.'라는 의미이므로 '~가 …하는 것을 막다'를 나타내는 〈keep+목적어+from v-ing〉를 써서 나타낸다.

11 〈On v-ing〉는 '~하자마자'라는 의미로 〈As soon as+주어+동사〉로 바꾸어 쓸 수 있다.

12 '~할 만큼 충분히 …하다'를 나타내는 〈형용사/부사+enough+to-v〉는 〈so+형용사/부사+that+주어+can〉으로 바꾸어 쓸 수 있으므로 so smart that he can이 와야 한다.

13 '(만약) ~이 없다면'은 〈Without[But for] ~〉 또는 〈If it were not for ~〉로 쓸 수 있으므로, 첫 번째 빈칸에는 for these batteries를 쓰고, 두 번째 빈칸에는 it were not for these batteries를 쓴다.

14 목적어가 that절인 문장을 수동태로 쓸 때는 〈It+be동사+v-ed that …〉의 형태로 써서 It is reported 뒤에 that절의 내용을 그대로 쓴다. 또는 that절의 주어를 수동태 문장의 주어로 쓸 수도 있는데, 이때 that절의 동사는 to부정사로 바뀌므로, 두 번째 빈칸에는 is reported to be를 쓴다.

15 '무엇을 ~하더라도'는 복합관계대명사 Whatever 또는 No matter what으로 나타낸다.

16 '~의 몇 배 …한[하게]'는 〈배수사+as+원급+as〉 또는 〈배수사+비교급+than〉으로 나타내므로 five times as many books as 또는 five times more books than이 와야 한다.

17 (a) '(전에는) ~이었다'라는 의미로 과거의 상태를 나타낼 때는 used to를 쓴다.
(c) ought to의 부정형은 ought not to이다.

18 관계대명사 that은 계속적 용법으로 쓸 수 없으므로 앞의 명사 his favorite game CD를 선행사로 하는 계속적 용법의 관계대명사 which로 고쳐야 한다.

19 '~하기를 고대하다'는 〈look forward to v-ing〉로 나타내므로 meet은 meeting으로 고쳐야 한다.

20 의문사가 없는 직접화법의 의문문을 간접화법으로 바꿀 때에는 〈ask(+목적어)+if[whether]+주어+동사〉형태로 쓴다. 직접화법에서 인칭대명사 you와 my는 I와 her로, 주절의 시제가 과거이므로 동사는 could로, this는 that으로 바꾸어 쓴다.

21 ⑤ 주어가 '놀란' 감정을 느끼게 되는 수동의 의미이므로 과거분사 surprised를 써야 한다.

22 (1) 문맥상 '조금 어지러워서 앉아서 쉬었다.'라는 의미가 알맞으므로 이유를 나타내는 분사구문 Being a little dizzy로 쓴다.

(2) 문맥상 '어젯밤에 숙제를 하지 않아서 오늘 꾸중을 들었다.'라는 의미가 알맞으므로 이유를 나타내는 분사구문을 쓴다. 분사구문의 부정은 분사 앞에 not이나 never를 붙이며, 부사절의 시제가 주절의 시제보다 앞서므로 완료형 분사구문을 써서 Not[Never] having done her homework last night로 쓴다.

(3) 문맥상 '고개를 끄덕이며 음악을 듣고 있다.'라는 의미가 알맞으므로, 동시동작을 나타내는 분사구문 nodding her head로 쓴다.

MEMO

MEMO

MEMO

MEMO

MEMO

문제로
마스터하는
중학영문법